IMAGINING A COMMON HORIZON FOR HUMANITY AND THE PLANET

، ، ،

EDITED BY
HASAN ALİ KARASAR
ŞAFAK OĞUZ

CAPPADOCIA
UNIVERSITY

2023

Cappadocia University Press: 67
Politics Book Series: 15
ISBN: 978-605-4448-58-6

© June 2023

Imagining a Common Horizon for Humanity and the Planet
Editors: Hasan Ali Karasar and Şafak Oğuz

Series Editor: Halil Burak Sakal
Cover Design: Nazile Arda Çakır
Page Design: ademşenel.com
Language Editor: Şafak Oğuz
Printing and Binding: Bizim Buro (Certificate No: 42488)

PRESIDENCY OF THE REPUBLIC OF TÜRKIYE
DIRECTORATE OF COMMUNICATIONS

This book is published with a support from Presidency of the Republic of Türkiye Directorate of Communications

Disclaimer
The opinions and comments presented in the book represent the personal views of the individual authors. The authors are individually responsible for the content of their chapters.

Karasar, H.A., Oğuz, Ş. (eds.) (2023). *Imagining a Common Horizon for Humanity and the Planet*. Nevşehir: Cappadocia University Press.
234 p. 16.5x23.5 cm.
ISBN: 978-605-4448-58-6
Keywords: 1. Humanity, 2. The Planet, 3. Common Horizon, 4. Climate Change, 5. Democracy.

CAPPADOCIA
UNIVERSITY
50420 Mustafapaşa, Ürgüp, Nevşehir
yayinevi@kapadokya.edu.tr
kapadokyayayinlari.kapadokya.edu.tr
0(384) 353 5009
www.kapadokya.edu.tr

IMAGINING A COMMON HORIZON FOR HUMANITY AND THE PLANET

, , ,

EDITED BY
HASAN ALİ KARASAR
ŞAFAK OĞUZ

CAPPADOCIA
UNIVERSITY

2023

TABLE OF CONTENTS

List of Abbreviations

ABM	Anti-Ballistic Missiles
CNN	Cable News Network
CPGS	Conventional Prompt Global Strike
EPAA	European Phased Adaptive Approach
GDP	Gross Domestic Product
IMF	International Monetary Fund
IPCC	Intergovernmental Panel on Climate Change
NASA	National Aeronautics and Space Administration
NATO	North Atlantic Treaty Organization
NMD	National Missile Defense
NPT	Non-proliferation Treaty
NWs	Nuclear Weapons
MAD	Mutual Assured Destruction
WMD	Weapons of Mass Destruction
PDG	Preimplantation Genetic Diagnosis
SALT	Strategic Arms Limitation Treaty
START	Strategic Arms Reduction Treaty
TNW	Tactical Nuclear Weapons
UDI	Unilateral Declaration of Independence
UNDRIP	United Nations Declaration of the Rights of Indigenous People
UNEP	United Nations Environment Program
UNESCO	United Nations Educational Scientific and Cultural
VUCA	Volatility, Uncertainty, Complexity, Ambiguity
WMO	World Meteorological Organization
WWI	World War I
WWII	World War II

List of Tables

List of Figures

Preface

Humanity and our planet have been undergoing difficult times. We have been witnessing state-level warfare that included a nuclear threat, an alarming development that had seemingly slipped from the world's consciousness. We have been witnessing civil wars, based on religious or ethnic rivalry, resulting in mass murders and internal and international mass migration. The figures amount to some 100 million displaced persons in the world, a new world record. Economic crises have reshaped the economic situation, resulting in income redistribution in favor of rich people and rich states, while aggravating economic conditions for those on the lower end of the scale. According to the UN World Food Programme, a record 349 million people across 79 countries are facing acute food insecurity, while more than 900,000 people worldwide are struggling to survive in famine-like conditions.

The COVID-19 pandemic changed the way of life around the world, and new pandemics are expected to emerge. Despite high-level standards in health systems, scenarios that include mass death in pandemics remain real and imminent. Recent pandemics, especially COVID-19, underscored how local or regional efforts are not sufficient to curb the effects of pandemics and cope with them. As we have endeavoured to highlight in our project, shared global cooperation is crucial in the fight against pandemics.

Respect and tolerance for diversity, including ethnicity and religion, has decreased to the extent that discrimination, hatred, and intolerance have become normal throughout the world. Provocateurs burn holy books, instigating social disruptions that might lead to new crises. We have witnessed a new form of slavery in the 21st century, and it appears to be worsening. Even in developed states, women are suffering, even though "motherhood" apparently retains its high status and value in the world. Despite international agreements and efforts, children are forced to work in jobs unsuitable for them, and in miserable conditions. Many children, especially young girls, are deprived of the education they deserve. Humanity has failed to provide common and proper prospects for them.

Insofar as we know, Earth is the only planet that hosts living creatures. Unfortunately, we have been experiencing a major crisis of climate change, caused by human beings. No living creature harms nature and the environment in any way comparable to humans, the living creatures supposedly regarded as the most intelligent. Human actions continue to result in the extinction of other species. Neither regional nor international efforts have yet proven sufficient to curb the crisis.

Recent developments clearly highlight that borders are not capable of containing local or regional crises. We must work together to cope with the problems we have been witnessing and suffering. We need to imagine a Common Horizon for the Humanity and the Planet, for our own future and especially for that of our children. The project *Imagining a Common Horizon for Humanity and the Planet,* organized by Cappadocia University and bringing together distinguished scholars constitutes a significant and valued effort to remind the international community that the future of humanity and indeed of the planet is tied to developing a global perspective to resolve these crises. It is our hope that more steps and efforts in this direction will follow suit.

Alev Alatlı

Chairman of the Board of Trustees

Cappadocia University

List of Contributors

Catarina Belo is Associate Professor at the Department of Philosophy of American University in Cairo in Eqypt.

Giorgos Kallis is a Professor at the Institute of Environmental Science and Technology of Universitat Autònoma de Barcelona in Spain.

Frank Furedi is Emeritus Professor of Sociology at the University of Kent in the UK.

Hasan Ali Karasar is a Professor of International Relations and Rector of Cappadocia University in Türkiye.

John Keane is Professor of Politics at the University of Sydney in Australia and at the Wissenschaftszentrum Berlin (WZB) in Germany.

Joseph Massad is Professor of Modern Arab Politics and Intellectual History at Columbia University in the US.

Masahiro Morioka is Professor at the Department of School of Human Sciences of Waseda University in Japan.

H. Nüzhet Dalfes is a retired Professor, formerly at Eurasia Institute of Earth Sciences of the Istanbul Technical University in Türkiye.

Ruslan Dzarasov is a Professor of Russian Financial University under the Government of the Russian Federation in Russia.

Simon Estok is a Professor and Senior Research Fellow in the Department of English Language and Literature at Sungkyunkwan University in South Korea.

Susan Buck-Morss is a distinguished Professor at the department of Political Science of City University of New York in the US.

Şafak Oğuz is an Associate Professor at the Department of International Relations at Cappadocia University.

Acknowledgement

Cappadocia University embarked on an international and interdisciplinary project on the future of humanity and our planet titled "**Imagining A Common Horizon for Humanity and the Planet**".

The Project convened intellectuals and thinkers from across the arts and sciences to consider one of the most fundamental issues of contemporary philosophy: **How can we build a common horizon for the future of the humanity and the planet**? It aimed to bring together the leading thinkers of the world, to create an international intellectual platform that draws its strength from human dignity, and that aims to build for the future of humanity and the planet with a holistic synergy with a view to offering humanity a common horizon. As Cappadocia University, our vision in this regard is to provide an academic platform from where esteemed intellectuals from around the world can share their visions for a common future of humanity and our planet, and to comment on the challenges and opportunities they envisage.

This book is a product of this project contributed by distinguished scholars who discussed and analyzed the topic from their expertise and perspectives.

Prof. Joseph Massad of University of Columbia University discusses white supremacist settler-colonialism and its effects which are regarded as some of the most important sources for crises all around the world.

Prof. Frank Furedi of Kent University explains how pandemics, especially COVID-19, have changed the perception of and life of population all around the world and advises us to learn how to live with pandemics.

Prof. Susan Buck-Morss of City University of New York sheds light to the historical background of philosophical life of human and presents a horizon for us in the context of philosophy.

Prof. Catarina Belo of the American University in Cairo discusses free will and determinism in classical Islamic Philosophy and provides us insight for the historical and contemporary problems in the Islamic world.

Prof. H. Nüzhet Dalfes focuses mainly on the problems of our Earth, such as Climate Change or Extinction of Species, and advocates for a solid bridge between science communities and the public-at-large to lay the foundations of a common horizon to save our planet.

Prof. Ruslan Dzarasov of Russian Financial University under the Government of the Russian Federation analyses contemporary economic crisis from the perspective of world system approach and discusses the problems created by global economic structure.

Prof. John Keane of Sydney University provides us a different perspective for interpreting the crises humans are facing, discussing the fate of certainty in times of uncertainty. While analysing the various reasons for the growing popularity of pessimism, he interrogates this mentality of catastrophism to show that uncertainty is a feature of our human condition on planet Earth.

Prof. Giorgos Kallis of Universitat Autònoma de Barcelona analyses the limits and scarcity of economic growth in the world from the perspective of Malthusian principles and discusses the effects of growth.

Prof. Simon Estok of Sungkyunkwan University argues that COVID-19 pandemic has resulted in the responses for the survival of the population, however, it also evoked panic and phobic reactions. Therefore, he highlights the need to recognize the long-term microbial effects of compulsive sanitizing and reflexive ecophobia.

Prof. Masahiro Morioka of Waseda University argues how contemporary civilization provided a pleasure and comfort for the society, defining it as painless civilization, and discusses the long term negative effects of this new form of life.

Assoc.Prof. Şafak OĞUZ of Cappadocia University analyzes the new security environment in the perspective of nuclear threat and questions if a world without nuclear weapons is possible.

Prof. Hasan Ali Karasar of Cappadocia University discusses the failure of the development of a new international order and underlines the level of readiness for a pessimistic scenario we may face.

We also thank to Prof. Ussama Makdisi of Rice University, Prof. Adom Getachew of Chicago University, Prof. Wendy Brown of Princeton University, Dr. Douglas Vakoch. Prof. Christopher Afoke Isike of University of Pretoria in S. Africa and Prof. Ebrahim Moosa of the University of Notre Dame for their valued contribution to our project as guest. We also thank to Prof. Cemil Aydın of North Carolina University, Prof. Banu Bargu of UC Santa

Cruz, Dr. Ethemcan Turhan of University of Groningen, Prof. Oktay Tanrı-sever of METU, Prof. Burak Özçetin of Bilgi University, Dr. Volkan İpek of Yeditepe University, Prof. Iskender Öksüz of Cappadocia University, Prof. Serpil Oppermann of Cappadocia University and Dr. Sinan Akıllı of Cappadocia University for their contribution as the moderator.

Cappadocia University will continue to provide a platform to discuss and analyze international crises and to offer solutions to mitigate the effects of the problems we face. Cappadocia University is determined to urge international community to **Imagine a Common Horizon for Humanity and the Planet.**

Hasan Ali Karasar and Şafak Oğuz

Editors

Independence: The Ruse of settler-Colonialism

Joseph Massad

One of the most remarkable aspects of the *independence* of states that remains ignored, elided, downplayed, and evaded in scholarly research, is the *white supremacist* settler-colonial origins of the very notion of a State's "independence." It was the establishment of the first *white supremacist* European colonial-settler State in 1776 by white colonists in what became the United States that inaugurated the age of "independence," a trajectory that ends with the Unilateral Declaration of Independence (UDI) by the European colonial settlers of Rhodesia on 11 November 1965. Indeed, the last *white supremacist* Declaration of Independence of Rhodesia's colonial settlers pays homage to the first in borrowing their North American counterparts' exact words to declare their own independence from the same mother country.[1]

The connection between the two independent *white supremacist* colonial-settler states was not lost on the British.[2] In 1963, the government of British Prime Minister Harold Macmillan's Conservative Party prepared contingency plans for intervening in Rhodesia to prevent a potential unilateral independence. The secret file containing the relevant British documents, as David Armitage has revealed, was titled "Boston Tea Party."[3]

The secession and subsequent independence of Europe's white colonists in the settler colonies of the Americas, Asia, Africa, and Oceania takes place during the almost two centuries that separate the independence of the first and last white supremacist colonial-settler states. During this period and after, "independence" would become the political and economic goal of the natives of Europe's colonies and settler-colonies, both within Europe (in Ireland and Poland) and across the globe. But, if the nineteenth century ushered in the

---

1 David Armitage, *The Declaration of Independence, A Global History*, Harvard University Press, Cambridge, 2007, p.135-136.

2 The American Declaration also traveled to another British white supremacist settler colony, namely South Africa, where it was reprinted in the South African Christian Recorder, 2, 8, (January 1837), p. 432, cited by Armitage, The Declaration 95.

3 ibid.,*p.* 136.

independence of the North, Central, and South American and Caribbean settler-colonies, and some of the Oceanian and African settler-colonies, and the
Christian "European" provinces of the Ottoman State, the momentum of independence advanced more rapidly in the wake of WWI, both for the white colonial settlers of North America, Africa, and Oceania as much as for the natives
of Asia, Africa, Europe, and the Americas. The pace became unstoppable after World War II. Aside from the independence of the European settler colonies of Israel (1948), South Africa (1961), and Rhodesia (1965), scores of Europe's colonies, Protectorates, and Mandated territories obtained independence,
ushering in the world of independent states across the globe.

Since "independence" as a concept and political practice, seems to equate
the now independent countries, whether controlled by natives or colonial-settlers, it simultaneously ends the era of formal colonialism and perpetuates
and legitimates not only economic imperialism, but also formal settler-colonialism, recognizing both as in possession of sovereignty ratified by the latest
global forum designed to grant such legitimacy, namely the United Nations.
Yet, independence, as both a political idea and practice of sovereignty, continues to be marketed by all these countries as a political and economic good
that ended the unjust rule of colonial powers in the case of the colonies or that
of the mother countries in the case of the settler-colonies, even and especially
if in the case of the latter it meant the continued subjugation of the indigenous
peoples-- from the first Nations of Canada and the Native Americans of the
United States and the indigenous populations across Central and South America, to the Aborigines of Australia, the Palestinians, the Maoris, the Kanaka
Maoli, and, not least, Black South Africans and Zimbabweans.

Whence arose this concept of independence? What was its historical and
geographic trajectory? How did this white European settler-colonial principle
also become the goal of the colonized natives and indigenous peoples of the
world? That the formal independence of white Protestant British colonial settlers resulted in outcomes vastly different from the formal independence of the
natives of Europe's colonies or even that of the Spanish and Portuguese colonial settlers and their mixed race descendants seemed to signal, to many European and white American commentators, less that the principle was invented
to benefit mainly Europe's English-speaking Protestant colonial settlers from
its inception, but the colonially-predicted "failure" of natives and non-English
settlers to manage their own affairs.

In the following, I trace some of the juridical, philosophical, and political histories of the concept and practice of independence in order to understand its global effects as the primary principle for the existence of the State system since the late 18th century, and how the concept of self-determination would join it during and after World War I, as a corollary, to institute white European colonial and settler-colonial privileges over the indigenous peoples of the colonies.

, , ,

Most accounts of "independence" depict it as an outcome of the European Enlightenment and Revolutionary thought, which is committed to "universal" human equality and freedom. In fact, the genealogy of "independence" is entirely inseparable from the 18th century new ideology of white supremacy and settler-colonialism, and that this deep co-foundationalism is what liberal Euro-American historians and theorists, and their disciples need to forget, repress, and deny.

Before the term "independence" came into existence and acquired political significance and legal status, other concepts were used to separate from or leave the control of a sovereign. The Dutch "Act of Abjuration" of 1581 is often referred to anachronistically to mean a "declaration of independence," especially as it is alleged that American colonial settlers would later cite it as an inspirational precedent to their own desire to declare independence, even though the Dutch "Plakkaat van Verlantige" was in fact a renunciation (the Dutch word means "abandonment") of the sovereignty of King Philip II of Spain, in effect a secession (itself a sixteenth century English term) and did not posit notions of dependence or independence as operative.[4] The Dutch abjuration was a religious one, of Protestants resisting the religious persecution of King Philip, but also a territorial and economic one, wherein sections of the Dutch nobility and bourgeoisie felt insecure about being part of a much larger empire and wanted to secure their interests from outside control.[5]

---

4   For claims that the *Plakkaat* was an inspirational source for the Declaration of Independence, see Stephen Lucas, "The 'Plakkaat van Verlatinge': A Neglected Model for the American Declaration of Independence," *Connecting Cultures: The Netherlands in Five Centuries of TransAtlantic Exchange*, (eds.) Rosemarijn Hoefte, Johanna C. Kardux, and Hans Bak, , Vrije Universiteit University Press, Amsterdam, 1994, p.187-207.

5   Immanuel Wallerstein, *The Modern World-System I, Capitalist Agriculture and the Origins of the European World-Economy in the Sixteenth Century*, University of California Press, Berkeley, 2011, p. 202-212.

Still the coupling of the whiteness and Protestantism of the English-speaking settlers would set them apart from all others in the course of the centuries to come, as they would be the only colonists to achieve both political *and* economic independence (the two other exceptions would be the British-sponsored settler colonies of South Africa and its Dutch and English white Protestant colonists and the European Jewish settler-colony of Israel, whose colonial project was designed by British Protestant evangelicals).

It is in the middle of the eighteenth century in the latest literature on "the law of nations," however, where the term is inaugurated and would soon acquire a juridical and technical sense, referring to the status of a State in what becomes the society of nations. The ancient Roman notion of *jus gentium,* which was "private law" that dealt with relations among individuals within the Roman imperium and not with foreign relations, was adopted in the first half of the seventeenth century to different ends and endowed with a different meaning by the Dutch jurist Hugo Grotius, inaugurating a new doctrine in juridical and political parlance also governing relations between States. *Jus gentium* was translated, but misapprehended, in the eighteenth century as the "Law of Nations" and later, "international law," and the new significations were often anachronistically applied to this ancient and medieval Roman notion, though Jeremy Bentham's later coinage of the term "international," rather than "interstatal" as Immanuel Kant had suggested, remained operative.[6]

Yet, the basis of what becomes modern international law was in fact created by the colonial encounter in the Americas in the sixteenth century through the major figure of Francisco de Vitoria, a precursor to Grotius, and wherein the questions of civilized and barbarian nations, of defensive and aggressive wars (later "just" and "unjust" war), were concretized and continue to inform the discipline through the present.[7]

However, the "independence" of States *tout court* did not become part of this legal lexicon for another century or so. According to the Oxford English Dictionary, the word "independent" is a seventeenth century English term that

---

6   For the translation and origins of *jus gentium*, see Arthur Nussbaum, *A Concise History of the Law of Nations,* The MacMillan Company, New York, 1947, p. 18-22, 135.

7   Antony Anghie, *Imperialism, Sovereignty, and the Making of International Law,* Cambridge University Press, Cambridge, 2004. Indeed, the Orient would be paramount in these early developments, especially of notions of "just war." De Vitoria supported as lawful the indiscriminate murder of Saracen male prisoners and that their wives and children be committed to slavery. See Nussbaum, A Concise History, p. 65.

begins to be used in a political sense in midcentury. Thomas Hobbes uses it in 1651 in *The Leviathan* to refer to the different branches of a "mixed monarchy" which led to civil war in England. Hobbes offered a contrary view to Grotius' and others' understanding of *jus gentium*, insisting on it being exclusively an affair between states and *not* individuals. In *The Leviathan*, he states that such a governing system as "mixed monarchy" is not "one independent commonwealth, but three independent factions."[8] It took another century before the term "indépendance" in French, or "independency" and/or "independence" in English, begins to acquire a political meaning akin to what it would refer by the last quarter of the eighteenth century.

The term remained in flux in the 1740s and beyond, especially so as Montesquieu himself did not use it in his 1748 *Spirit of the Laws* in this technical sense. In contrast to its later political signification, Montesquieu used the term in reference to an unconstrained individual not governed by laws or one who lived in a state of nature; he seemed to equate "independence" with "unlimited freedom," which he insisted was not the same as "liberty." This aside, Montesquieu does not apply the term "independence" to states, nor to individuals who live within them. He elaborates on this when he explains that "We must continually have present to our minds the difference between independence and liberty. Liberty is a right of doing whatever the laws permit, and if a citizen could do what they forbid he would be no longer possessed of liberty, because all his fellow-citizens would have the same power."[9] In line with the reigning climatology of the times, Montesquieu worried that in warmer climates, bodies are more susceptible to vice, including love and passion than they are in colder ones where people "have few vices," so much so that "in southern countries a machine of a delicate frame but strong sensibility resigns itself either to a love which rises and is incessantly laid in a seraglio, or to a passion which leaves women in greater *independence*, and is consequently exposed to a thousand inquietudes [emphasis added]."[10]

For Montesquieu, not only are Muslim societies endowed with such climatological inclinations towards vice but so are Catholic ones. It is in this context that he understands liberty as the sole endowment of northern European

---

8   Thomas Hobbes, *Leviathan,* edited by J.C. A. Gaskin, Oxford University Press, Oxford, 1996), Part II, [paragraph 172], p. 219.

9   Baron de Montesquieu, *The Spirit of the Laws*, translated by Thomas Nugent, Two volumes in one, Hafner Publishing Company, New York, 1949, 150 of volume 1.

10   Ibid.,*p.* 223-224.

Protestants: "When the Christian religion, two centuries ago, became unhappily divided into Catholic and Protestant, the people of the North embraced the Protestant, and those of the South adhered still to the Catholic...The reason is plain: the people of the North have, and will forever have a spirit of liberty and independence, which the people of the South have not; and therefore a religion which has no visible head is more agreeable to the independence of the climate than that which has one."[11]

It is in the German Christian von Wolff's book *The Law of Nations*, published in 1749, a year after Montesquieu's book, that we find the early transformation of the term "independent" into its later technical signification in a few scattered references.[12] Whereas there is no reference in the book to the "independence" of states, the adjective "independent" is used in relation to nations and peoples: "By nature nations are free and therefore the civil power, consequently the mode of exercising it, or the form of the state, is quite *independent* of other nations" (emphasis added).[13]

A decade later, it was the Swiss Emer de Vattel, a student of Wolff, who would use the term in such a manner that instituted it as the new technical term that came to be known as the *independence* of a State. In his 1758 *Le droit de gens*, Vattel mentions a state's "independence" of other states when he speaks of the ability of a state to "discharge the duties she owes to herself and to her citizens."[14] In his enumeration of the laws of nations, Vattel lists "the liberty and independence" of nations as his second general law, explaining that "nations being *free and independent* of each other, in the same manner as men are naturally free and independent."[15] He adds that "after having established the position that foreign nations have no right to interfere in the government of an independent state, it is not difficult to prove that the latter has a right to oppose such interference. To govern herself according to her own pleasure, is a necessary part of her independence."[16]

---

11 Ibid., Volume 2, p.31,
12 Christian Wolff, *Jus Gentium: Methodo Scientifica Pertractatum*, translated by Joseph H. Drake, Volume Two, Clarendon Pres, Oxford, 1934.
13 Ibid., Volume 1, p. 123.
14 Emer de Vattel, "The Law of Nations, or, Principles of the law of nature, applied to the conduct and affairs of nations and sovereigns, with three early essays on the origin and nature of natural law and on luxury", edited and with an introduction by Bela Kapossy and Richard Whatmore; translated by Thomas Nugent, Liberty Fund, Indianapolis, 2008, p. 15.
15 Ibid., p. 74.
16 Ibid., p. 292.

The question of settler colonialism is paramount in the mind and thought of Vattel, which may explain his later popularity among the white Protestant English-speaking colonists and their descendants in the thirteen British colonies of North America. In the tradition of John Locke and other liberal political theorists, Vattel was intent on justifying white European colonization of the lands of non-Europeans and registered his support specifically for English-speaking settler-colonists, as he was more discriminatory than others in refusing to grant legitimacy to *all* settler-colonization:

Those who still pursue this idle mode of life, usurp more extensive territories than, with a reasonable share of labour, they would have occasion for, and have therefore no reason to complain, if other nations, more industrious, and too closely confined, come to take possession of a part of those lands. Thus, though the conquest of the civilized empires of Peru and Mexico was a notorious usurpation, the establishment of many colonies on the continent of North America, might, on their confining themselves within just bounds, be extremely lawful. The people of those extensive tracts rather ranged through than inhabited them.[17]

His notion of independence indeed focuses on settler-colonialism as its principal example. He tells us that "an independent individual, whether he has been driven from his country, or has legally quitted it of his own accord, may settle in a country which he finds without an owner, and there possess an independent domain. Whosoever would afterwards make himself master of the entire country, could not do it with justice without respecting the rights and independence of this person. But if he himself finds a sufficient number of men who are willing to live under his laws, he may form a new state within the country he has discovered, and possess there both the domain and the empire."[18]

Vattel's outright justification of the colonization of North America is relentless, even as he also justifies the colonization of the land of "pastoral Arabs" or nomadic Bedouins:

The savages of North America had no right to appropriate all that vast continent to themselves: and since they were unable to inhabit the whole of those regions, other nations might without injustice settle in some parts of them, provided they left the natives a sufficiency of land. If the pastoral Arabs would carefully cultivate the soil, a less space might be sufficient for them. Nevertheless,

---

17   Ibid., p.130.
18   Ibid., p. 309-310.

no other nation has a right to narrow their boundaries, unless she be under an absolute want of land. For, in short, they possess their country; they make use of it after their manner; they reap from it an advantage suitable to their manner of life, respecting which, they have no laws to receive from any one. In a case of pressing necessity, I think people might without injustice settle in a part of that country, on teaching the Arabs the means of rendering it, by the cultivation of the earth, sufficient for their own wants and those of the new inhabitants.[19]

Vattel's influence on North American figures who led the thirteen colonies to "independence" was most pronounced. While the first translation of his book into English appeared in 1760,[20] Benjamin Franklin informed the Swiss publisher in December 1775 that the book "has been continuously in the hands of our congress, now sitting."[21] Vattel's book became a staple textbook at American colleges "and after the establishment of the Republic, the favorite authority in American theory of international law."[22]

The white settler-colonists' disenchantment with the British Crown was on account of increasing concentration of wealth in the hands of English capitalists at home who were competing with the settler merchants after the major improvement in economic conditions which prevailed after 1720, but especially after 1745.[23] This was followed by a series of taxes imposed on the settlers, especially the Sugar Act and the Currency Act of 1764 and the Stamp Act of 1765, which reduced their profits further in favor of the Crown, profits made possible by continued colonization of the land of Native-Americans and slave labor. This was all the more poignant as it came on the heel of the 1763 Royal Proclamation prohibiting the white colonists from colonizing lands west of Appalachia, in the Ohio Valley, which were reserved for Native Americans, and forcing those colonists who had done so to evacuate the colonized lands and move east. This infuriated the white colonists and created a major schism with the British Crown.[24] It also led a large number of Native Americans to

---

19 Ibid.,p. 310-311.
20 See Charles G. Fenwick, "The Authority of Vattel," *American Political Science Review*, Vol. 7, No. 3, (Aug., 1913), p.406.
21 Armitage, "The Declaration", *p. 41.*
22 Nussbaum, *op.cit.,* p. 161.
23 Immanuel Wallerstein, *The Modern World-System III: The Second Era of Great Expansion of the Capitalist World-Economy, 1730s–1840s,* University of California Press, Berkeley, 2011, p.196.
24 Woody Holton, "The Ohio Indians and the Coming of the American Revolution in Virginia," *The Journal of Southern History,* Vol. 60, No. 3 (Aug., 1994), p. 453-478.

fight alongside the British against the white colonists during the "Revolutionary War" due to their sober assessment that a victory for the white colonists meant more devastation for them.

In *Prelude to Independence*, Arthur Schlesinger describes the pre-Revolutionary meanings of key words, including independence:

The stigmatizing of British policy as 'tyranny,' 'oppression' and 'slavery' had little or no objective reality, at least prior to the [British-imposed] Intolerable Acts [of 1774] but ceaseless repetition of the charge kept emotions at fever pitch … On the other hand, soul-stirring words like 'liberty,' 'freedom' and 'independence,' though at first they connotated nothing more than the status the colonies had enjoyed before 1763 [prior to the Sugar Act and the Currency Act of 1764 and the Stamp Act of 1765], came in time to pack a revolutionary meaning. Correspondingly, the magic term 'American,' implying a nationality and allegiance apart from the mother country, gradually replaced the oldest separatist designations of 'New Yorker,' 'Virginian' and so on."[25]

The emergence of the term "American" that came to be increasingly used in the 1760s by the white settler-colonists, also replacing the earlier terms of "colonists" and "settlers,"[26] is most important in this regard, as it signals a major transformation in the term and its generative power for indigenizing the colonists and the invention of a national identity. It is in this context that Benedict Anderson noted in *Imagined Communities* that colonial-settlers in the Americas were the progenitors of the concept of national identity and nationalism that would later have worldwide resonance.[27] Most important to stress, however, is that notions of freedom, liberty, and independence for the white Protestant male colonists, slave-owning or not, essentially meant little more than safeguarding their property, including slaves, and businesses from the encroachment of Britain and its taxation, which to them seemed like a form of slavery. Independence for the white Protestant settler-colonists therefore had centrally an economic sense, with the corresponding political sense ensuring the economic one. This would change considerably when, less than two decades later, independence reached the revolutionary and newly independent

25   Arthur M. Schlesinger, *Prelude to Independence, The Newspaper War on Britain, 1764-1776,* Alfred A. Knopf, New York, 1958, p. 34.

26   See Christopher K. Brooks, "Controlling the Metaphor: Language and Self-Definition in Revolutionary America," *Clio,* Vol. 25, No. 3, 1996, p. 233-254.

27   Benedict Anderson, *Imagined Communities, Reflections on the Origin and Spread of Nationalism,* Verso, London, 2016.

Haiti whose black and "colored" peoples overthrew colonial slavery but were subjected to an economic siege by the US and Europe and forced to pay indemnities to France. When independence reached Spanish America four decades later, the new states' indebtedness to Britain would saddle their independence from its inception. In line with this application of independence to non-English speaking colonists, let alone the Black and Colored former slaves of Saint Domingue, after World War I, and especially WWII, the national "independence" of non-white peoples would become operatively political and anything but economic.

It would be left to the English-born white colonial settler Thomas Paine, who arrived in the British American colonies in 1774, to elaborate on what he called "the doctrine of independence" in his mass-circulated pamphlet *Common Sense,* which he addressed to "the inhabitants of America" and published on 14 February 1776.[28] In *Common Sense,* Paine defines the term "independency" as follows: "Is the power who is jealous of our prosperity, a proper power to govern us? Whoever says *No* to this question is an *independent,* for independency means no more, than, whether we shall make our own laws, or whether the king, the greatest enemy this continent hath, or can have, shall tell us, *'there shall be no laws but such as I like.'*"

Paine identifies the enemies of the idea of independence as enemies of settler colonialism: "Ye that oppose independence now, ye know not what ye do; ye are opening a door to eternal tyranny, by keeping vacant the seat of government. There are thousands, and tens of thousands, who would think it glorious to expel from the continent, that barbarous and hellish power, which hath stirred up the Indians and Negroes to destroy us, the cruelty hath a double guilt, it is dealing brutally by us, and treacherously by them."

Despite his opposition to slavery and recognition of the theft of Native American lands and livelihoods, Paine's understanding of independence was exclusive to the white colonial settlers within the rubric of English-speaking Protestant white supremacy.[29] During the "Revolutionary War," both the northern

---

28   The text of the pamphlet is available here: https://www.learner.org/workshops/primarysources/revolution/docs/Common_Sense.pdf

29   Paine does expose the irony of the white colonists' opposition to tyranny. He wrote to a newspaper in March 1775 asking: "With what consistency, or decency," could the white settler-colonists "complain so loudly of attempts to enslave them, while they hold so many hundred thousand in slavery." Cited in Eric Foner, *Tom Paine and Revolutionary America, Updated version with a new preface,* Oxford University Press, Oxford, 2005, p. 73. Paine also ridiculed

colonists and the British crown promised Black slaves freedom if they joined their respective armies, but tens of thousands of slaves preferred to support the British and thousands fought for them.[30] In the case of the rebel southern colonies, in contrast with the north, Virginia, Georgia, and the Carolinas promised land and a slave to go with it to white men who would volunteer to fight in the struggle against the British.[31]

This legacy of independence would not only be espoused by white French slave-owning Saint Domingans, or the white Creoles of Spanish America, but also the Dutch setters of South Africa, Black American colonists of West Africa, and by the end of the 19th century, the English and French colonists of Canada, Australia, and New Zealand, the mixed race *Indische* European colonists of Batavia in Indonesia, not to mention the Anglo-Indians, the Rehoboth Basters of Namibia, the French *colons* of Algeria, the Zionist Jewish colonists of Palestine, and the British colonists of Rhodesia and even Kenya. They will be joined at the turn of the twentieth century by the colonized peoples of the world, those living in colonies and settler-colonies, who would use a more recent concept to achieve independence that came to be known as "self-determination."

, , ,

It is often claimed that anti-colonial nationalism and self-determination have a coeval history, indeed, that self-determination is the principle through which anti-colonialists would achieve their declared goal of *independence* from

the role of Christian missionaries trying to proselytize the Native American Osage tribe, yet he did not propose that the independence he sought for the American colonies include them. See Christopher Hitchens, *Thomas Paine's Rights of Man: A Biography,* Atlantic Books, London, 2006, p. 107.

30   On the numbers of runaway slaves who joined the British and were freed and evacuated with them and the controversy about their actual numbers, see Cassandra Pybus, "Jefferson's Faulty Math: The Question of Slave Defections in the American Revolution," *William and Mary Quarterly, Third Series*, Vol. 62, No. 2, (April 2005), p. 243-264. See also Woody Holton, *Black Americans in the Revolutionary Era: A Brief History with Documents,* Bedford/St. Martin's, Boston, 2009.

31   Robin Blackburn, *The Overthrow of Colonial Slavery, 1776-1848*, Verso, London, 1988, p. 116. Thomas Jefferson had included an anti-slavery paragraph in the original Declaration, which at the request of delegates from South Carolina, Georgia, Massachusetts, Connecticut, and Rhode Island, had to be deleted in the final copy. See Herbert Aptheker, *The American Revolution, 1763-1783,* International Publishers, New York, 1960, p. 213. Aptheker includes the text of the deleted paragraph. See also Arthur Zilversmit, *The First Emancipation: The Abolition of Slavery in the North,* University of Chicago Press, Chicago, 1967, p.7.

colonialism.[32] The story goes that not only have anti-colonialism and self-determination emerged around the same historical juncture, but that they are also imbricated in one another, indeed, that the colonial recognition of one automatically leads to the colonial recognition of the other. Yet, on closer inspection, this seems to be a misleading narrative. Not only does the dominant form of self-determination seem to be a principle designed to limit the claims of anti-colonial nationalism and to enhance the claims of colonialism, especially the settler-colonial variety and its "right of conquest," but even more importantly colonial and settler-colonial resistance and reticence to recognizing the colonized as nations that deserve independence would only be mitigated once self-determination became the operative criterion by which substantive political, let alone economic, independence can be negated. In the case of settler-colonialism, the settler-colonists would only accede to a recognition that the indigenous peoples whose lands they usurped are *nations* is the moment self-determination is introduced as a principle or a right that not only would *not* lead to the declared goal of "independence" from settler-colonialism, but rather one that would effectively *obstruct* it.

This can be observed in settler-colonies around the globe. From the Americas to Australia, from Palestine and Algeria to Rhodesia and South Africa, the colonial settlers fought and mostly preserved their "right of conquest" as a right to "self-determination." European colonial nationalism was predicated on the understanding that colonizing countries, like Britain and France, formed nations, which were judged as a civilized form of community and even as a political achievement that many among the colonized did not constitute, let alone were able to achieve. It was in this context that the British denied that the Egyptians or the Indians constituted nations rather than a motley of different communities, tribes, clans, castes, sects, etc. The French too denied that the Algerians were a nation. Egypt's English ruler, Lord Cromer, identified Egyptians as "the dwellers in Egypt," insisting that there were no such things as "true Egyptians," rather a bunch of Fellahin, Bedouin, Copts, Turks, Syrians, Jews, Azhar Sheikhs, Circassians, Levantine nondescripts "whose ethnological status defies diagnosis," Greeks, Armenians, Tunisians, Algerians, "Soudanese,"

---

32   This is an assertion found in Palestinian anti-colonial literature, as in other anti-colonial settings. See for example Shafiq al-Rushaydat, *Al-Muqawamah al-Filastiniyyah wa Haqq Taqrir al-Masir (Palestinian Resistance and the Right of Self-Determination)*, Matba'at Awlad 'Abduh Ahmad, Cairo, 1970. This section on self-determination is based on my article "Against Self-Determination," *Humanity: An International Journal of Human Rights, Humanitarianism, and Development*, Vol. 9, No. 2, (Summer 2018).

Maltese, and "half-breeds of every description." Unlike "the Englishmen, the Frenchmen, or Germans," whom one could tell by looking at their faces, the "dwellers in Egypt" were no nation politically or physiognomically, let alone a single race.[33] The French racial colonial policy in Algeria before 1954 aimed specifically to diminish the commonalities among Algerians and to stress instead their differences. For French colonialism, the Algerians consisted of grande Kabylie, petite Kabylie, Aurés (mixed Berbers and Arabs), Arabs, and Blacks. In the case of India, it was Winston Churchill who declared: "India is an abstraction...India is a geographical term. It is no more a united nation than the Equator."[34] Golda Meir (née Mabovitch), the Ukrainian leader of the European Jewish colonists of Palestine declared as late as 1969 that "It was not as though there was a Palestinian people in Palestine considering itself as a Palestinian people and we came and threw them out and took their country away from them. They did not exist."[35] The denial of the national identity of those colonized by European colonists should be contrasted with the support European powers gave in the nineteenth century to nationalisms within the Ottoman Empire for the purpose of breaking it up –here European support for Christian Greek and Bulgarian nationalisms are prime examples.

It was in the context of the Scramble for Africa and the Berlin Conference of 1884-85 that discussions among the attendees supported indigenous Africans' right to dispose of their lands to European colonists. Indeed, the Scramble had been increasingly put into effect through negotiating treaties with native sovereigns. One of the American delegates to the Berlin Conference, John Kasson, insisted that modern international law was leading to the recognition "of the right of native tribes to dispose freely of themselves and of their hereditary territory," and that this right was to be "extended" to require the "voluntary consent of the natives whose country is taken possession of, in all cases where they had not provoked the aggression."[36] It is this right of the colonized

---

33 See The Earl of Cromer, *Modern Egypt*, Vol. 2, Macmillan Company, London, 1916, p. 126, 127, and 128.

34 Cited in William Manchester, *The Last Lion: Winston Spencer Churchill: Visions of Glory, 1874-1932*, Bantam, New York, 1984, p. 836.

35 London Sunday Times, June 15, 1969.

36 Protocol of 31 January 1885, Parliamentary Paper, c. 4361, 209; Gavin & Betley, 1973, p. 240, cited in Matthew Craven, "Between law and history: the Berlin Conference of 1884-1885 and the logic of free trade", *The London Review of International Law*, Vol.3, No. 1, 2015, p. 47. See also Siba N'Zatioula Grovogui, *Sovereigns, Quasi Sovereigns, and Africans, Race and Self-Determination in International Law*, University of Minnesota Press, Minneapolis, 1996, p. 80.

to dispose of themselves, argues Siba N'Zatioula Grovogui, that was construed in the twentieth century as "self-determination."[37]

The rise of anti-colonial nationalisms in the WWI period forced a major concession on colonizing powers, one that could threaten colonial rule altogether. Coeval with this development, European colonial settlers in Africa and Asia were also looking for an arrangement that would limit the authority of the colonial mother country while at the same time preserve and expand European colonial-settler privileges. In the case of the European colonists of southern Africa, this began since the middle of the 19th century with some success but was defeated by the British in the Boer Wars. In the case of European Jewish colonists of Palestine, it awaited the end of World War I. The French colonists in Algeria sought independence in the late 19th century but could not achieve it. They staged a coup in 1961 against the French government when they realized it was about to concede independence to the Algerian National Liberation Front.[38]

A new colonial formula was needed to appease anti-colonial nationalist demands for *independence* while prolonging colonial and settler-colonial rule indefinitely. But as self-determination had emerged in the late 1890s as a socialist principle, espoused by Karl Kautsky, but more importantly by Vladimir Lenin as an anti-colonial right par excellence, colonizing countries and the settler-colonists became concerned with its increasing popularity. It was in the context of the Russian Revolution which quickly moved to apply self-determination to the non-Russian subjects of the former Russian Empire, that Woodrow Wilson hijacked this socialist concept and deployed it at the Paris Peace Conference as a right to be granted only to the colonies of the defeated empires of WWI, but certainly *not* to those colonized by the victorious empires.

Lenin agreed with Rosa Luxemburg that nationalism could never bring economic independence nor grant economic agency to the national working class, but unlike Luxemburg, he insisted on the importance of political self-determination against the chauvinism of colonizing peoples, like the Great Russians, and distinguished between the nationalism of "oppressor" and "oppressed" nations, supporting the latter. Wilson's concept of self-determination, unlike Lenin's, was one that granted political agency not only to the colonized in

---

37   Ibid.

38   Alistair Horne, *A Savage War of Peace: Algeria 1954-1962*, Macmillan, London, 1977, p. 436-460.

the defeated empires but also to the colonizers and sought to balance the two equally –"the interests of the populations concerned must have equal weight with the equitable government whose title is to be determined." Here Wilson's explicit aim was to equate the powerful and the powerless (or as Lenin would have it "the oppressor nations" with the "oppressed nations") and seemed to posit self-determination as a mask for the "right of conquest" rather as its undoing.[39] Wilson's support for the Mandate system that was answerable to the new League of Nations, was essentially support for a new institutional cover for imperial conquests.

This assessment was shared across Europe by the victors. The post-WWI territorial rearrangements by the victors relied on the *right of conquest* and not on the right of self-determination, primarily in order to prevent the emergence of a German superstate encompassing all the German-speaking populations of Europe.[40] Thus while the socialist and Leninist pedigree of self-determination was now being coopted for the purpose of an American and European imperial propaganda war, in reality what triumphed after WWI, especially through the League of Nations, was a *right of conquest* through which the territorial spoils of the war would be redistributed.

Like independence, self-determination in the colonial world was also first demanded by white colonial settlers in South Africa following the Boer War. Here, we need to pay special attention to settler-colonies as *a model* that was also extended to non-settler colonies. It was the South African Afrikaner leader Jan Smuts who articulated the colonial principle of self-rule for the white settler colonies in the form of "Dominions" as well as the weaponizing

---

39   In attempting to elevate the importance of Wilson's self-determination and downplay the importance of Lenin's, Erez Manela correctly states that it was the position of the United States, emerging as a world power after WWI, that gave more weight to the Wilsonian principle around the colonized world. His claim however that Lenin's influence would only come later, after the end of the civil war in the emerging Soviet Union and the waning of what he calls the "Wilsonian moment," downplays the colossal impact that the triumph of the Russian Revolution had at the time among the colonized worldwide, not to mention the Russian communists' convening of the Congress of the Peoples of the East in Baku in September 1920 which called for and declared solidarity with anti-colonial struggles. See Manela, The Wilsonian Moment, p. 7, 10. See also Eric D. Weitz's critique of the elision of Lenin's influence in academic literature on the post-WWI usage of self-determination in Weitz, "Self-Determination, How a German Enlightenment Idea Became the Slogan of National Liberation and a Human Right," *American Historical Review*, Vol. 120, No. 2, 2015, p. 485.

40   Jörg Fisch, *The Right of Self-Determination of Peoples-The Domestication of an Illusion,* (trans.) Anita Mage, Cambridge University Publishing, Cambridge, 2015, p.147-159.

of "self-determination" attributed to Woodrow Wilson.[41] The earlier principle of "self-rule" had been in use by European settler-colonists, particularly across the British Empire, but as it did not include the indigenous populations in its purview, it did not acquire the universal appeal that the Wilsonian definition of "self-determination" would after WWI, primarily due to the latter's application to colonists and natives alike and equalizing non-equals in a move to undermine Lenin's definition.

The British Lord Curzon was explicit at a cabinet meeting when he declared in December 1918 that Britain "will play self-determination for whatever it is worth" to maintain colonial gains;[42] or more precisely, to use self-determination as a cover for the right of conquest. Former British governor of Nigeria and British representative to the Permanent Mandates Commission of the League of Nations, Lord Frederick Lugard, adopted this strategy and ran with it. He articulated it in his classic guide to British colonial officials: "the tropics are the heritage of mankind, and neither, on the one hand, has the suzerain Power a right to their exclusive exploitation, nor, on the other hand have the races that inhabit them a right to deny their bounties to those who need them."[43] His method, reminiscent of de Vattel's justifications of colonial conquests, worked well for the non-settler colonies, where he supported "native rulers and their councils" but not representative government.[44] In the settler-colonies, however, as in Kenya and Rhodesia (let alone South Africa and Palestine), the European settlers had a different set of local priorities not directly attached to the mother country.

Rhodesia is most similar to Palestine in that its colonization by white colonial settlers begins in the 1890s, rather than earlier as is the case with South Africa and Algeria or the Americas and Australia, and indeed the colonists acquire a great deal of power in the early 1920s just like the Zionists did, though

---

41 J. C. Smuts, *The League of Nations: A Practical Suggestion*, The Nation Pres, Inc., New York, 1919. On his position on Ireland see Marie Coleman, *The Irish Revolution, 1916-1923*, Routledge, London, 2014, p.48-50.

42 Susan, Pedersen, *The Guardians, The League of Nations and the Crisis of Empire*, Oxford University Press, Oxford, 2015, p.27. British colonial diplomat Mark Sykes of "Sykes-Picot Agreement" fame would express similar sentiments about how the British should rule Mesopotamia. See Joseph Massad, *Islam in Liberalism*, University of Chicago Press, Chicago, 2015, p. 94.

43 Frederick Lugard, *The Dual Mandate in British Tropical Africa*, 5th ed., Archon Books, Hamden, 1965, p. 61.

44 Ibid., 195.

Rhodesia's colonists were the first to become a self-governing colony with their own parliament, army and police, exercising a Wilsonian "self-determination" as early as 1923 through what was called "responsible government."[45] All in all, Lugard's influence, as Susan Pedersen states, "consolidated and legitimated a reaction against 'self-determination.'"[46] This is true, however, if self-determination is understood in its Leninist rather than its reformulated Wilsonian version. If the latter, then Lugard's influence in fact consolidated the imperial definition of what self-determination meant. Thus, self-determination for Europe and the US moved from support for white colonial settlers in the American, African, Asian, and Oceanian colonial settlements to accommodate collaborating and/or co-optable colonized nationalist elites, something that would be put to practice across the globe following World War II, and which became the basis for the Fanonian critique of anti-colonial nationalism.[47]

The hegemonic idea that "self-determination" is some progressive principle that has always had a socialist and/or anti-colonial history which grants the colonized political agency is consequently erroneous, as it ignores how "self-determination" was imperially coopted and transformed from its socialist context early on and continued to be adopted by imperial and colonial-settler powers for the express purpose of maintaining colonial gains, especially in the case of settler-colonies where agency is granted differentially to the colonists at the expense of the colonized. It should be remembered that even Hitler and the Nazis, like Wilson and Lloyd George before them, found the concept of self-determination an excellent mask for the right of conquest which they used to annex territories with German speakers to the Third Reich, most famously Austria and the Sudetenland.[48]

, , ,

While varieties of nationalism as ideology identified language, religion, economy, territory, ethnicity, race, and blood as bases for common identity and difference, the national and the foreigner were defined juridically across colonial nation-states since the inception of laws of nationality in the last quarter of the nineteenth century in relation to two exclusive bonds: blood and soil.

---

45 See Larry W. Bowman, *Politics in Rhodesia, White Power in an African State*, Harvard University Press, Cambridge, 1973.

46 Pedersen, *The Guardians*, p.109.

47 See Frantz Fanon, *The Wretched of the Earth*, Grove Press, New York, 2004.

48 For the Nazi use of self-determination, see Fisch, "The Right", p. 160-172.

The Germans had been the forerunners of *jus sanguinis*, often seen as an essentialist concept, while the French historically opted for *jus soli*, seen as anti-essentialist. Post-colonial states followed suit with laws replicating verbatim those of their colonial masters, often with a combination of *jus soli* and *jus sanguinis*. What colonial-settlers were able to achieve is the conjuring up of this connection for themselves and its severance for the indigenous and colonized under the capacious umbrella of "self-determination." This is as true for Canada's First Nations as it is for Australian Aborigines, South African and Zimbabwean Blacks, United States' Native Americans, and the Palestinians, inter alia.

After WWII, European colonizers and colonists slowly accepted that there was no escape from recognizing that the colonized too were nations and were entitled to self-determination. Such recognition became the colonial mechanism that navigated which blood-and-soil schematization is prioritized over others. The strategy followed across settler-colonies was as follows: recognize *jus soli* and *jus sanguinis* for all European colonial-settlers to ensure their control of all the land they stole and steal but concede that the indigenous are nations in the sense of *jus sanguinis,* which the colonizers and colonists had previously denied; this would grant the indigenous no more than national cultural and identity rights. Simultaneously, the colonizers and the colonists, in keeping with John Locke, de Vattel, Wilson, Lloyd George, and Lugard would insist on denying the indigenous peoples *jus soli*, to keep their lands in the hand of colonial settlers.

This became the operative criterion since the 1960s both in specific cases of the settler-colonies of Algeria, Kenya, and Zimbabwe where the rights of the settlers had to be preserved even after independence, as well as in South Africa and Palestine. But more importantly, it was generalized through the United Nations Declaration of the Rights of Indigenous Peoples issued in 2007, which cemented this understanding. The preamble to UNDRIP states explicitly that "nothing in this Declaration may be used to deny any peoples their right to self-determination, exercised in conformity with international law," which could easily apply to colonial-settlers, as it often has. The Obama administration who voted against UNDRIP in 2007, decided to accept it in 2010 through affirming Article 46, which ensures that UNDRIP does not threaten territories colonized by European colonial settlers.[49] The article stipulates that "Nothing in this Declaration may be interpreted as implying for any State, people, group or person any right to engage in any activity or to perform any act

---

49   See http://www.state.gov/documents/organization/184099.pdf

contrary to the Charter of the United Nations or construed as authorizing or encouraging any action which would dismember or impair, totally or in part, the territorial integrity or political unity of sovereign and independent States." As such, the Declaration has limited the general understanding of self-determination in international law further as one that used to grant the right to *independence* by transforming this right when applied to indigenous populations as one that grants them only the right to "self-government" and political participation within existing states and not outside their sovereignty.[50]

Therein lies the historical and contemporary *form* of the problem of self-determination and its legal and rhetorical links to anti-colonial nationalism and the quest for independence, but most especially to the European settler-colonies. The situation of the Palestinians, where the European Jewish colonial settlers continue to rule, seems to instantiate one form, or perhaps functions as one of its many iterations --think of the Maoris, the Australian Aborigines, the First Nations of Canada, US Native Americans, and Native peoples across Latin America. Yet, another form of the problem would be that of Rhodesia and South Africa. In the case of Rhodesia, upon the imminent defeat of the White colonists, through the Lancaster House Agreement of 1979, which facilitated the "independence" of Zimbabwe, the British government undertook to safeguard all the settlers' colonially acquired land. The Agreement tied the hands of the post-independence government of Zimbabwe from initiating land reform in the country for ten years initially, while the British government (as well as the US government under Jimmy Carter) provided funds to "compensate" white colonists on a "willing seller, willing buyer" basis, ensuring that *jus soli* would be preserved for the white colonists and would continue to be denied to Zimbabwe's native Black population. This situation would end up holding for two decades, until the year 2000 when the government initiated a forced take-over of white-owned farms without compensation. The Western response to this violation of the right of conquest of white settlers was swift. Sanctions were immediately imposed on Zimbabwe by the United States, the United Kingdom, and the European Union.[51]

In the case of South Africa, the moment political self-determination was granted to the majority non-white population in 1994, international economic

---

50   On the new possible innovations of self-determination as a result of UNDRIP, see Helen Quane, "The UN Declaration on the Rights of Indigenous Peoples: New Directions for Self-Determination and Participatoty Rights," *in Allen and Xanthaki, Reflections...,* p. 259-287.

51   See Richard Bourne, *Catastrophe: What Went Wrong in Zimbabwe*, Zed Books, London, 2011, p.160-193.

bodies and instruments took away economic self-determination and limited the new state's sovereign ability to exercise it by insisting that economic decisions related to property remain in the hands of the white colonial-settler population who owns it, the IMF, and the World Bank. Here Lenin's understanding of self-determination as "political" in nature and Luxemburg's understanding that it could never be "economic" come into play, but in a more insidious form, wherein whatever erstwhile pretensions about political and economic sovereignty existed before have now been done away with. In this case, the interplay between *jus soli* and *jus sanguinis* to undo the right to self-determination is camouflaged as an exchange of political rights, which every South African regardless of race now has, for economic ones wherein white South Africans in alliance with (white) international capital possess almost exclusively (not unlike what the Évian Accords achieved in Algeria and the Lancaster House Conferences achieved in Kenya in the early 1960s, the Lancaster House Agreement achieved in Zimbabwe in the late 1970s, or UNDRIP insists on now in the Americas and Oceania). Here self-determination guarantees white colonial settlers' *right of conquest* of the land and its wealth based on a white supremacist *jus sanguinis* at the moment that it equalizes them politically with the non-white natives regarding *jus soli*, while prohibiting the newly equalized Blacks, Indians, and Coloreds from using self-determination as an anti-dote to the landed (and other) wealth acquired through the right of conquest.[52]

What the story of the Palestinians, Black South Africans and Zimbabweans, and indigenous peoples in the Americas and Oceania, clarifies is that self-determination is not only *not the only* route to political and economic "independence," but that it is also the legal and rhetorical strategy and the principle that has blocked it from ever being realized. In short, whereas self-determination led to political independence of some European states after WWI and of the European colonies in Asia and Africa after WWII, in the settler-colonies, and in line with the ideas circulating at the Berlin Conference more than 130 years ago, self-determination has mostly been and continues to be the enemy of the political and economic goals of "independence" from settler-colonial rule. As ruses of settler-colonialism, the principles of independence and self-determination have exclusively served white colonial-settlers who deployed them against the non-white colonized and indigenous peoples of the world, and they continue to do so with impunity.

---

52 On the details of the South African case, see Naomi Klein, *The Shock Doctrine: The Rise of Disaster Capitalism*, Picador, New York, 2008.

References

Al-Rushaydat, Shafiq, *Al-Muqawamah al-Filastiniyyah wa Haqq Taqrir al-Masir (Palestinian Resistance and the Right of Self-Determination)*, Matba'at Awlad Abduh Ahmad, Cairo, 1970.

Anderson, Benedict, *Imagined Communities, Reflections on the Origin and Spread of Nationalism*, Verso, London, 2016.

Anghie, Antony, *Imperialism, Sovereignty, and the Making of International Law*, Cambridge University Press, Cambridge, 2004.

Aptheker, Herbert, *The American Revolution, 1763-1783*, International Publishers, New York, 1960.

Armitage, David, *The Declaration of Independence, A Global History*, Harvard University Press, Cambridge, 2007.

Blackburn, Robin, *The Overthrow of Colonial Slavery, 1776-1848*, Verso, London, 1988.

Bourne, Richard, *Catastrophe: What Went Wrong in Zimbabwe*, Zed Books, 2011, pp.160-193.

Bowman, Larry W., *Politics in Rhodesia, White Power in an African State*, Harvard University Press, Cambridge, 1973.

Brooks, Christopher K., "Controlling the Metaphor: Language and Self-Definition in Revolutionary America," *Clio*, Vol. 25, No. 3, 1996, pp. 233-254.

Christian Recorder, Vol. 2, No. 8, (January 1837), pp. 432, cited by Armitage, The Declaration 95.

Coleman, Marie, *The Irish Revolution, 1916-1923*, Routledge, London, 2014.

Craven, Matthew, "Between law and history: the Berlin Conference of 1884-1885 and the logic of free trade", *The London Review of international Law,* Vol.3 ,No. 1, 2015.

Fanon, Frantz, *The Wretched of the Earth*, Grove Press, New York, 2004.

Fenwick, Charles G., "The Authority of Vattel," *American Political Science Review*, Vol. 7, No. 3 (Aug., 1913), pp.380-406

Fisch, Jörg, "The Right of Self-Determination of Peoples-The Domestication of an Illusion", (trans.) Anita Mage, Cambridge University Publishing, Cambridge, 2015.

Hitchens, Christopher, *Thomas Paine's Rights of Man: A Biography*, Atlantic Books, London, 2006.

Hobbes, Thomas, *Leviathan*, edited by J.C. A. Gaskin, Oxford University Press, Oxford, 1996, Part II, [paragraph 172].

Holton, Woody, "Black Americans in the Revolutionary Era: A Brief History with Documents", Bedford/St. Martin's, Boston, 2009.

Holton, Woody, "The Ohio Indians and the Coming of the American Revolution in Virginia," *The Journal of Southern History*, Vol. 60, No. 3 (Aug., 1994), pp. 453-478.

Horne, Alistair, *A Savage War of Peace: Algeria 1954-1962*, Macmillan, London, 1977, pp. 436-460.

Klein, Naomi, *The Shock Doctrine: The Rise of Disaster Capitalism*, Picador, New York, 2008.

Lucas, Stephen, *The 'Plakkaat van Verlatinge': A Neglected Model for the American Declaration of Independence,"* in Rosemarijn Hoefte, Johanna C. Kardux, and Hans Bak, eds.,

Connecting Cultures: The Netherlands in Five Centuries of TransAtlantic Exchange, Vrije Universiteit University Press, Amsterdam, 1994

Lugard, Frederick, *The Dual Mandate in British Tropical Africa,* 5th ed., Archon Books, Hamden, CT, 1965.

Manchester, William, *The Last Lion: Winston Spencer Churchill: Visions of Glory, 1874-1932,* Bantam, New York, 1984.

Massad, Joseph, "Against Self-Determination," *Humanity: An International Journal of Human Rights, Humanitarianism, and Development,* Vol. 9, No. 2, Summer 2018.

Massad, Joseph, *Islam in Liberalism,* University of Chicago Press, Chicago, 2015.

Montesquieu, Baron de, *The Spirit of the Laws,* translated by Thomas Nugent, Two volumes in one, Hafner Publishing Company, New York, 1949, 150 of volume 1.

Nussbaum, Arthur, *A Concise History of the Law of Nation,* The MacMillan Company, New York, 1947.

Pedersen, Susan, *The Guardians, The League of Nations and the Crisis of Empire,* Oxford University Press, Oxford, 2015.

Pybus, Cassandra, "Jefferson's Faulty Math: The Question of Slave Defections in the American Revolution," *William and Mary Quarterly, Third Series,* Vol. 62, No. 2, April 2005, pp. 243-264.

Quane, "The UN Declaration on the Rights of Indigenous Peoples: New Directions for Self-Determination and Participatoty Rights," in Allen and Xanthaki, Reflections..., pp.259-287.

Schlesinger, Arthur M., *Prelude to Independence, The Newspaper War on Britain, 1764-1776,* Alfred A. Knopf, New York, 1958.

Siba N'Zatioula, *Sovereigns, Quasi Sovereigns, and Africans, Race and Self-Determination in International Law,* University of Minnesota Press, Minneapolis, 1996.

Smuts J.C., *The League of Nations: A Practical Suggestion,* The Nation Pres, New York, 1919.

The Earl of Cromer, *Modern Egypt,* Vol. 2, Macmillan Company, London, 1916.

Vattel, Emer de, *The Law of Nations, or, Principles of the law of nature, applied to the conduct and affairs of nations and sovereigns, with three early essays on the origin and nature of natural law and on luxury,* edited and with an introduction by Bela Kapossy and Richard Whatmore; translated by Thomas Nugent, Liberty Fund, Indianapolis, 2008.

Wallerstein, Immanuel, *The Modern World-System I, Capitalist Agriculture and the Origins of the European World-Economy in the Sixteenth Century,* University of California Press, Berkeley, 2011.

Wallerstein, Immanuel, *The Modern World-System III: The Second Era of Great Expansion of the Capitalist World-Economy, 1730s–1840s,* University of California Press, Berkeley, 2011.

Wolff, Christian, *Jus Gentium: Methodo Scientifica Pertractatum,* translated by Joseph H. Drake, Volume Two, Clarendon Pres, Oxford, 1934.

Zilversmit, Arthur, *The First Emancipation: The Abolition of Slavery in the North,* University of Chicago Press, Chicago, 1967.

Year 1: A Philosophical Recounting in Light of a Common Future

Susan Buck-Morss

Philosophy's Planetary Horizon

Figure 1. Earth from space December 7, 1972[1] (NASA, Apollo 17)

Images of earth from space have challenged philosophical conceptions of our world. Heidegger expressed anxiety that this changed perspective meant that man would no longer be able to confront the essence of his being. This speaks against Heidegger, not the planet, and demonstrates the defectiveness of the essentialist ontology that he championed. We are obliged to accept a diminution of our supremacy. Scientists tell us there are more than 100 billion planets in our galaxy alone. This almost inconceivable number converges with a growing awareness of the fragility of planet earth, caused precisely by those

---

1   https://www.nasa.gov/content/blue-marble-image-of-the-earth-from-apollo-17

industrial and technological advances that have enabled perceptions on a planetary scale. The industrial and technological revolutions that define modernity have led to the profound realization that the very success of modern progress threatens to endanger life itself. No horizon of thought can ignore this reality. It determines the parameters of policy in our time.

Historical progress was the central organizing principle of the twentieth century. Economic growth produced a grid of geographies marking temporal differentiations. Time was a sequential ordering of stages. Certain countries were "advanced." Others were "underdeveloped." The world was divided between two blocs, capitalist and socialist, but both marked historical time in terms of progress in industrialization, mechanization, and modernization. It is the great Cold War irony that these mortal enemies, capable of mutual destruction, accepted the same criteria of material development. Socialist industrialization mimicked Western forms. Stalin saw himself in a battle with time, a need to "race like the wind" to catch up with the West that defined the terms of progress in time. We must ask: What if the Soviet experiment had chosen an ecologically sound approach to forms of development – solar energy and green cities (both proposed by Bolshevik visionary Konstantin Melnikov), decentralized production, alternative infrastructures? What if socialist countries had refused to compete in an arms race that no human collective can survive unscathed?

The advances of modern science are awe-inspiring. But it is a philosophical error to superimpose that progress onto historical time. A fundamental theoretical problem is to understand the relationship between "sciences" of society, economics, and politics that claim to grasp reality in its predictability, and the unpredictability of historical change, in which conscious agency, hence human freedom plays a role. Science deals in laws of repetition. The ancient Greek word for this repetitive time is chronos. In contrast is kairos, unpredictable time, not knowable by science, and this indicates the philosophical task: how can we recognize the unpredictable moments of possibility in the present, signaling an opening for conscious change? What method, what approach, will be adequate to a planetary focus today?[2]

---

2   Susan Buck-Morss, *The Dialectics of Seeing Walter Benjamin and the Arcades Project,* The MIT Press, Cambridge, 1991.

Figure 2. Post-colonial map of the world.[3]

Depictions of space are also documents of time.

Figure 2 is post-colonial map of the world. After the break-up of empires, the boundaries of former colonies were transformed into the borders of exclusionary and sovereign nation-states. These lines are politico-historical impositions creating a world-imaginary that attributes to geographically bounded populations a separate identity in terms of history, culture, and a sovereign right to the land. Figure 3 is the world as seen from space without the divisions of national sovereignties. The significant elements are deserts and mountains, water sheds and river basins, oceans and ice caps. Satellite maps view the natural world as it changes over time, documenting the fact that nature, too, has a history. The Anthropocene names our era of geological time in which nature and history converge. The imaginary frame of the post-colonial map is outmoded. National political frames, national histories and the limitation of ethical responsibility to national borders are inadequate given the interconnectedness of our fates. Nature changes with, and because of human actions.

---

3   https://www.nationalgeographic.com/maps/article/about-maps

Figure 3. World Map.[4]

New knowledge is demanded: oceanology, atmospheric chemistry, species preservation, desertology (eremology), water study, land-change science. These fields of research demand transnational cooperation and trust among scientists, whose first responsibility is accuracy and reliability of their investigations regardless of national or religious differences. They cannot thrive when political boundaries intervene.

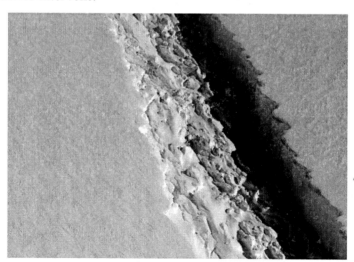

Figure 4. Rift in Larsen B, Antartica, photo by NASA 10 November 2016[5]

4   https://www.natgeomaps.com/re-world-satellite
5   http://earthobservatory.nasa.gov/IOTD/view.php?id=89257

Major chunks of the Antartica Peninsula's Larsen Ice Shelf — which had been stable for more than 10,000 years — disintegrated within days in 1995, and again in 2022.

Figure 5. The container ship *Ever Given* stuck in the Suez Canal in Egypt, viewed from the International Space Station, 27 March 2021.[6]

Dilemma: The problems are planetary. Pandemics, droughts, floods, deforestation, warming temperatures and rising seas - not to speak of radioactive fallout - cross national lines with impunity. And yet nation-states are the stability of political life. Philosophical work is situated in the midst of this dilemma, that exposes the nation-state order as itself unstable, because it cannot provide the most basic security needs.

Globalization as a policy goal reflects the contradictions of the moment by limiting planetary consciousness to material profit and economic gain. Mediated by resource extraction and commodity production, global space becomes a wild zone where the lack of regulation in wealth accumulation intensifies the compulsion to destroy the biosphere, while nation-states strive to gain competitive advantage for themselves (figures 4 and 5). A planetary ethics of environmental justice is demanded, one that respects non-human forms of life. All religions have recognized the need for humans to be the stewards of creation. How is this wisdom to be sustained in a common world? What is the relationship

6   https://eol.jsc.nasa.gov/SearchPhotos/photo.pl?mission=ISS064&roll=E&frame=48480

between the new idea of planetary commons and the old idea of human universality? How do our present geopolitical imaginaries lock us in? What shift in epistemological perspectives will lead toward a planetary consciousness?

Knowledge in the age of the Anthropocene approaches the future by examining the past. Scientists have learned to look backward to gage the future. I am suggesting that philosophers do the same and consider what might be gained philosophically by *facing backwards*, working historically (with one's back to the future) as a way of opening the horizon of our shared time. Consider the marking of global time today as Year 2022, counting forward from an originary Year 1. It is an artificial nomenclature, an *ex post facto* construct not even proposed by Christian institutions until the 10th century. Its subsequent global acceptance is a political marker of Western dominance. The remedy for this imperial act is not the renaming of time. (If, for example, we were to substitute Hijra dating, we could not count the chaotic ignorance of time *before* the Hijra at all.) Rather, it is to move the imaginary of universal history sideways, off-center, focusing on diasporas rather than imperial centers, rejecting present claims to "own" a time or a space as an exclusionary possession, and "tilting the hermeneutic mirror" of historical knowledge until it reflects something other than ourselves.

Figure 6. Temple of Augustus in Ankara.[7]

---

7   https://www.cornucopia.net/guide/listings/sights/haci-bayram-pasha-and-the-temple-of-augustus/

Figure 6 is a monument to history as multiplicity. It is a first-century temple in present-day Ankara, built to worship the first Roman Emperor Augustus Caesar. On its wall is inscribed Augustus' post-humous testimony to his accomplishments, the "Deeds of the God Augustus" (*Res Gestae Divi Augusti*). This Roman imperial document survives only in Ankara, the 20th-century, secular capital of the Turkish nation. The reason we possess any copy at all is the fact that the pagan temple on which it was inscribed was transformed into a Byzantine Church (sixth century CE) and then, in the fifteenth century, into a Muslim Mosque. The history of the temple's survival demands that all of these layers of belonging be included. A focus on the material, historical object demonstrates not only the arbitrariness of exclusionary claims to ownership of the past, but also the necessity of collaboration internationally among scholars if accurate knowledge of our shared past is to be achieved.

There may be no progress in history in the sense that 20th-century philosophers believed. But there is progress in history-writing. Challenging myths of historical uniqueness by working across boundaries of disciplinary specializations and collective identities can provide a philosophical reorientation to knowledge. This is the central methodological contribution of *YEAR 1: A Philosophical Recounting* (2021).[8] Rather than approaching human universality as an abstraction, a least common denominator of humanity, the book insists on historical concreteness that reveals universality as a sharing across borders, and origins as multiplicity. We cannot separate out the strands of our collective past—nor should we try.

The sharing of time across every line of difference suggests a shift in the perspectival axis along which differences are charted and with it, a corresponding shift in the ethical orientation of knowledge production. History need not be treated like a motherless child in need of the protective wisdom of Solomon (سليمان Sulaymān[9]) against those who would cut it into particularized, privatized terrains. Approaching the present as a common temporal matrix, shared by those alive today, suggests that those inhabiting an earlier era belong together in time and therefore not to us. In other words, Christians today do not own a certain slice of Antiquity; secular classicists another, Jews yet a third slice, and Muslims a fourth, all competing with each other to stake out

---

8   Susan Buck-Morss, *Year 1: A Philosophical Recounting*, The MIT Press, Cambridge, 2021.

9   According to the Qur'an (27:18), Solomon could understand the language of animals, even of ants, and especially the song-language of birds.

their claims. The actions and accomplishments of history cannot be appropriated today by any part of humanity as its exclusive and exclusionary possession. Against the pretension that the laws of property make sense in the realm of history, we insist on a common, un-owned, indeed, *communist* inheritance of the past.

Following al-Qaida's attack on the World Trade Center in 2001 and US military retaliation against Afghanistan, a global discourse of the "clash of civilizations" led to multiple projects initiated by UNESCO and other nation-based organizations to foster a "dialogue of civilizations." A decade of attending such conferences (two were in Türkiye) convinced me that I have more in common with academic counterparts met on these travels than with any putative Western civilization. Representing "the West" in such a context is no more possible than philosophizing from a "United States point of view." Knowledge is partial, not partisan. There are no alternative facts, only additional ones. Academics globally share readings and debates, values and concerns, as part of a long-distance intellectual community, that since the 18th-century Enlightenment has been called a Republic of Letters.

This universalizing practice of scholarship is not limited to Western modernity. Ancient libraries in Alexandria and Pergamon [Bergama], and Muslim Houses of Wisdom in Baghdad, Fustat, and Cordoba were inclusive in their assemblages of scholars who came from long distances to share knowledge and learn from others. It was self-understood that philosophers would need to travel in search of wisdom, based on the understanding that no one *ethnos*, no one part of the world held a monopoly of truth. This centuries-old commitment to learning from others has shaped the history of universities. National governments sense with reason that universities, for which autonomy is fundamental, can be a threat to their interests. Boundaries are inimicable to learning, and the independent search for truth is a university's uncompromisable vocation.

Translation is the life-blood of knowledge, and diasporic sensibility is the litmus test of truth. The universally human is reached only through translation, the opening up of languages to each other, as well as diverse epistemological frames. Souleymane Bachir Diagne, a Senegalese, French-speaking Muslim philosopher at Columbia University, writes of linguistic translation: "Philosophy can *only* be universal if it moves across differences." And: "It is distance that constitutes philosophy."   Working independently, the philosopher Agata Bielik-Robson, a Polish Professor of Jewish Studies at the University of Nottingham, concurs: "The only way to reach universality is horizontal, never pretending to abandon the realm of particularity"; philosophy's path leads through translation, "making various languages clash, marry, meet, befriend, mingle with, and confront one another." Indeed, being mono-lingual is a decided disadvantage not only for philosophers, but for any planetary citizen today.

I have been arguing that planetary consciousness is a philosophical matter, requiring a new idea of universality drawn from the particulars of the past, the transient, shared history of humans and nature. Free exchange of knowledge is vital to this shared task, turning competitive principles inside out. The governing ethic of this work is the non-partisan attempt to speak freely and truthfully. It is not a dialogue between, but a conversation among those whose first responsibility is to responsible speech itself. Material support of intellectual projects cannot be accepted with inhibiting strings attached. The privileged freedom of our work demands a deep commitment to democratic inclusion, in pursuit of the public good. A planetary consciousness must exceed national interests. It must eschew subsumption under the profit motive.

I do not speak of the "secular" university in this context, because the ethical demands of our work, as well as the humility it inspires, require recognition of the limits to human knowledge. Plato speaks of a realm of transcendent ideas; Kant's entire philosophy delineates the limits of human reason, and thereby makes room for faith. But sectarian struggles over which faith is the true one is not a philosophical project. Philosophy concerns human multiplicity, not God's singularity. *Philo-sophia* means, literally, love of wisdom, the pursuit of truth with passion, but without secure possession. I am skeptical of Plato's republic where philosophers are kings. Politicians make bad philosophers (and bad theologians), and perhaps philosophers make bad politicians as well. There is an institutional distinction among these tasks. And yet, rarely, the situated practice of individuals has been able to combine all three. Exemplary are: the Persian Muslim philosopher, Ali Shariati, who defied the brutal autocracy of the Shah of Iran and whose teaching inspired a generation of students; the Peruvian Jesuit philosopher Gustavo Gutierrez, who articulated a Theology of Liberation in the name of the landless and the poor; the African-American, Baptist theologian Martin Luther King who, as leader of the civil rights movement in the United States, sacrificed his life in the struggle for social justice. The work of these men achieved universality of meaning precisely through attunement to the historical specificity of their actions. They addressed the potential of the moment with every capacity that they had.

Here is the most radical thing I am saying from a philosophical perspective: Historical concreteness is indispensable to the theory and practice of universality. Concepts kill the life of truth. So much of theory today believes that it becomes deeper by bracketing out the empirics of analysis. Governmentality, bare life, states of exception—these concepts emerged from specific historical analyses, but then were considered philosophically deeper by ridding themselves of their historical baggage so that they could travel unhindered around the globe. This method confuses abstraction with universality. As philosophers, we cannot do without the specificities that historical knowledge provides.

Consider the abstract rendering of positions in political discourse, distributed along a spectrum of Left versus Right. These terms refer to a specific moment of history, the French Revolution, when the party whose delegates to the National Assembly supported the revolution sat on the king's left, and those against it on his right. As those on the left became more extreme, pushing the center to the right, the supporters of monarchy were led with the king to the guillotine. When historical progress becomes equated with the physical elimination of one's opponents, the intolerance of secular politics mirrors that of the religious intolerance it (rightfully) deplored. It might be argued that we need the idea of the Left in order to distinguish the global spread of reactionary movements from those rightfully called progressive. But the distinction already exists if the goal is a planetary consciousness. From a planetary perspective, constituencies of racial purists or ethnic supremacists are, by definition, only possible as a minority. Exclusionary nationalists can mimic each other, but global solidarity cannot survive in nationalist terms.

What about the terms "liberal," "radical," and "conservative"? I might question the philosophical benefit of these distinctions as well. Or, I would say that universality of thought has to have the qualities of all three: liberal in the sense of open and non-exclusionary; radical as a horizon of courage in times of change (Lenin speaks of the need to be "as radical as reality itself"; Raymond Williams says to be truly radical is to make hope possible), but also conservative, because the wisdom that can move us forward requires rescue of past culture from its use by history's victors as an ideological legitimation for their crimes. I do not subscribe to the position that theorists as revolutionary leaders know in advance the right way for people to be led. Rather, our contribution to a planetary consciousness is fulfilled best by paying attention to what human beings themselves are creating when they act together toward a common goal. Let us consider recent examples.

Figure 7. Mass anti-war demonstration Hyde Park, London, February 15, 2003.[10]

In February 15, 2003, as the United States was poised to invade the sovereign nation of Iraq, close to 30 million people appeared in the public squares and streets of nearly 800 cities around the globe to protest against the war (figure 7). The rallies followed the sun, circling the earth: Australia, Asia, Africa, Middle East, Europe, the Americas. This was the first simultaneous, planetary action in the name of humanity at peace. Participants took photos to document the crowds, uploaded and shared them online, as a grass-roots action using new computer technology (several years before smart-phones). As the planet turned, ordinary citizens world-wide saw each other acting in concert, across political boundaries, joining an inclusive, peaceful mass movement, with a cohesion and commonality not seen on the planet before.

The movement was unsuccessful. Within weeks, the US began its bombing of Iraq. The war here, as well as in Afghanistan dragged on with devastating violence against the people and natural environments of these countries. And yet, despite its failure as instrumental politics, the planetary protest was pivotal. The visibility of the globe inhabited by people determined to stand together against mutual slaughter created images in the minds of millions of participants that did not go away.

10   https://www.iwm.org.uk/history/5-photographs-from-the-day-the-world-said-no-to-war

Figure 8. Tahrir Square February 8, 2011.[11]

In 2011 many of the same people returned to the streets, initiating multiple demonstrations that bear the name Arab Spring. In city after city – Tunis, Cairo, Damascus, Bahrain, Sana'a, people flooded into public squares to demand a reckoning from their governments. The mass occupation of Tahrir Square lasted 18 days. Live video coverage was streamed around the world. These regional events converged with others - Athens, Madrid, New York, Tel Aviv. They spread trans-locally in the ensuing years: Santiago, Istanbul, Rio, Bangkok, Maidan, Hong Kong, Moscow, Darfur. No part of the world was excluded. No protest was barred from visibility. No acts of suppression escaped witnessing by others.

The issues that sparked these demonstrations were local, but the global context was shared. When the neo-liberal, capitalist order confronted a worldwide financial collapse in 2008, the private interests of economic elites were given priority. Governments repaid their loans and bailed out the banks, while societies paid. Populations already suffering massive unemployment and economic hardships were forced to accept "austerity measures" that depleted social welfare. These policies revivified the precarious system that had produced the crisis, while leaving its destabilizing structures unchanged. The exception

11   https://tr.wikipedia.org/wiki/2011_Mısır_Devrimi

was China, where autocratic control of banks and local governments avoided chaos and a massive infrastructure program quickened recovery, but a previous move toward democratic reforms was halted, shaping the subsequent movement in Hong Kong as a call for "genuine universal suffrage."

When people come out together in protest, performing acts of solidarity with strangers, they are visible evidence of a society which, according to neo-liberal dogma, does not exist. These non-violent urban occupations practiced a new sociality, turning the privatization of public space inside-out. What was that momentary vision of a transformed society that became apparent to a watching world? People protected others as they prayed. They shared food, music and social care. They self-organized for common tasks. They claimed a democratic voice for rights in the public sphere. These ephemeral enactments of collective life were celebrations of diversity in terms of sex, religion, ethnicity, occupation, and even political belief. Protesters protected public green spaces from development projects. The promise of globalization was deemed as not identical to a shopping mall.

Figure 9. Fasters celebrate *iftar* at an "earth table" on Istiklal Caddesi pedestrian avenue in Istanbul, July 9, 2013. - Muhsin Akgun ("An earth table for equality, justice, freedom and fraternity")[12]

In terms of old-order revolutions, these movements failed, in some cases tragically. Thousands of demonstrators were killed and thousands more imprisoned. Even where governments were pressured to step down, even when

---

12 https://www.al-monitor.com/originals

democratic reforms were enacted, the catastrophic twinning of economic inequalities and political corruption intensified. The spirit of Maidan, like that of Damascus before it, succumbed to civil war. Refugees were forced to flee for safety worldwide.

Still, the transient triumph of the protests was the public performance itself, filling the gaping hole where society should have been. Their script was the enactment of societal democracy, peaceful and inclusive, a celebration of diversity in microcosm, an egalitarian ethics of collective will. In 2019, Chilean women massed in public space to sing together, "Un violador en tu camino" ("A Rapist in your Path") written by the women's collective Las Tesis to protest against the impunity of gender-based violence. Their song echoed on the streets of Paris, San Francisco, Auckland, Oslo, Leipzig, and elsewhere. The ongoing global movements to protest against environmental degradation included the global climate strike of 2019 that involved 150 countries. The examples are multiple. They need to be judged, not in instrumental political terms, but in terms of the change of consciousness that is permeating an entire generation with a new vision of human solidarity, a new way of doing our work and living our lives. Are these movements "socialist"? Yes, but socialism of a new kind. Are they "anarchist"? Only because, for the moment, new structures of rule are not yet possible to establish. Will they be successful? In a sense, by communicating a new political sensibility, they already are.

These trans-local enactments of sociality – let us call them planetary societies in microcosm – have been passed on to us in images that stretch our political imagination beyond the boundaries of nation-states, inaugurating a cosmopolitanism from below (Figures 9-13). The demonstrators communicated through the specificities of their situations precisely to a global audience—anyone, anywhere—in a practice of solidarity and a call for global judging of the rightness of their action. It moves us to change our political understanding of community. Even if the experience of community was fleeting, it mattered.

Figure 10. May 15, Madrid, 2011: "Real democracy now!
We are not merchandise in the hands of politicians and bankers"
(non somos mercancía en manos de politicos y banqueros)[13]

Figure 11. Oct. 28, 2014, pro-democracy protesters.[14]

Pro-democracy protesters spread a yellow banner with the words reading: "I want genuine universal suffrage" at a rally in the occupied areas outside government headquarters in Hong Kong's Admiralty. (Kin Cheung/AP) The

---

13   https://commons.wikimedia.org/wiki/File:Democracia_real_YA_Madrid.jpg
14   https://www.voanews.com/a/hong-kong-marks-one-month-anniversary-of-student-pro-tests/2499296/p1.html

Yellow Umbrella movement of passive resistance for "citizen power" (Gōng mín 公民) culminated in massive government arrests.

Figure 12. Demonstrations to support the right for independent candidates to run for the Duma Assembly: "Power – it's ourselves! Give us the right to a voice," Moscow, Russia 2019[15]

Figure 13. Protests for "freedom, peace and justice," and against military rule, in which women played a major role. Darfur, 2019[16]

15 https://euromaidanpress.com/2019/09/09/protests-in-moscow-its-no-longer-just-a-game/?share=reddit.

16 https://www.jpost.com/International/Sudanese-woman-in-iconic-protest-image-reports-getting-death-threats-586666.

Conclusion

We are not mere onlookers to historical events. The justness of those who struggle against oppression is undeniable. No person should go to prison for signing a letter for peace. No university should be denied autonomy of practice. The US invasion of Iraq and the Russian invasion of Ukraine both deserve our condemnation as violations of international law. The loyalty of a Republic of Letters is to support civil society, civil rights, and civil protections of refugees, insisting that simply being human cannot be considered a criminal act.

The movements that began in 2011 spoke in resonance with each other, and the lessons they taught us were these: Real democracy demands responsibility to the needs of the people. Without the bonds of society, democracy cannot flourish. When politicians collude with global oligarchs, the people suffer. When the profit motive dominates globally, the planet suffers. Accumulation of wealth as the highest goal of individual achievement is not good for people, or for any living thing. And: Consciousness changes. Sometimes faster than we think.

Perceptions of the horizon are ephemeral, moving with time. Collective actions embrace a revolving world. Cosmopolitanism from below suggests a radical idea of community, no longer based on an exclusionary national past but on our co-inhabitation of the planet, here and now.

References

Buck-Morss, Susan, *Dreamworld and Catastrophe: The Passing of Mass Utopia in East and West*, The MIT Press, Cambridge, 2002.

Buck-Morss, Susan, *Günümüzde Devrim (Revolution Today)*, çev. Onur Yıldız, Nika Yayınevi, Ankara, 2021.

Buck-Morss, Susan, *Hegel, Haiti ve Evrensel Tarih*, çev. Erkal Ünal. Metis Yayıncılık. İstanbul, 2012.

Buck-Morss, Susan, *Küresel Bir Karşı Kültür: Eleştirel Teori ve İslamcılık, Küresel Bir Sol Olabilir mi? (Thinking Past Terror: Islamism and Critical Theory on the Left)*, çev. Süreyya Evren, Versus Kitap Yayınları, İstanbul, 2007.

Buck-Morss, Susan, *Rüya Alemi ve Felaket: Doğu'da ve Batı'da Kitlesel Ütopyanın Karışması*, çev. Tuncay Birkan, Metis Yayıncılık, İstanbul, 2004.

Buck-Morss, Susan, *The Dialectics of Seeing Walter Benjamin and the Arcades Project*, The MIT Press, Cambridge, 1991.

Buck-Morss, Susan, *Year 1: A Philosophical Recounting*, The MIT Press, Cambridge, 2021.

https://www.nasa.gov/content/blue-marble-image-of-the-earth-from-apollo-1

https://www.al-monitor.com/originals/2013/07/turkey-gezi-park-protesters-observe-ramadan-iftars.html#ixzz7VM1f16IW

https://www.susanbuckmorss.info/

https://www.iwm.org.uk/history/5-photographs-from-the-day-the-world-said-no-to-war

https://commons.wikimedia.org/wiki/File:Democracia_real_YA_Madrid.jpg.

https://www.nationalgeographic.com/maps/article/about-maps

https://www.voanews.com/a/hong-kong-marks-one-month-anniversary-of-student-protests/2499296/p1.html.

http://earthobservatory.nasa.gov/IOTD/view.php?id=89257

https://tr.wikipedia.org/wiki/2011_Mısır_Devrimi

https://eol.jsc.nasa.gov/SearchPhotos/photo.pl?mission=ISS064&roll=E&frame=48480

https://www.natgeomaps.com/re-world-satellite

https://www.cornucopia.net/guide/listings/sights/haci-bayram-pasha-and-the-temple-of-augustus/

https://www.jpost.com/International/Sudanese-woman-in-iconic-protest-image-reports-getting-death-threats-586666

https://euromaidanpress.com/2019/09/09/protests-in-moscow-its-no-longer-just-a-game/?share=reddit.

Painless Civilization and the Fate of Humanity: A Philosophical Investigation

Masahiro Morioka

Introduction

Painless civilization is a term I coined in my Japanese book of the same title, which was published in 2003. Contemporary civilization aims to provide pleasure and comfort and eliminate pain and suffering as much as possible. This is especially evident in advanced countries. Contemporary civilization is moving toward a painless civilization. However, in a painless civilization, we are deprived of the joy of life, which is considered a fundamental source of meaning in life, and we are led toward the situation of drowning in a sea of pleasure. This is a kind of dystopia, and we cannot find an easy way to escape from it. It is important to pay special attention to this aspect of contemporary civilization when we think about the future of our planet.

The reasons that I came up with the idea of a painless civilization were as follows. The first was an episode in which a patient was in a deep coma in intensive care. A nurse was caring for the patient, who did not feel any pain or suffering, just slept peacefully and comfortably in a clean, temperature-controlled hospital room. The nurse said to me, "In the end, isn't this the form of human existence modern civilization is trying to create?" I was shocked to hear this and began to think that we might be destined to be peaceful, happy, and painless inhabitants of modern cities surrounded by advanced technologies.

The second was the paradox of addictive experiences. When people are absorbed in addictive experiences, such as gambling, alcohol, pornography, and self-injury, many of them have contradictory emotions: on the one hand, they feel strong pleasure, but on the other hand, they have the sense that what they really want to pursue is not that kind of pleasure. Here, pursuing pleasure does not lead to true happiness and fulfillment. However, because they are deeply trapped by addictive and repetitive pleasure, they cannot find an escape from this tragic, vicious cycle.

Third, I was confronted with a philosophical problem concerning pleasure and pain. Looking back on my past experiences, I cannot but feel that pleasure seeking and pain elimination do not necessarily lead to true joy and happiness. Engaging in these pursuits made me lose sight of something very important that is necessary for living a meaningful life. I could not find deep fulfillment in life just by increasing pleasure and decreasing pain. However, strangely enough, many people did not agree with me. They argued that it was a good thing to increase pleasure and decrease pain in almost all situations. I sensed a major philosophical problem here.

The fourth is the problem of the environmental crisis and capitalism. In the 1980s, I studied the ethics of global environmental problems. I read many books that argued that one of the fundamental causes of today's environmental crisis is global capitalism. Some of these books became bestsellers in Japan, driven by the power of capitalism. I was surprised that the books that criticized the movement of global capitalism were printed in large numbers and worked as driving forces for advancing the movement of capitalism itself. I thought something new was happening. I sensed that this was a problem that should be examined from a civilizational perspective.

The Desire of the Body

The book *Painless Civilization* was published in Japanese in 2003 and has been translated into English (Chapters One through Three are available on the internet),[1] Korean (the entire book)[2], and Turkish (Chapter One, under the title of *Acısız Medeniyet*)[3].

A painless civilization is a civilization in which the system of enhancing pleasure and comfort and eliminating pain and suffering extends to every corner of society. Today's society has not reached this stage, but it is certain that contemporary civilization is heading toward a painless civilization. We can see a variety of signs of painless civilization in many cities in advanced countries. It is hard to criticize a painless civilization because an act of criticism

---

1   Masahiro Morioka, "Painless Civilization 1." Tokyo Philosophy Project, 2003, 2021. Downloadable from: https://www.philosophyoflife.org/tpp/painless01.pdf

2   Masahiro Morioka, "The Concept of Painless Civilization and the Philosophy of Biological Evolution: With Reference to Jonas, Freud, and Bataille", *The Review of Life Studies*, Vol.13, 2022, p.16-34. http://www.lifestudies.org/press/rls1304.pdf

3   Masahiro Morioka, "Painless Civilization 2." Tokyo Philosophy Project, 2003, 2023. Downloadable from: https://www.philosophyoflife.org/tpp/painless02.pdf

can be utilized by a painless civilization itself as a tool for further advancing its movement.

In order to better understand what a painless civilization is, let us look at the history of human civilization. A painless civilization is an evolutionary form of self-domestication, a concept proposed by Egon von Eickstedt in the 1930s. Von Eickstedt argued that humans domesticated not only animals but also themselves in the process of forming human civilizations. This means that humans have modified themselves in the same manner as they have modified animals, such as goats and sheep.

The following are the main characteristics of self-domestication, expanded and redefined by me:

a. Humans have placed themselves in an artificial environment.

b. Humans have built a system that can automatically supply food.

c. Technology has enabled humans to overcome natural threats.

d. Humans have learned to manage their reproduction (e.g., family planning and reproductive medicine).

e. Humans have tried to improve their quality of life (e.g., eugenics and recent reproductive technologies).

f. Humans have gradually gained control over death (e.g., elimination of unexpected deaths and death with dignity).

g. The emergence of voluntary subordination (voluntary subordination to a comfortable modern civilization).

We can easily find these phenomena in advanced countries around the world today. A painless civilization is a civilization in which the self-domestication of humans develops to the highest possible degree. Our society is heading toward a painless civilization, and all of us are being forcibly incorporated into the current of painlessness. The four episodes described in the beginning of this paper are examples of self-domestication that are growing in a society moving toward a painless civilization. However, what is the driving force that is moving us toward this development?

I proposed the hypothesis that there is a basic desire inside human beings—the "desire of the body"—and it drove humans to domesticate themselves. The desire of the body has five aspects:

a. Seeking pleasure and avoiding pain.

b. Maintaining the current state of affairs and planning for stability.

c. Expanding and increasing itself if there is an opening.

d. Sacrificing other people.

e. Controlling (human) lives, (biological) life, and nature.

The desire of the body is deeply imprinted into human life. We cannot easily escape from this desire.

A painless civilization is a civilization whose movement is driven by these five aspects of the "desire of the body," which are inscribed in the deepest layer of our existence. Let us examine these aspects one by one.

First, in a painless civilization, we seek pleasure and comfort and avoid pain and suffering. Social systems that support these actions extend into every corner of our society.

Second, in a painless civilization, we maintain the current state of affairs if it is considered beneficial to us, and we seek to protect the stability of this state.

Third, in a painless civilization, we seek to expand our territory and sphere of influence if there is a chance.

Fourth, in a painless civilization, we sometimes seek to benefit by sacrificing others, and we close our eyes to such exploitative actions, and many technologies that help turn our eyes from them have been invented.

Fifth, in a painless civilization, we control our lives' itineraries, the lives and deaths of creatures (including humans), and the natural environment as much as possible. This control is made possible by scientific and social technologies. This is the most important characteristic of a painless civilization.

The five aspects of the "desire of the body" are deeply inscribed in humans. This is because four of the five were created long before the human race appeared on Earth. We must take the history of biological evolution into account when we think about the "desire of the body." Its second characteristic, "maintaining the current state of affairs and planning for stability," was formed when primitive cells, which were the ancestors of all creatures on Earth, appeared four billion years ago. They began maintaining their cell structures by exchanging particles through their membranes. This is called metabolism. The third characteristic, "expanding and increasing itself if there is an opening," was formed when the primitive cells began dividing themselves and proliferating. The fourth characteristic, "sacrificing other people," was formed when unicellular organisms began eating other unicellular organisms on ancient Earth. This is called phagocytosis. (In this context, we should say, "sacrificing other *creatures*"). This behavior was handed down to other multicellular creatures through biological evolution. The first characteristic, "seeking pleasure and avoiding pain," was formed when animals equipped with central nervous systems appeared on Earth. In addition to the above, the fifth characteristic, "controlling (human) lives, (biological) life, and nature," was formed when the human race appeared and created civilizations by making use of controlling technologies.[4]

It is striking that four of the five characteristics of the "desire of the body" were formed before the appearance of the human race. We have four billion years of biological evolution inside our bodies and are heavily bound by it. I believe that this is why the "desire of the body" is so deeply inscribed in us and it is very difficult for us to escape from the movement toward painless civilization.

Technologies in a Painless Civilization

The fifth characteristic of the desire of the body, "controlling (human) lives, (biological) life, and nature," has led to the creation of a network of technologies that seek to control everything in society and society's relationship with the surrounding nature. These technologies function as fundamental driving forces for advancing painless civilization.

Technologies in a painless civilization have at least three important characteristics: a. preventive pain elimination, b. double-controlled structures, and c. pain elimination devices.

The first is "preventive pain elimination." This is a preventive or preemptive action that seeks to eliminate future pain before it actually emerges. In the book *Painless Civilization 1,* I wrote, "This is a system that not only eliminates suffering that already exists but carefully predicts suffering that could arise to threaten us in the future and preventatively eradicates here and now whatever seems likely to be a cause of this future suffering" (p. 30). A good example is cancer screenings; if we find cancer in its early stages, we can remove it quickly. This is a typical act of preventive pain elimination.

---

4   For a detailed discussion of the relationship between the desire of the body and biological evolution, see my 2022 paper "The Concept of Painless Civilization and the Philosophy of Biological Evolution: With Reference to Jonas, Freud, and Bataille".

Another example is selective abortion. Today, we can test amniotic fluids to see whether a fetus has severe disabilities, and if it has, we can abort it under certain conditions. This technology can also be applied to fertilized eggs that are artificially made outside a woman's body. Eggs that have disabilities will simply be discarded. The number of human traits that can be tested is expected to radically increase in the future. A painless civilization is a civilization where these kinds of technologies can be found throughout society.

At first sight, it is unclear what the problem with preventive pain elimination is.

The problem arises when technologies for preventive pain elimination accumulate in society. In such a society, where we are surrounded by a variety of preventive pain elimination technologies, we realize for the first time that we are being deprived of the possibilities of encountering otherness and being reborn, which are very important for living an authentic life.

However, painless civilization is clever. It deceives us by using double-controlled structures. So, what is a double-controlled structure?

A double-controlled structure is a structure that a painless civilization creates in our society. A painless civilization never tries to erase all pain and suffering from our lives. It seeks to eliminate pain and suffering from society as a whole, but at the same time, it intentionally leaves pain and suffering in small corners of our society, and it even positively brings our attention to them. A painless civilization positively leaves room for us to be able to enjoy small amounts of pain and the expectation of risks there.

A good example of this is the human-centered, wise control of the environment that will be found in future nature parks in which we can enjoy the wilderness and the sense of risk of losing our lives in untamed nature, but in reality, we never lose our lives and seldom injure ourselves because the natural environment in the area is wisely controlled as a whole by painless technologies. Because these painless technologies are sophisticatedly hidden within the controlled environment, we do not recognize their existence during the period we are enjoying the natural park.

A nature park that extends to a planet scale is the goal of the environmental protection that a painless civilization seeks to advance. I call this a "double-controlled structure": here and there, we can encounter the uncontrolled violence of nature, but true dangers are almost completely suppressed by technologies.

Inside such a double-controlled structure, we are encouraged to actively enjoy a sense of risk and to experience pain and accidents in nature. At the same time, we are allowed to forget that the whole system is skillfully controlled. This shows that a painless civilization never seeks to eliminate all the pain and suffering we encounter in our daily lives. On the contrary, it makes us concentrate on the non-severe pains, and in exchange, it makes us forget that the whole system is sophisticatedly controlled.

In other words, a double-controlled structure is a structure in which people's freedom to escape from society's control is secured in small parts of society, whereas in society as a whole, such freedom is almost completely controlled. A painless civilization tries to deceive us as much as possible by using pain elimination devices. So, what is a pain elimination device?

A pain elimination device is a device that seeks to eliminate pain and suffering from our lives and make us forget that we are being controlled by a painless civilization's double-controlled structures. Painkillers, alcohol, and narcotics can work as pain elimination devices at the physical level. At the psychological level, psychotherapy and religion can work as pain elimination devices that reduce mental and spiritual pain.

However, the most important devices are 1) mass media, 2) discourses that influence our way of thinking, and 3) entertainment industries, such as TV shows, movies, dramas, and music, that can divert our attention away from the vague anxieties that we sometimes feel in a society moving toward a painless civilization. These entertainment devices circulate various moving stories of love and compassion and argue that although it is true that we live in a society full of pain and suffering, we will finally be able to reach a state of happiness and fulfillment through the power of love and compassion. And finally, we are guided toward the opinion that the basic framework of a painless civilization does not have to be altered and that there is no problem with living there.

What Is Wrong with a Painless Civilization?

Readers may think, "Okay, I understand the essence of painless civilization, but what is wrong with it?" I believe there is a big problem with living in a painless civilization. I would like to shed light on one important aspect and try to clarify its essence.

A painless civilization is a civilization that encourages us to seek pleasure and comfort, eliminate pain and suffering, maintain a current framework
that is beneficial to us, and control our lives so that they can proceed the way
we planned beforehand. What is missing here is the possibility of rebirth after experiencing unpredicted, grave suffering. In our lives, we sometimes encounter unpredicted, grave suffering: we may lose a beloved family member,
we may have severe disabilities from a traffic accident, our business may fail
and leave us without money, or our children may commit a significant crime.

In such cases, we are thrown to the bottom of our lives. We think that our
life is over and that there is no way out. We experience huge pain and scream
in agony. However, sometimes a very strange thing occurs to us—after having
gone through such pain, the psychological framework we have strongly main-
tained is dismantled, and a new framework, or a new view of life that has been
unknown to us, appears in front of us. The place that we considered a hell becomes another good place in which to live. A huge reformation of our worldview occurs to us. We are reborn at the bottom of our life. We feel an unexpected sense of joy.

I have called this kind of unexpected joy that we feel after going through
huge suffering the "joy of life." This "joy of life" is indispensable to being able
to lead an authentic and meaningful life. Because we are not robots that maintain the same framework throughout our lives, this kind of rebirth experience
plays an extremely important role in our lives. Without the "joy of life," many
of us feel suffocated as if we were drowning in a sea of sugar, unable to escape from the framework of a painless civilization.

The central problem of a painless civilization is that it systematically erases
the possibility of this "joy of life" from the lives of the people there.

However, we must pay special attention to the fact that there remains another desire within us that seeks to dismantle the "desire of the body." I have
called this the "desire of life." The "desire of life" is a desire to dismantle our
current framework and see a new world or a new framework that we have not
imagined before. In a society moving toward a painless civilization, we are
faced with a battle in our inner world between the "desire of the body" and
the "desire of life." This battle causes various types of pathology in a painless
civilization, for example, self-injury. However, self-injury is not necessarily an
illness to be healed. Instead, it is a form of hope, because self-injury is an act
of courageous attack of the "desire of life" against the "desire of the body."

What is needed is to guide the energy of the "desire of life" in another direction and to try to find ways of escaping from a painless civilization.

The "desire of life" is a key concept in the theory of painless civilization. True hope is breathing inside the "desire of life." The interesting point is that the "desire of life" is actually a transformation of the "desire of the body." Philosophically speaking, the "desire of life" is a desire that attempts to transcend the realm of the "desire of the body." This is because the "desire of the body" has the desire to expand itself beyond its limits, and this leads to the attempt to transcend the desire of the body's inclination to protect its own framework. Here, the "desire of the body" transforms into another desire, a desire to dismantle the "desire of the body," which I call the "desire of life." The "desire of life" is a desire that strongly supports the possibility of the "joy of life," which is an indispensable element for us to be able to acquire the meaning of life in a society moving toward a painless civilization. In the relationship between the two desires, we can see an interesting dialectic of life. However, the "desire of life" is not an almighty counter-concept to the "desire of the body." We need a more detailed analysis of our desires in contemporary civilization. (I have discussed the dialectic relationship between these two desires in Chapter Five of *Painless Civilization*.)[5]

The power of the "desire of the body" is very strong. The basis of our existence is made of this desire. Therefore, the battle against the "desire of the body" means a battle against oneself. In order to escape from a painless civilization, we have to fight against an intertwined system of preventive pain elimination, double-controlled structures, and pain elimination devices, which are deeply inscribed into current civilization. There is no easy way out.

There is no prescription for dismantling the negative side of a painless civilization. This is because if there were such a prescription, a painless civilization would jump on it, spreading the discourse on the prescription as an attractive commodity throughout society, and by doing so, a painless civilization would try to reduce the power of our act of dismantling. (This is similar to a situation in which, no matter how many books on environmental issues may be published, the actual environmental issues are not solved.) An argument

---

5   The "desire of life" is different from the "joy of life." In this paper, I do not discuss this point much further. Those who have interest are encouraged to read forthcoming translated chapters of Painless Civilization.

alone will not solve the problem of painless civilization. We must be careful lest our arguments be utilized by a painless civilization.

In a society moving toward a painless civilization, it is not those who do not have power or money who need to be aware of the problem of painless civilization. It is those who do have power and money that need such awareness. This is because those who have power and money are more deeply bound by their "desire of the body" than those who do not. They seek pleasure, comfort, painless situations, the maintenance of the current framework, and the maintenance of their preferable lives. These lives look gorgeous, but they have almost lost the possibility of experiencing the "joy of life," which can only be granted when their stable framework is destroyed by encountering the Other or the advent of otherness.

I am frequently asked, "Why do we have to fight against a painless civilization? Isn't it okay to lead a pleasurable and painless life?" My answer is that it might be okay for you to live such a life in the short term, but in the long term, it is likely that our society will become more and more painless, and it will become very hard for us to escape from the situation of "drowning in the sea of sugar." What is needed is to broaden your imagination and think, from the bottom of your heart, what kind of society you would like to live in.

In this sense, the theory of painless civilization is an endeavor to think deeply about ourselves and try to remember what the meaning of life was when we were younger and more sensitive than today. What was the meaning of life when we were younger and less bound by our "desire of the body"? As an adult man who has lived long, I recognize that I have also been heavily bound by my own "desire of the body," and in this regard, my life has had a significant problem. However, I am always saying to myself that I will never turn my eyes away from the fact that I am heavily bound by my "desire of the body."

Of course, it is clear that just blaming myself in this way does not solve any problems arising from the "desire of the body" and painless civilization. The theory of painless civilization is a call for readers from me. I would like you to deeply reconsider your own life in a "civilized" society and think about what sort of life you wish to live, sharing hope with other people in this society. Sometimes I am asked why I am talking about people who are living pleasantly and comfortably, while many people are struggling with painful and miserable lives. Yes, it is true that there are many people who are in great suffering. However, what would these people wish for after escaping from their painful lives? Would they not wish for a life full of comfort, pleasantness, less pain, and stability supported by modern technologies and medicine? This implies that the problem of painless civilization is a problem not only for rich and successful people, but potentially also for poor and suffering people. It is a problem for the entire human race.

Love in a Painless Civilization

One thing that is destined to disappear in a painless civilization is the possibility of unconditional love. To love someone without placing any conditions on them has always been very hard to do, from ancient times to the present. A painless civilization seeks to completely erase the possibility of unconditional love from society. We can see one of the symptoms in today's reproductive medicine.

Let us imagine contemporary reproductive technologies, such as selective abortion and preimplantation genetic diagnosis (PDG). By using these technologies, we can select healthy, non-disabled embryos or fetuses to give birth to. This is a typical example of the previously discussed "preventive pain elimination." Most parents believe that the life of a child with a severe disability is unhappy and that raising such a child is a heavy burden to them. Indeed, almost all parents who discover a severe disability in their fetus choose abortion. As discussed in Section Three, this is a preventive or preemptive action that seeks to eliminate future pain before it actually emerges. A painless civilization is a civilization where various types of "preventive pain elimination," such as this, permeate every corner of society.

This creates a society in which a human being is only allowed to be born when they have met certain conditions that their parents have placed on them. People place conditions on their children, and when these children grow up, they find partners and place conditions on their own offspring. What is systematically lacking in such a society is the possibility of unconditional love: the love of fully accepting someone's existence, no matter how disabled, ugly, undesirable, unfavorable, or burdensome they might be. Such unconditionality constitutes the necessary foundation of human love. However, the love found in a painless civilization is radically different from what we imagine when we hear the word "love."

In *Painless Civilization 2*, I wrote the following:

To be loved is to be given the belief that your existence is affirmed by someone even if you do not meet certain criteria. The belief that my existence, simply being here, right now, in whatever state I may find myself, is being affirmed by someone else. To be given this kind of belief is to be loved.

This future society is one that systematically removes this kind of belief in love from the depths of every human heart. It is a society that minimizes suffering and burdens on the basis of the elimination of the possibility of love. It is a society in which everyone lives their everyday lives, forming human relationships and trying to preserve a stable way of life, while carrying deep within their hearts a vague unease: "It may be that I am not actually loved by anyone." "It may be that I am not actually loved by anyone" is the fundamental feeling that lies submerged at the bottom of this society. (pp. 62–63)

The fundamental sense that people are forced to have in this society, which is deeply embedded in their minds, will be this: "The person existing here right now didn't have to be this 'me.' Anyone else would have done just as well if they'd satisfied the conditions." However, because living in a society that is moving toward a painless civilization is full of pleasure and comfort, people are apt to turn their eyes away from this fundamental problem and deceive themselves.

Love in a painless civilization is a type of love that protects our own pleasant frameworks and seeks to care about someone as long as our "love" does not destroy them. This is conditional love, but people in a painless civilization mistakenly believe that this kind of love is what they actually wish to receive from their partners. Because we are heavily brainwashed by the ways of thinking provided by painless civilization, simply singling out the problem of conditional love and seeking ways to overcome it do not lead to meaningful resolutions. What is needed are attempts to solve the problem of love in connection with the entire problem of the painless civilization, into which all of us are deeply incorporated. The problem of painless civilization lies not only in the infrastructure of society but also in our inner realities and the mindsets that we cling to in our daily lives. In *Painless Civilization 2*, I linked the concept of love to that of the "fundamental sense of security." I wrote, "A fundamental sense of security is a social foundation upon which people can live their lives peacefully and meaningfully. It is something like trust or confidence in the world and a society that supports the existence of human beings" (p.65).

I believe that this concept should be one of the foundations of morality in the age of painless civilization.

The concept of my own death is another important subject in the theory of painless civilization because at a deep layer of our "desire of the body" there is a strong urge to attain immortality in this world or some other world. "I do not want to die" is one of the driving forces that develop a painless civilization. Therefore, overcoming painless civilization is to overcome our desire to live forever in this world, in the next world, or in heaven. This implies that we should seriously reconsider the worldview of religions that say that we will be able to acquire eternal life somewhere outside of this world. In this sense, the criticism of religions may be one of the main subject matters of the theory of painless civilization. The point is not that religions should be negated in our society, but that any religion, Christianity, Islam, Buddhism, or Hinduism, can serve as a painless device to lure us into the realm of painless civilization. I would like religions to think deeply about their possible relationship to a painless civilization in contemporary society. Of course, it is true that religions have the potential to dismantle the movement toward a painless civilization. I would like to discuss this further with readers who are interested in the theory of painless civilization.

Conclusion

There are a number of other topics that should be discussed from the perspective of the theory of painless civilization. The book *Painless Civilization* is currently being translated into English, chapter by chapter, so readers will be able to see the whole picture of my argument in the near future. I hope that you will join our discussion on the future of our civilization and the fate of the human race.

There have been many previous studies on the painlessness of modern civilization. Aldous Huxley's book *Brave New World* (1932)[6] depicts a dystopian world in which people's pleasure and pain are cleverly controlled by advanced scientific technologies. Ernst Jünger's book *On Pain*[7] discusses the philosophical meaning of pain and its relation to modern technology and war. In his book *The Heart of Man: Its Genius for Good and Evil* (1964), Erich Fromm[8]

---

6   Aldous Huxley, *Brave New World*, Vintage Books, 1932.

7   Ernst Jünger, *On Pain (Über den Schmerz)*, Telos Press Publishing, 1934.

8   Erich Fromm, *The Heart of Man: Its Genius for Good and Evil*, Lantern Books, 1964.

discusses the fate of humans in modern society, who are deprived of the energy of life and mesmerized by necrophilia. Karl Marx's *Capital* (*Das Kapital,* 1867) is considered to be one of the first studies to deal with the incessant movement of painless civilization. Japanese philosopher Shozo Fujita's book *Totalitarianism Toward 'Comfort'* (1995)[9] gives an interesting discussion of pleasure, pain, and joy, which was a precursor of my theory of painless civilization. Leon Kass et al.'s book *Beyond Therapy: Biotechnology and the Pursuit of Happiness* (2003)[10] deals with a painless civilization appearing in the medical world. Byung-Chul Han's book *The Palliative Society: Pain Today*[11] which was published after the publication of my *Painless Civilization,* discusses the same subject from a post-modern perspective. Although it was published in 2003, my book *Painless Civilization* remains unfinished. I am now trying to write a long, final chapter (Chapter Nine) in Japanese and complete my argument on painless civilization.

Although there is no easy answer to the problem of painless civilization, we must tackle it from various angles and try to find ways of escaping from the painless stream swirling through society. Recall the five aspects of the desire of the body: seeking pleasure and avoiding pain, maintaining the current state of affairs and planning for stability, expanding and increasing itself if there is an opening, sacrificing other people, and controlling (human) lives, (biological) life, and nature. These five aspects of the "desire of the body," which have been propelling the progress of painless civilization, are all incorporated deep inside each of us living in a society moving toward painlessness.

What I want to stress is that, in order to envision a better future for our civilization, we must seriously reexamine our understanding of the meaning of life and the meaning of having been born. A philosophical re-examination of ourselves is what is truly required now.

---

9   Fujita Shozo, "Totalitarianism Toward 'Comfort*'*, 1995.
10   Leon Kass, Elizabeth H. Blackburn, Rebecca S. Dresser, Daniel W. Foster, Francis Fukuyama, et al., *Beyond Therapy: Biotechnology and the Pursuit of Happiness*, Dana Press, 2003.
11   Byung-Chul Han, "The Palliative Society: Pain Today, (*Palliativgesellschaft: Schmerz heute*)", *Polity*, 2020.

References

Fromm, Erich, *The Heart of Man: Its Genius for Good and Evil*, Lantern Books, 1964.

Fujita, Shozo, *Totalitarianism Toward 'Comfort'*, 1995, (in Japanese).

Han, Byung-Chul, "The Palliative Society: Pain Today (*Palliativgesellschaft: Schmerz heute*)", Polity, 2020.

Huxley, Aldous, *Brave New World,* Vintage Books, 1932.

Jünger, Ernst, *On Pain (Über den Schmerz),* Telos Press Publishing, 1934.

Kass, Leon; Blackburn, Elizabeth H.; Dresser, Rebecca S.; Foster, Daniel W.; Fukuyama, Francis; et al., *Beyond Therapy: Biotechnology and the Pursuit of Happiness,* Dana Press, 2003.

Morioka, Masahiro, *Painless Civilization 1*, Tokyo Philosophy Project, 2003, 2021. Downloadable from: https://www.philosophyoflife.org/tpp/painless01.pdf

Morioka, Masahiro, "The Concept of Painless Civilization and the Philosophy of Biological Evolution: With Reference to Jonas, Freud, and Bataille", *The Review of Life Studies*, Vol.13, 2022, pp. 16-34. http://www.lifestudies.org/press/rls1304.pdf

Morioka, Masahiro, *Painless Civilization 2*, Tokyo Philosophy Project, 2003, 2023. Downloadable from: https://www.philosophyoflife.org/tpp/painless02.pdf

The Fate of Certainty in Times of Growing Uncertainty

John Keane

There seems to be growing agreement among scholars and citizens that our planet and its peoples are passing through an era of grave political uncertainty. Floods and fires, global pestilence, species destruction, unending wars, shrinking US power, talk of the spiritual decadence of the West, disaffection with democracy, and the birth of a new Chinese global empire are among the forces said to be responsible for the rising tides of uncertainty. They are doomsayers' delights. Some pessimists speak of a great leap backwards, a regression towards catastrophe, a rebirth of the disquiet and fear and violent breakdowns that marked the world of the 1920s and 1930s. They are sure not only that we are gripped by VUCA – volatility, uncertainty, complexity, ambiguity, to use the current managerial acronym - but also that the future will bring only threats, rather than new opportunities to live well. Conservative scholars not known for their optimism speak of the 'devastation we have made together'. They suggest that human foolishness and stupidity have joined forces to ensure the irreversibility of current trends. 'It may well be too late to avert a global catastrophe', it is said.[1] 'Unlike the great extra-human threats of the past, earthquakes, tsunamis, volcanoes, asteroid strikes, we have brought this one on ourselves and show every sign of intending to go on doing so.' This style of catastrophist thinking is growing in popularity. Schopenhauer is again fashionable. While there is no agreement about the root causes of the unfolding tragedy, pessimism is the new cool, given wings by the 'if it bleeds, it leads' mentality of breaking news journalism, and by the information-spreading dynamics of networked, communicative abundance. The combined effect is to ensure that a collective sense of doom is enjoying an unprecedented boom. Or so it seems.

How are we to judge the plausibility or veracity of the new pessimism? Is the gloom really without precedent? Things are indeed serious, but dogmatically

---

1   Remarks made by John Dunn in his review of Adam Przeworski, 'Crises of Democracy', (Dunn 2021). Niall Ferguson's *Doom: The Politics of Catastrophe* (Ferguson 2021) provides many examples of past and present tragedies while adding his own hawkish prediction of a coming cold war with China.

pessimistic claims about a new age of hyper-uncertainty come shrouded in doubts. When seen historically, for instance, it is unclear whether, and to what extent, the new uncertainty exceeds or even matches previous periods of calamity. Are the difficulties of our era and fears of an uninhabitable planet comparable in scale and depth to the disasters of the first half of the twentieth century, with its economic crises, a pestilence that killed 5 per cent of the world's population, failed empires, the destruction of parliamentary democracy, totalitarianism and catastrophic global wars that robbed more than 100 million soldiers and civilians of their lives? Or how do the uncertainties of our age compare with the great religious turmoil of the late medieval and early modern period, masterfully analysed by the French historian Jean Delumeau: the guilt and terror of damnation and death whipped up by the Church and compounded by episodes of military violence, famine, disease and widespread end-of-the-world fears of witchcraft and other sinister forces of magic?[2]

We don't really know how to respond straightforwardly to these challenging, unsettling questions. When comparing whole epochs, and contrasting our own difficulties with their misfortunes, classifying and measuring the experience of uncertainty is done with difficulty. Even the definition of uncertainty remains uncertain. That should come as no surprise, for only life unaffected by flows of time can be defined with any certainty. We could even say that uncertainty is a fickle character, a capricious tormenter of human yearnings for certitude, an irritable doubter of certainty and - as several previous important studies of certainty and uncertainty have pointed out – a chronic feature of all human action. A century ago, in his *Psychologie der Weltanschauungen* (1919), the German philosopher Karl Jaspers[3] pointed out that those moments when we are gripped by uncertainty and face basic 'limit situations' can remind us that we are fragile and finite beings for whom dignity, freedom, happiness and meaningful living become truly precious. The sociologist Hartmut Rosa has recently said much the same thing: our sense that life is uncontrollable is a precondition of feeling alive and 'resonating' with the world.[4]

Here there is something of a rule: when times are felt to be out of joint questions about how best to classify and measure the experience of uncertainty flourish. Think of John Dewey's *The Quest For Certainty*. First delivered as the Gifford Lectures at the University of Edinburgh in 1928/29, it acknowledged

---

2   Jean Delumeau, *Sin and Fear: The Emergence of a Western Guilt Culture, 13th-18th Centuries,* Palgrave Macmillan, London, 1990.

3   Karl Jaspers, *Psychologie der Weltanschauungen,* Springer, Berlin, 1919.

4   Hartmut Rosa, *The Uncontrollability of the World*, Polity Press, Cambridge, 2021.

the omnipresence of uncertainty in human affairs and the flawed efforts of previous ('primitive') attempts to 'escape from peril' and eliminate hazards by means of 'supplication, sacrifice, ceremonial rite and magical cult.'[5] Dewey went further. He implicated the whole Western philosophical tradition in the foolish quest for definite knowledge of an ultimate and immutable reality. The search presumed that 'certainty, security can be found only in the fixed and unchanging' and that 'knowledge is the only road to that which is intrinsically stable and certain' backed by the conviction that 'practical activity is an inferior sort of thing.'[6] The consequent split between the quest for contemplative knowledge of antecedent timeless essences and the mundane realm of everyday action is crippling, Dewey reasoned. It limits human progress, which now requires their pragmatic joining so that the search for knowledge supports efforts to live well and to act rightly. Dewey urged philosophy to rid itself of theology and to put its feet firmly on the ground by abandoning disembodied and 'passionless reason' and its 'isolation from contemporary life.'[7] Experimental scientific methods should hereon be our trusted guide to intelligent living protected by a strong measure of certainty. Certain knowledge, he emphasised, isn't a 'photograph' of 'a reality beyond.'[8] It is rather tested in experience by experimental means that are measured against test outcomes and actual experience. Just as astronomers study stars from afar and must interpret their behaviour from generalisable observations, so philosophy and other human sciences can help dispel uncertainties by using experimental scientific methods to garner testable 'reflective knowledge applied to human experience'.

Dewey emphasised that the elimination of uncertainty from human affairs isn't possible, not only because nature is a fickle mixture of regularity and unknown surprises, but also because since 'uncertainty is primarily a practical matter' human action is always risky.[9] Referring to Heisenberg's principle of uncertainty, Dewey proposed that indeterminacy in human affairs is double-edged: it can bring good things, as well as bad, 'evil or…good fortune.'[10] Human action is 'fraught with future peril.'[11] There is no escaping the 'gnawing

---

5   John Dewey, *The Quest for Certainty: A Study of the Relation of Knowledge and Action*, Minton, Balch & Company, New York, 1929, p.3.

6   Ibid, p.51.

7   Ibid, p.35,70.

8   Ibid, p.137-139.

9   Ibid, p.223.

10   Ibid, p.223.

11   Ibid, p.223.

tooth of time' and 'vicissitude and uncertainty.'[12] But it's the experimental method applied to socio-economic and political life that can help us tame the wild horses of uncertainty and bring a 'greater meed [share] of security' to citizens' lives.[13]

The Quest For Certainty's attack on Western metaphysics was formidable. The practical formulations were less so. They suffered vagueness, but elsewhere, during a long life well lived as America's most prominent public intellectual, Dewey made clear his attachments to such political principles as the independence of universities, the public regulation of markets and corporations, life-long education, opposition to bigotry and fanaticism, and affection for power-sharing democracy. But given these commitments, it's worth noting the strangely technocratic or managerialist bias within his political commitment in these lectures to what he variously called 'operational thinking', 'pragmatic instrumentalism' and 'intelligent methods of regulation', 'orderly social reconstruction' and 'adjusting things as means, as resources, to other things as ends'. Dewey was a firm believer in the Progressive vision of good government as policy formulation and implementation based on evidence gathered by expert bureaucracies and other agencies. The role of democratic politics in the book's vision remained unclear. Equally questionable for a similar reason was his early twentieth-century belief in the conquest of nature: 'science advances by adopting the instruments and doings of directed practice, and the knowledge thus gained becomes a means of the development of arts which bring nature still further into actual and potential service of human purposes and valuations.'[14] A century later, the whole human project of manipulating and conquering 'nature' conceived as external to humans is suffering a profound crisis. Growing numbers of scientists and citizens and their representatives have turned their backs on the vandalisation of our planetary biosphere. They are instead embracing principles and methods guided by precautionary sensibilities. Contrary to Dewey, many people are insisting, rightly in my view, that the 'operative intelligence' of scientific-technical reasons is making things worse, compounding the uncertainties of our times. They are saying that humans aren't the measure of all things, and that our universe is not to be regarded as a stockpile of resources to be plundered by humans at will,

12   İbid, p.292-296.
13   İbid, p.307.
14   Ibid, p.85.

for our self-aggrandisement and selfish pleasure. Humility in the face of the new uncertainties - humans as wise shepherds rather than arrogant masters of the biosphere – is now mandatory. So is the re-imagining of democracy as a project of protecting humans and their biomes against the ravages of power exercised arbitrarily.[15]

Everyday Life

A more philosophically radical approach to the subject of certainty and uncertainty is on display in the extraordinary set of 676 aphorisms known as *On Certainty* (*Über Gewissheit*), a classic work penned and typed by Ludwig Wittgenstein during the final 18 months of his life, on the move, from Ithaca to Vienna and Oxford, from mid-1949 to his death at the end of April 1951.[16]

On Certainty is an anthem against the human will to certitude and mastery of the world. To begin with, it reminds us that certainty and uncertainty are intimate, everyday matters. There is an embodied, personal dimension of the experience of not knowing exactly who we are, what our world is and where we and our world are heading. Big talk of global spikes and planetary uncertainty is one thing. Daily living with uncertainty is another. And it is a political matter.

We typically cope with uncertainty by setting it aside and hiding away from it, if we can. There are times and places where it is impossible to do so. Think of recent worst-case settings, for instance the many thousands of Afghan people abandoned at Kabul airport by an empire in retreat; a city (Mariupol) whose remaining people live amidst rubble in fear of starvation and death; or reflect for a moment on the lives of more than two million Beirutis ripped apart by one of the largest non-nuclear explosions ever recorded; or think of the people of Haiti, nearly all of whom are currently suffering the back-to-back lethal effects of earthquakes and aftershocks, battering by tropical depression Grace, landslides, the assassination of President Jovenel Moïse, gang violence, cholera, severe food shortages and child malnutrition. In catastrophe zones of these kinds, uncertainty rules absolutely. People's everyday lives enjoy only one kind of certainty: disarray and death.

---

15 John Keane, *Power and Humility: The Future of Monitory Democracy*, Cambridge University Press, Cambridge and New York, 2018. See also concluding sections of John Keane, *The Shortest History of Democracy,* Black Inc., London, New York and Melbourne, 2022.

16 Ludwig Wittgenstein, *Über Gewissheit/On Certainty,* ed. G.E.M.Anscombe and G.H. von Wright, (trans. Denis Paul and G.E.M.Anscombe), Harper and Row, New York, 1972.

When people are luckier, and circumstances are kinder, Wittgenstein pointed out, they have the luxury of imagining that uncertainty has little or no grip on our daily lives. We hedge ourselves with certainties. We build nests of pre-dictability. We do so by supposing things to be fixed, certain, settled. 'The game of doubting itself presupposes certainty', wrote Wittgenstein.[17] Just as a child 'learns by believing the adult' and suspending doubt, which 'comes *af-ter* belief'[18], so in our daily lives all of us arm ourselves with unshakeable be-liefs and cocoon ourselves within language-shaped practices that we suppose to be indubitable, 'true' and morally 'right'. 'I act with complete certainty', re-marks Wittgenstein. 'But this certainty is my own'.[19]

We doze, pillow talk, spring from our beds the same side every morning. We sit on the toilet; wash our faces, peer in the mirror at our bodies while brushing our teeth. We boil kettles, make tea, drink coffee, kiss goodbye our loved ones, catch buses, walk, mount our bicycles, send text messages, scan breaking news, doom scroll, say good morning, daydream before wielding the word 'absolutely' in our first morning conversations. Certainty is our mantra against lost bearings. But it's not just a stop-gap remedy for confusion and dis-empowerment: contrived certainty is a condition of possibility of our being-in-the-world. It is otherwise known as habit: learned dispositions that function as stabilisers and enablers within everyday life. Habits - what Aristotle called *hexis* and Maurice Merleau-Ponty called *habitude* and Pierre Bourdieu called *habitus* – are not blind anchors that dull the pains of uncertainty by mechan-ically weighing down and constraining our daily actions. Friedrich Nietzsche mused that a life without habits would hellishly require constant 'improvisa-tion', but he also worried that their nourishing effects could become so habit-ual - 'enduring' - that habits turn into 'tyrants'.[20] He had a point. Habits come inside us. They become us. They may in consequence have harmful effects on our propensity to act in the world, as well as damage the lives of others. Bad diet, no exercise, racist talk, masculinist arrogance, domestic violence, and rac-ist talk are disabling habits, and thoroughly political matters; in the fields of everyday life and beyond, they arbitrarily shape who gets how much, when, and how. But habits can be positively enabling. Far from reducing us to lazy

17 Wittgenstein, ibid, p.115.
18 Wittgenstein, ibid, p.160.
19 Wittgenstein, ibid, p.174.
20 Friedrich Nietzsche, *The Gay Science*, (ed. Bernard Williams), (trans. Josefine Nauckhoff), Cambridge University Press", Cambridge, 2001.

slobs or turning us into bigots, habits function as internalised experiences that strengthen our creative ability to navigate life's vicissitudes. They serve as regularities that augment our being: empower us (and other living species), render us fit and such fitness, as Ghassan Hage has noted, enables us to handle the challenges thrown our way by the social milieux in which we dwell and evolve.[21]

The Uncertainties of Certainty

So much for habits. Wittgenstein's thoughts on the contingent and fabricated quality of what counts as certain knowledge are just as important. They have profound implications for the way we scholars of the political think about such matters as the role of universities, empirical research, truth, and the meaning and functional role of expertise in a democracy. Consider, for instance, the way in which Wittgenstein's reflections help us to see the need to abandon the orthodox view that experts are those blessed with incontrovertible truths, as if they are substitutes for priests and shamans, and instead to re-imagine experts as specialists who know from long experience some of the worst mistakes that can be made in their field. Genuine expertise is incredulity towards meta-narratives of truth-as-knowledge. It is opposition to grand illusions of certainty, big lies and bone-headed nonsense. Experts, seen in this new way, operate as contrarians. They are specialists in contrapuntal reasoning. The expert is someone who wisely sets out to avoid mistakes, humbly imploring others not to be foolish in their arrogant ignorance. When they live up to their own standards, experts fling counter-perspectives into the face of established authority. Their contrariness is often said to involve speaking 'truth' to power, but given the philosophical and political difficulties with that arrogant weasel word, wisdom counsels against its use. It is much better to see experts as people who know that they do not fully know. Experts have a strong sense of wonder about the world. They are aware that their judgments always teeter on the brink of error. Their expertise is an unending adventure into the lands of uncertainty. Experts are trained to expect the unexpected, and they are aware of the quantum weirdness of the world.[22]

---

21 Ghassan Hage, "Eavesdropping on Bourdieu's Philosophers", *Thesis Eleven,* Vol. 114, No. 1, 2013.

22 See my remarks on the changing meaning of expertise, and why experts are best considered as experienced practitioners who admit the limits of their own knowledge and warn the powerful to exercise caution, in Keane 2021.

Wittgenstein's emphasis on the contingent and fabricated quality of our think-ing has more general implications. By arguing with and against G.E. Moore, the Cambridge Apostle defender of 'here is one hand, here is another' com-mon sense, Wittgenstein pointed out in his aphorisms that the word certainty (*Gewissheit*) belongs to a family of terms linked to a set of meanings that in-clude determined, reliable, sure (Latin: *certus*: settled, sure), not variable, not to be doubted, established as a 'fact', or (more strongly) as 'truth'. Consoling and comforting they all may be, he wanted to say, but all these words serve to obfuscate the thoroughly contextual and contingent quality of what we take for granted, or what we agree upon.

'Knowledge is in the end based on acknowledgement [*Anerkennung*]'[23], said Wittgenstein. The thought is more daring than Max Weber's earlier ob-servation that 'all our "knowledge" is related to a categorially formed reality' and that even '"causality" is a category of "our" thought.'[24] Wittgenstein's re-mark certainly has continuing relevance for what counts as political science: what we take to be true, factual, evidential, certain and incontrovertible is al-ways and everywhere anchored, positioned and defined within rules-struc-tured 'language games'.

Though he used different words, Wittgenstein in effect revived a now-ob-solete verb from the early sixteenth century with older roots: to certain, which means to make certain, or to certify something as beyond doubt.[25] The point goes beyond Dewey's pragmatism, for according to Wittgenstein all truth claims are assertions made from within the confines of a given language game. What counts as evidence and 'the facts', and all testing, confirmation and dis-confirmation of truth claims based on 'evidence' and 'the facts', takes place within the scaffolding (*Gerüst*) of a language game.[26] 'The reason why the use of the expression "true or false" has something misleading about it', Wittgen-stein noted, 'is that it is like saying "it tallies with the facts or it doesn't", and the very thing that is in question here is what counts as "tallying" [*Überein-stimmung*].[27] In other words: certainty about ourselves and the world derives

23   Wittgenstein, ibid, p.378.
24   Max Weber, *The Methodology of the Social Sciences*, Free Press, Glencoe, Ill, 1949, p.188.
25   The verb is traceable back through Middle English *certeyn, certayne*, borrowed from Anglo-French *certein, certain*, going back to the Latin *certānus*, from *certus* 'indisputable, settled, fixed', which was originally the past participle of *cernere* 'to discern, decide, determine, sift', with roots back to the Greek *krīnein* 'to separate, choose, decide'.
26   Wittgenstein, ibid, p.105.
27   Ibid, p.199.

from our efforts to make things certain, to certify them. Evidence is adduced. Facts are artifacts. Truth is claimed. Certainty is fabricated, and it thus has a time-bounded quality. It follows that 'what men and women consider reasonable alters', said Wittgenstein. 'At certain periods, they find reasonable what at other periods they found unreasonable. And vice versa'. He added: 'When language-games change, then there is a change in concepts, and with the concepts the meanings of words change'.[28]

Over the years, I've tried in various ways to follow this rule, for instance by making a case for the revival and reconstruction of the language of civil society, developing the theory of monitory democracy and deploying the old term despotism to make new sense of the power dynamics, sources of resilience and weaknesses of phantom democratic regimes such as Russia, China, Hungary, Türkiye, and Vietnam. My efforts to bring together history and democracy and to underscore the punk quality of democracy - its defiance of fixed ways of living and refusal of all forms of top-down power masquerading as 'normal' or 'natural' - are similarly wedded to Wittgenstein's insight that things are never forever, and that uncertainty, the twin of certainty, can't be banished from human affairs.[29] Amidst the present-day doom and gloom, Wittgenstein's wisdom exudes a fresh pertinence. For it turns out (pace Benjamin Franklin) that not even taxes and death are certain. Nothing is certain but the uncertainty of the unforeseen and the unexpected. This may be cold comfort. Uncertainty can be ruthlessly cruel; misfortunes greater than anybody expected regularly happen. Yet uncertainty is capable of kindness; and, as Chinese people like to say, bad outcomes can be blessings in disguise (*sài wēng shī mǎ yān zhī fēi fú*). In either case, or anywhere in between these extreme opposites, uncertainty keeps its cards close to its chest. There are even times, as José Saramago reminded us in his wonderfully satirical account of a dictator felled by a collapsing deckchair while relaxing at his summer house, when small moments produce great surprises of historic significance. Saramago's allegory referred to the bizarre fate of Portugal's António de Oliveira Salazar, who after suffering a cerebral haemorrhage caused by an accidental fall was removed from the office of prime minister by the president of Portugal, but then lived on for another twenty-three months, unexpectedly recovered

---

28 Wittgenstein, ibid, p.65;256.
29 John Keane, *The New Despotism,* Mass., London and Cambridge, 2020; and "Why History Matters for Democracy", *Democratic Theory,* Vol. 6, No. 2 (December 2019), p. 96-110.

his mental powers and, with the help of his obliging staff, carried on supposing that he was still at the helm of his country, until death (in July 1970) finally put an end to his illusion.[30] That's why, in opposition to human snobbery and swagger, Wittgenstein appealed for greater humility about what we claim to know, or what we think we're capable of knowing. He asked us to imagine language games in which an understanding of 'knowledge' and even the word 'know' are entirely absent[31]. And he urged believers in hard evidence, facts and truth to think twice, to acknowledge the contingency of their beliefs. 'Suppose it were forbidden to say "I know"', he wrote. Imagine we were 'only allowed to say "I believe I know"?'[32].

Pessimism

On Certainty may be read today as a timely assault on all forms of human intellectual vanity. It's a warning against literal mindedness and cock-sure claims based on claimed 'evidence', 'facts' and 'objective reality'. But here we encounter a corollary that was not spelled out by Wittgenstein: gloomy convictions that we are living in a doomed age headed for hell are the conjoined twin of know-all certainty. Pessimism is optimism turned upside down. Part of the appeal of gloomy catastrophism is its cock-sure seductiveness. Its propositions and judgments appear to be in accordance with 'the facts'. But as we've seen, to repeat Wittgenstein, what counts as 'facts' or 'reality' is always controversial. That's why the form, content and genealogy of dogmatically pessimistic perspectives must be of interest to those who study the political.

Here we encounter a paradox. We can say that catastrophism is a type of certainty that sets out to crush and destroy uncertainty. It knows that everything is shit. It's sure that unless everything somehow changes things are bound to become shittier. Albert Hirschman called it 'fracasomania', the manic obsession with failure and decline, and his objection to its grip on our thinking about the political was that it had no room for ingenuity, amelioration, problem solving and policy adaptation to evolving conditions. His rejection of catastrophism was pragmatic. 'Possibilism' was his mantra. He once said that the core aim of his work was to 'broaden the limits of what is or is considered possible, even at the expense of reducing our ability, real or imagined, to discern

---

30   José Saramago, *The Lives of Things,* Verso, London and New York, 2013, p.96-110.
31   Wittgenstein, ibid, p.443;562.
32   Ibid, p.366.

the probable'[33]. For Hirschman, determinism of every kind must be challenged. The social sciences have to pay attention to the fluidity and open-endedness of the fields of power they investigate. Researchers must embrace methods that steel their sense of uncertainty. They must cast doubt on arrogant truth claims, question big-picture stories, probe the uniqueness of situations and concentrate on unexpected dynamics. Their brief is to look for countervailing trends, signs of improvement and unintended consequences. They must ask counterfactual questions about how things might have been and whether new ways of turning historical corners are possible. Social scientists ought never make the mistake of supposing that the growing pains of change are equivalent to the collapse of entire social systems.

Hirschman's rejection of pessimism was a social science version of Oscar Wilde's well-known remark that a pessimist is somebody who complains about the noise when opportunity knocks. He was right to say that our political imaginations are damaged when we are lured towards the sirens of either nothing-can-be-done fatalism or total change. But more needs to be said about the metaphysical ingredients of the catastrophism he rejected. Just as early modern geological theories of how our planet has been shaped periodically by sudden devastating events (mountain chain upheavals, vast floods, and the extinction of species) were sometimes inspired by Old Testament accounts of the great flood ordered by God, the mentality of today's catastrophism usually comes tainted by metaphysics. The key point in need of further research is that catastrophe thinking enjoys no innocence or 'objectivity': not only is catastrophism typically attached to a form of dogmatic belief in certainty, but its dogmatism often draws on deeper, older, often-forgotten metaphysical presumptions. Eschatology is its guide. Think of the way Christian notions of baptism as purification were anchored in a catastrophe fable: a grand flood (40 days long according to Genesis 7:17, or 150 days according to Genesis 7:24) that ended when lucky Noah, raised to new life and salvation after waters had buried the old world, set free a raven which 'went to and fro until the waters were dried up'. Now consider a contemporary version of this catastrophe fable evident in the writings and speeches of Rupert Read, a prominent spokesperson of Extinction Rebellion. 'It is beyond reasonable doubt', he says, 'that we are at present driving ourselves toward a cliff, maybe one with a fatally larger drop below it than our best current science suggests.' Our

33   Albert O. Hirschman, *Desarrollo y América Latina. Obstinación por la Esperanza*, Fondo de Cultura Economica, México, 1973, p.36.

'industrial-growthist civilisation...is going down...one way or another, *this* civilisation is finished.'[34] The apocalyptic formulations on the fate of capitalism peddled by German political sociologist Wolfgang Streeck are another recent example of a style of dogmatic thinking with theological affinities. Certain that we have already passed through the gates of purgatory, sure that we are now living through times tottering on the edge of hell or paradise, Streeck urges us to admit that 'capitalism is facing its *Götterdämmerung* [catastrophic collapse marked by disorder and violence].'[35] It's not socialism or barbarism – Rosa Luxemburg's famous formulation in her 1915 prison pamphlet *The Crisis in German Social Democracy* – but we're now facing the unopposed self-destruction of capitalism, whose 'master technicians have no clue today how to make the system whole again.[36] 'In our time, democracy doesn't stand a chance. Declining growth rates and rising household and state indebtedness and widening income and wealth gaps are now pushing capitalism to the brink. Uncertainty and decadence are mushrooming. We're in for a painful extended period of cumulative decay, quite probably on a scale comparable to the global breakdown of the 1920s and 1930s, or worse. Capitalism is on its way to hell, he says in *How Will Capitalism End?*, but 'it will for the foreseeable future hang in limbo, dead or about to die from an overdose of itself but still very much around, as nobody will have the power to move its decaying body out of the way.'[37]

Lurking inside these lines is a kind of sublimated Calvinism, a this-worldly faith in predestination: the disposition of an intellectual blessed with certain knowledge that our world is corrupted and condemned to downfall, and certain in this dark hour of the sure pathway to salvation - ridding the world of capitalism - even if for the moment we are forced to await the apocalypse. The point here is not that Read and Streeck are religious figures dressed in secular clothing. It is to note the homologies between their eschatological mode of political thinking and apocalyptic religiosity, their dogmatic conviction that in these turbulent times of mounting uncertainty what is needed is a great purification – total solutions that miraculously rescue humanity from its fatal ignorance and stupidity.

---

34 Rupert Read and Samuel Alexander, *This Civilisation is Finished: Conversations on the end of Empire – and what lies beyond,* Simplicity Institute, Melbourne, 2019, p.45-, 7-8.
35 Wolfgang Streeck, "How Will Capitalism End?", *New Left Review 87,* (May-June), 2014, p. 46.
36 Ibid.
37 Streeck, Ibid, p. 36.

Democracy

Albert Hirschman liked to point out that pessimistic disregard of complexity and uncertainty are antithetical to the spirit and substance of democracy, and so I would like to round out this essay with some thoughts about the rather tricky relationship between certainty, uncertainty and democracy.

All regimes, including the new despotisms of our day, try to handle uncertainty by hiding it away. Tyrannies of the past imposed certainty through tough public order measures that had the unintended effect of triggering disquiet and fear among their subjects and, as Lucian's famous tract on the Sicilian tyrant Phalaris reminds us[38], endless sleepless nights for their rulers gripped by fears of plots, assassinations and popular rebellions. Early modern European monarchies handled uncertainty quite differently. They were a form of government guided by God-given rules that explained why superior blood lineage entitled a few to rule, how crowns were to be passed on, and why loyal subjects were obliged to cope in peace with their daily uncertainties.

Measured in terms of certainty and uncertainty, democracy is a different, and unique form of political rule. Considered as a type of self-government of people who treat each other as equals, it is the only political form that publicly admits of uncertainty as well as enables people to deal constructively with its potentially damaging effects. We owe to the Polish-American political scientist Adam Przeworski the insight that democracies are systems of 'ruled open-endedness, or organized uncertainty.'[39] But uncertainty is not only or principally the effect of elections, as he thought. Under the post-1945 conditions of monitory democracy, uncertainty is the combined effect of periodic elections and the continuous public scrutiny of power by watchdog institutions and social media platforms that together breed unpredictability in matters of deciding who gets how much, when and how. Democracy is good at whipping up political uncertainties. It has a *sauvage* (wild) quality, as the French thinker Claude Lefort liked to say. It tears up certainties, transgresses boundaries and isn't easily tamed. Democracy denatures power. There's a French proverb that runs *rien n'est sûr que la chose incertaine* (Nothing's certain but uncertainty). This

38 Lucian, "*Phalaris' in Phalaris, Hippias or The Bath and other works*", *Loeb Classical Library 14,* Vol. 1, Harvard University Press, Cambridge, 1913.

39 Compare his 'Some Problems in the Study of the Transition to Democracy': 'The process of establishing a democracy is a process of institutionalizing uncertainty, of subjecting all interests to uncertainty' (Przeworski 1979: 14). The theme of democracy and uncertainty is applied in Jan-Werner Müller, *Democracy Rules* (Müller 2021).

could easily be a motto for monitory democracy. The value placed by democracy on public openness, institutional pluralism and continuous public scrutiny of arbitrary power enables individuals, groups and whole organizations to question and overturn the supposedly 'natural' order of things. With the help of bodies such as anti-corruption agencies, investigative journalism, independent courts and periodic elections, monitory democracy promotes indeterminacy. It heightens people's awareness that the way things are now isn't necessarily how they will be in future. The spirit of monitory democracy challenges people to see that their worlds can be changed. Sometimes it sparks revolution.

But there's an emotionally deeper, less obvious connection between democracy and uncertainty. Inasmuch as democracy regularly demonstrates the fallibility of those who exercise power, it tutors citizens' everyday sense of the malleability of the world. When it works well, monitory democracy casts public doubts on what Wittgenstein called 'complete conviction, the total absence of doubt'.[40] We could say that it helps trigger a long-term mood swing, a transformation of people's perceptions of the world. The metaphysical idea of an objective, out-there-at-a-distance 'reality' is weakened; so too is the presumption that stubborn 'factual truth' is superior to power. The fabled distinction between what people can see with their eyes and what they are told about the emperor's clothes breaks down. Especially under media-saturated conditions, when vibrant democracies are marked by dynamism, pluralism and a multiverse of competing stories told about how the world works, 'information' ceases to be a fixed category with incontrovertible content. What counts as information is less and less understood by citizens and their representatives as 'brute facts'[41], or as chunks of unassailable 'reality'. Talk of 'truth' lingers, but the sense that it has variable and contestable meanings gets the upper hand. Zones of verification featuring different criteria of what counts as truth multiply. The quest for truth in courts of law isn't the same, say, as what is said about truth in mosques, churches and synagogues, or what counts as 'fact' and 'knowledge' in the field of quantum physics.[42] The upshot is that what is called 'reality', including the 'reality' peddled and promoted by the powerful, comes to be understood as always 'reported reality', as 'reality' produced by some for others, in other words, as mediated veracity claims that are shaped and reshaped and re-shaped again in complex processes of production and transmission

---

40   Wittgenstein, ibid, p.194.
41   John R. Searle, *The Social Construction of Reality*, Free Press, New York, 1997.
42   Bruno Latour, *An Inquiry into Modes of Existence: An Anthropology of the Moderns*, trans. Catherine Porter, Harvard University Press, Cambridge, 2013.

of truth claims. Reality is robbed of its reality, which is why political efforts by leaders to privilege their own certainties and to seduce and manipulate citizens using smoke and mirrors, lying and bombast, are deemed unwelcome, and dangerous. Democracy serves reminders that 'truth' rests upon acknowledgment, and that 'truth' has many faces. It nudges citizens into thinking for themselves; to see the same world in different ways, from different angles; and to sharpen their overall sense that prevailing power relationships are not 'natural', but contingent. Reality is multiple and mutable, a matter of re-description and interpretation - and of the power marshalled by wise citizens and their representatives to prevent one-sided interpretations of the world from being forced down others' throats.

Precautions

It is customary to say that resilient democracies provide citizens with secure lifeboats in seas of uncertainty: protective mechanisms such as written constitutions and rule of law procedures; fixed-term elections and election monitoring; integrity watchdogs; bridge doctors (a South Korean invention) and other health and safety bodies; future generations commissions; and public enquiries. By means of these and other institutions, it is said, democracy affords citizens and their representatives a measure of reassurance that power will not be exercised arbitrarily, in ways abusive and offensive to citizens. They feel safer, more secure. But here there's a less obvious and more pressing sense in which democracies engage and reduce uncertainty. When reimagined in terms of precaution, monitory democracy, the most power-sensitive form of self-government in the history of democracy, is the best weapon so far invented for guarding against the illusions of certainty by breaking up monopolies of unaccountable and dangerous power, wherever and however they operate. Democracy protects people against those who deny their own ignorance. Amidst the 'noise' of public life, as Daniel Kahneman and his co-authors have noted, decisionmakers *who believe themselves capable of an impossibly high level of predictive accuracy are not just overconfident. They don't merely deny the risk of noise and bias in their judgments. Nor do they simply deem themselves superior to other mortals. They also believe in the predictability of events that are in fact unpredictable, implicitly denying the reality of uncertainty.*[43]

---

43   Daniel Kahneman, et. al., *Noise: A Flaw in Human Judgment,* Little Brown Spark, New York, Boston, London, 2021, p.145.

Gripped by a strong sense of reality as fluid and alterable, democracy is thus a fair-minded defender of caution, a prudent friend of perplexity when in the company of those who exercise power with cocksure certainty. Nothing about human behaviour comes as a surprise: it sees that humans are capable of the best, and perpetrators of the worst. For that reason, democracy stands against every form of hubris. It considers concentrated power blindly hazardous; it reckons that humans are not to be entrusted with unchecked rule over their fellows, or the biomes in which they dwell. It upends the old complaint that democracy resembles a ship of fools, or a rollicking circus run by monkeys. A great threat to democracy is rulers who are blind fools.

When it works well, democracy stands against stupidity and dissembling; it is opposed to silent arrogance and has no truck with bossing, bullying and violence. Its role as an early warning system – spotting and countering the sources of destructive uncertainty, like reckless submarine purchases and military adventures, wanton destruction of species, market failures, including risky and fool-headed efforts to monetise uncertainty using such financial instruments as derivative securities, indemnities and catastrophe bonds - makes it attuned to conundrums and alive to difficulties. When democratic mechanisms function properly, they warn citizens and their representatives about the possible dangers of unknown consequences of consequences of consequences. In this way, by getting serious about the calamities of our times, and by tracking the possible calamities to come, democracy is the harbinger of certainty. It offers reassurance and comfort to the afflicted lives of citizens.

Pathologies

Speaking of calamities: the general proposition that democracy is a form of government that handles uncertainty with aplomb needs to be handled with care. The key reason is to be found buried within the aphorisms of *On Certainty*, where Wittgenstein remarks that the 'groundlessness [*Grundlosigkeit*] of our believing'[44] poses a great difficulty for our era, especially for anybody clinging dogmatically to rigid habits or simple-minded, commonsense beliefs in fact-based Truth. Rephrased in more nuanced terms that go well beyond his limited political horizons, we could say that one of the special challenges faced by democracy when it works well is the way it forces citizens to cope with a double challenge: to live their lives with a tolerable measure of certainty while at the same time admitting that their different beliefs and various ways

---

44 Wittgenstein, ibid, p.166.

of being-in-the-world have no absolute foundations - that they are 'groundless' and, hence, susceptible to change and haunted by grinding uncertainty.

Wittgenstein seemed to think that once a sense of doubt and contingency grip people's lives, uncertainty would irreversibly trump certainty. Perhaps *On Certainty* was right: it may be that all the king's horses and all the king's men are unlikely to reverse the fallibilist trend, the long goodbye to absolute certainty. Present-day dynamics suggest we should be less certain.

Democracy can live without dogmatic Truths and other absolute certainties, but it requires *wise citizens* and *wise representatives*: experienced and humble people who know they don't know everything, and who therefore are suspicious of those who think they do, especially when they try to use alibis to camouflage or enforce their arrogant will to power on others. But historians of democracy teach us that there have been many times in the past when the political form known as democracy destroys wisdom in this sense. When things go well, democracy provides spaces and mechanisms for people to articulate with some certainty their own insecurities. When things go badly, democracy does the opposite: it produces feelings of uncertainty that grip millions of people, sometimes with pathological effects.

Pressured by outside forces and internal dynamics, democracies can stumble, paralyse their own workings, drown in surpluses of uncertainty. They can nurture feelings that there's too much confusion, too little relief, too much talk and too little being done by leaders and governments. All regimes can suffer that fate, of course but, as Max Scheler long ago pointed out, democracy is peculiarly vulnerable to violations of its professed commitment to the principles of equality.[45] Whether measured by actual social conditions or considered as an ethical postulate, the ethos of equality is the carrier of *ressentiment*. Easily disappointed, perceived violations of equality breed fears of being marginalised, feelings of anger, indignation and envy, sour grapes yearnings for revenge against those who are more fortunate and more privileged.

The case of contemporary India shows that if *ressentiment* takes root in a democracy, demagoguery comes into season.[46] When famished children cry themselves to sleep at night, when millions of women feel unsafe and multitudes of migrant workers living on slave wages are forced to flee for their lives in a medical emergency, the victims are unlikely to believe themselves worthy

---

45 Max Scheler, *Ressentiment,* Schocken Books, New York, 1972, p.143-144.
46 Debasish Roy Chowdhury and John Keane, *To Kill a Democracy: India's Passage to Despotism*, Oxford University Press, Oxford, New York and Delhi, 2021.

of rights, or capable as citizens of fighting for their own entitlements, or for the rights of others. Large-scale social suffering renders the democratic principle utterly utopian. Or it turns into a grotesque farce. No doubt, citizens' ability to strike back, to deliver millions of mutinies against the rich and powerful, is in principle never to be underestimated in a democracy. But the brute fact is that social indignity undermines citizens' capacity to take an active interest in public affairs, and to check and humble and wallop the powerful.

But the scandal doesn't end there. For when millions of citizens are daily victimised by social indignities, the powerful are granted a licence to rule arbitrarily. Millions of humiliated people become sitting targets. Some at the bottom and many in the middle and upper classes turn their backs on public affairs. They bellyache in unison against politicians and politics. But the disaffected may do nothing. Complacency and cynical indifference breed voluntary servitude. But there is another possibility: amidst the deepening uncertainties, the disgruntled begin to yearn for political redeemers and steel-fisted government. Fantasists sure of their ground and power mongers armed with their Big Truth grow bold. The powerless and the privileged join hands to wish for messiahs - Yogi Adityanath, Mamata Banerjee, K. Chandrashekhar Rao (KCR), Narendra Modi - who promise to defend the poor, protect the rich, drive out the demons of corruption and disorder, and purify the soul of 'the people'. These loud-mouthed leaders who 'talk rather more about certain things than the rest of us' (the words of Wittgenstein[47]) boast of their power to put an end to uncertainty.

Citizens brimming with ressentiment begin to pay attention. The old seventeenth-century proverb then applies: 'He that leaves *certainty* and sticks to chance, when fools pipe he may dance.'[48] That is the moment when despots make their appearance and offer their poisonous gifts to the confused, the perplexed sufferers of unbearable uncertainty.

In these times of global pestilence and mounting anxieties about cascading disasters, might the moment of popular submission to big-mouthed demagogues and strong-armed despots promising redemption to 'the people' once again be heading our way?

---

47   Wittgenstein, ibid, p.338.

48   John Ray, "A collection of English proverbs digested into a convenient method for the speedy finding any one upon occasion: with short annotations: whereunto are added local proverbs with their explications, old proverbial rhythms, less known or exotic proverbial sentences, and Scottish proverbs", John Hayes, Cambridge, 1678.

References

Delumeau, Jean (1990), *Sin and Fear: The Emergence of a Western Guilt Culture, 13th-18th Centuries*, London: Palgrave Macmillan.

Dewey, John (1929), *The Quest for Certainty: A Study of the Relation of Knowledge and Action*, New York: Minton, Balch & Company. Available online at https://archive.org/details/questforcertaint032529mbp/page/n7/mode/2up (last accessed 30 October 2021)

Dunn, John (2021), Review of Adam Przeworski, *Crises of Democracy*, *Society* 58, pp.153-155.

Ferguson, Niall (2021), *Doom: The Politics of Catastrophe*, London: Penguin.

Hage, Ghassan (2013), 'Eavesdropping on Bourdieu's Philosophers,' *Thesis Eleven*, 114: 1, 76-93.

Hirschman, Albert O. (1973 [1971]), *Desarrollo y América Latina. Obstinación por la Esperanza*, México: Fondo de Cultura Economica.

Jaspers, Karl (1919). *Psychologie der Weltanschauungen*, Berlin: Springer.

Kahneman, Daniel et. al. (2021), *Noise: A Flaw in Human Judgment,* New York, Boston, London: Little Brown Spark.

Keane, John (2018), *Power and Humility: The Future of Monitory Democracy*, Cambridge and New York: Cambridge University Press.

------------------(2019), 'Why History Matters for Democracy', *Democratic Theory*, 6: 2 pp. 96-110.

------------------(2020), *The New Despotism* (London and Cambridge, Mass.Harvard University Press:

------------------(2021) ,'Breve historia del conocimiento expert, y su creciente importancia para la democracia', **Institución Libre de Enseñanza** (ILE), Madrid (10 March 2021), at: https://www.johnkeane.net/a-brief-history-of-expertise-and-its-growing-importance-for-democracy-fundacion-giner-madrid/ (last accessed 17 July 2022)

------------------(2022), *The Shortest History of Democracy* (London, New York and Melbourne: Black Inc.

Latour, Bruno (2013 [2012]), An Inquiry into Modes of Existence: An Anthropology of the Moderns, trans. Catherine Porter, Cambridge, Mass.: Harvard University Press, 2013.

Lucian (1913), 'Phalaris' in *Phalaris, Hippias or The Bath and other* works, Cambridge, Mass.: Harvard University Press, Loeb Classical Library 14, Lucian, Volume 1.

Müller, Jan-Werner (2021), *Democracy Rules*, New York and London: Allen Lane.

Nietzsche, Friedrich (2001), The Gay Science ed. Bernard Williams, trans. Josefine Nauckhoff, Cambridge: Cambridge University Press.

Przeworski, Adam (1979), 'Some Problems in the Study of the Transition to Democracy,' Working Paper 61, Washington, D.C.: Latin American Program of the Woodrow Wilson International Center for Scholars, Smithsonian Institution.

----------------------(1991), *Democracy and the Market, Political Economic Reforms in Eastern Europe and Latin America*, Cambridge, UK: Cambridge University Press.

Ray, John (1678), *A collection of English proverbs digested into a convenient method for the speedy finding any one upon occasion: with short annotations: whereunto are added local proverbs with their explications, old proverbial rhythmes, less known or exotick proverbial sentences, and Scottish proverbs*, Cambridge: John Hayes.

Read, Rupert and Samuel Alexander (2019), *This Civilisation is Finished: Conversations on the end of Empire – and what lies beyond*, Melbourne: Simplicity Institute.

Rosa, Hartmut (2021). *The Uncontrollability of the World*, Cambridge: Polity Press

Roy Chowdhury, Debasish and John Keane (2021), *To Kill A Democracy: India's Passage to Despotism*, Oxford, New York and Delhi: Oxford University Press.

Saramago, José (2013), *The Lives of Things* (London and New York: Verso.

Scheler, Max (1972), *Ressentiment,* New York: Schocken Books.

Searle, John R. (1997), *The Social Construction of Reality*, New York: Free Press.

Streeck, Wolfgang (2014), 'How Will Capitalism End?', *New Left Review* 87 (May-June), pp. 35-64.

----------------------(2016), *How Will Capitalism End?* (London and New York: Verso.

Weber, Max (1949), *The Methodology of the Social Sciences*, Glencoe, Ill.: Free Press.

Wittgenstein, Ludwig (1972), *Über Gewissheit/On Certainty,* ed. G.E.M.Anscombe and G.H.von Wright, trans. Denis Paul and G.E.M.Anscombe, New York: Harper and Row.

Refusing to Defer to the New Normal -
The Need to uphold the Spirit of Humanism

Frank Furedi

Time and again you hear political leaders and their experts and media commentators hold forth about the new normal. Although the meaning of this term is rarely defined, it conveys the connotation that the way we lived and worked in the past is likely to be very different to what the world will look like in the post COVID pandemic future.

There are numerous versions of the theme of the new normal. Public Health experts frequently claim that we will have embrace many of the anti-COVID measures into the indefinite future. Some of them argue that western societies should adopt the cultural practices of their Asian peers and routinely wear masks in public as well continue to practice social distancing measures.

Numerous commentators and experts have placed a positive spin on the new normal. They claim that the nature of work will change as millions of people continue to work from their home. They often attribute new forms of digital working with positive qualities such as the time people will save by not having to commute. In education, blended learning is frequently advocated as a superior alternative to what is presented as old-fashioned face to face teaching.

The New Normal is often framed in the language of environmentalism. From this perspective the pandemic serves as an argument against international travel. Green campaigners assert that the old normal way of feeding ourselves and organising economic life is at least indirectly responsible for the outbreak of the COVID pandemic. Their vision of the new normal is one where human activity and aspiration is subordinated to the ideological dogma of a zero-carbon society

Advocates of the New Normal in the sphere of economics argue that capitalism itself will have to be restructured. One World Bank blog asserts that Multinational Enterprises will take 'greater responsibility 'towards the environment and adopt an 'increased focus on sustainability and green initiative'[1]. The achievement of decarbonisation is projected as the ultimate ambition of the new normal culture. This is an outlook advocated by the globalist oligarchy associated with the World Economic Forum[2].

The idea of The Great Reset associated with this institution attempts to provide a positive spin to its model of the new normal. They claim that the application of new technology under the benevolent guidance of technocratic experts will create a more just and world. As far these experts are concerned the new normal in the years ahead will be 'far more tech-driven' than is the case today[3].

In the sphere of politics, the new normal would lead to the subordination of democratic decision making to the imperative of technocratic governance. This sentiment is most stridently expressed through the demand of public health operatives for a greater say in the management of society[4]. The past two years has seen an unprecedented trend towards the medicalisation of politics. For some advocates the new normal implies more of the same.

Unlike the technocratic promoters of the Great Reset, who at least project into the future a new technologically driven world, public health experts offer a down-beat pessimistic scenario, where the current conditions that were imposed during the past 18 months serve as a model for the future. It often appears that from their standpoint it is not human society but a virus who will determine our future direction of travel. A scenario that elevates the power of *virus determination* diminishes the status of human agency.

The term new normal is used to convey the conviction, that life, as we lived in the past has irrevocably given way to fundamentally different era. As Jennifer Ashton, the author of *The New Normal* (2021) explained, after the Covid pandemic 'we will never be the same again'. She added, 'The virus has changed our world, transformed how we live, and upended our sense of normality[5]. The assumption that 'we will never be the same again' is closely linked to the conviction that life as we have known it in the past has come to an end.

1   https://blogs.worldbank.org/psd/long-road-new-normal-economy
2   https://www.weforum.org/focus/the-great-reset
3   https://www.pewresearch.org/internet/2021/02/18/experts-say-the-new-normal-in-2025-will-be-far-more-tech-driven-presenting-more-big-challenges/
4   https://reliefweb.int/report/world/creating-new-normal-new-global-public-health-system
5   Jennifer Ashton, *The New Normal* [edition missing], Harper Collins, 2021. Available at: https://www.perlego.com/book/2100434/the-new-normal-pdf

It speaks to a mood of historical closure and evokes a sense of terminus. The ways of the old have become redundant in the new world of the new normal.

The declaration that society has become subject to a New Normal follows the well-trodden fatalistic path laid out by commentators insisting that history has come to an end. The claim that history has come to an end, views change as an autonomous force to which people must adjust. In its current version the end has come about because of the behaviour and impact of a virus. It is not people making their way in society but a virus that is responsible for the trajectory laid out for human-kind.

The New Normal is the accomplishment of human effort. Society has very little say about its arrival. It has no choice but to adapt to this condition. The end of the 'old normal' can be interpreted as integral to a zeitgeist wedded to the outlook of endism. In his study *Politics and Fate* (2013) the political theorist Andrew Gamble wrote about the 'outbreak of "endism"'[6]. Gamble links the outbreak of endism to the mood of fatalism prevailing in society. He wrote; *'There is now a deep pessimism about the ability of human beings to control anything very much, least of all through politics. This new fatalism about the human condition claims we are living through a major watershed in human affairs. It reflects the disillusion of political hopes in liberal and socialist utopias in the twentieth century and a widespread disenchantment with the grand narratives of the Enlightenment about reason and progress, and with modernity itself. Its most characteristic expression is the endless discourses on endism – the end of history, the end of ideology, the end of the nation-state, the end of authority, the end of the public domain, the end of politics itself – all have been proclaimed in recent years[7].'*

If one were to believe all the claims made on this score, it would be difficult to avoid the conclusion that just about everything that mattered in the days of the old normal has come to an end. We have the end of ideology, the end of the nation state and some now some suggest that we have the end of globalism[8]. Others write about the end of sovereignty, the end of authority, the end of the West and the end of politics. Commentators declare 'the end of

---

6   A. Gamble, *Politics and Fate*, 1st edn, Wiley, 2013. Available at: https://www.perlego.com/book/1535657/politics-and-fate-pdf (last accessed on 25 September 2021).

7   Ibid.

8   See https://www.foreignaffairs.com/articles/united-states/2016-12-09/end-globalism .

the book', which will hopefully materialise once you have finished this text[9]. Even science is recruited to the cause of endism by the author of *The End of Science: Facing the Limits of Knowledge In The Twilight Of The Scientific Age*[10]. Numerous commentators reflect on the end of the world and wonder 'how the world ends'[11].

That this endist imagination projects a dispirited outlook toward the future is summed up by the title of the book; *The End of Future: The Waning of a High-Tech World.*[12] A similar sentiment is communicated by James Bridle in his, *New Dark Age: Technology and the End of the Future*[13]. According to the sociologist Zygmunt Bauman this endist orientation towards the future has as its premise the absence of an agency able to 'move the world forward'[14]. According to Bauman it is the absence of 'self-confidence of the present' that encourages the belief that 'time is on our side' and that we are the ones who 'make things happen'[15]. It is precisely the absence of the conviction that we are *not* the ones who make things happen that has led to the passive acquiescence to the idea, that whether we like it or not, living in the new normal is out destiny.

In a world where crisis has become a far too overused term it is tempting to draw the conclusion that humanity has lost its capacity to influence its destiny. Warnings of a financial meltdown, cataclysmic climate change, antibiotic resistant superbugs and catastrophic super-terrorists all communicate the idea that the magnitude of the threats facing humanity call into question its survival. In such circumstances the cultural zeitgeist is hospitable to ideas that stress the powerlessness of human beings to control their fate. Indeed, not since the Renaissance has the conviction that human beings lack the capacity for self-determination has enjoyed such a powerful resonance as today.

For thousands of years humanity's capacity to influence its destiny has been a subject of philosophical and scientific debate. When the Romans coined the phrase 'Fortune favours the brave' they expressed a powerful belief in people's

---

9   https://www.theatlantic.com/magazine/archive/1994/09/the-end-of-the-book/376361/
10   https://www.amazon.com/End-Science-Knowledge-Twilight-Scientific/dp/0465065929/
11   https://www.livescience.com/65633-climate-change-dooms-humans-by-2050.html
12   https://www.amazon.co.uk/s?k=The+End+of+the+Future%3A+The+Waning+of+the+H
      igh-Tech+World&i=stripbooks&crid=2L6MK1Q8Z54I2&sprefix=the+end+of+the+fu-
      ture+the+waning+of+the+high-tech+world%2Cstripbooks%2C61&ref=nb_sb_noss
13   https://www.amazon.com/New-Dark-Age-Technology-Future/dp/178663547X
14   Zygmunt Bauman, *Liquid Modernity*, Polity Press, Cambridge, 2000, p.133.
15   Bauman, 2000, p.132.

potential to exercise their will and shape their future. With the ascendancy of the Enlightenment and the commanding influence of science and knowledge, belief in creative and transformative potential of humanity flourished. When US President Franklin Roosevelt stated in 1939, 'Men are not prisoners of Fate, but only prisoners of their own minds' he echoed the belief that people possessed the power to make their own way in the world. That Roosevelt could express such a positive construction of the human condition in the dark days of 1939 is testimony to an admirable quality of refusing to defer to fate.

The New Normal – A Destiny Without a Subject

Compared to the dark days of 1939, western culture's representation of humanity in the twenty-first century is distinctively unflattering. Virtually every domain of culture is devoted to drawing attention to human powerlessness and vulnerability. One of the most disturbing developments is the tendency to divest people of the capacity to make conscious decisions about their life. Indeed the idea that human beings act on the basis of reflection and weighing up alternatives has given way to the dogma that people are the product of their genes and biological make up. These days virtually every personality trait is represented as a consequence of how their brain works.

It is tempting to blame the current state of political *stasis* on the behaviour of politicians, their parties or some malevolent force. However, the loss of agency and sense of terminus are not the direct outcome of any specific errors or conscious strategy. They have surfaced alongside the ascendancy of widespread disappointment and disbelief in the promise of modernity. One important dimension of 21st century fatalism relevant for making sense of the disenchantment with politics is the tendency to question the capacity of people to possess the wisdom to both understand and shape their circumstances. Such a pessimistic cultural account of the relationship between people and the making of history has important implications for the way that the life of politics is experienced. Perversely political commentators often write of the end of deference. What they overlook is that the decline of deference to traditional authority has been replaced by a far more powerful sense of deference to Fate.[16]

---

16 'Individuals increasingly expect greater personal autonomy and are as a result less subservient to authority' notes a major study commissioned by the British Government. See Performance and Innovation Unit; Social Capital; A Discussion Paper, April 2002, p.43.

Political analyst frequently draw attention to the decline of the politics of class and to the politics of community. However, this erosion of previous forms of solidarity is paralleled by a far more important and fundamental process – the loss in the belief that people can shape or alter their circumstances through political action. Instead of perceiving themselves as political subjects individuals frequently experience their role as the objects of policy making. This process of **declining subjectivity** has intensified the sense of powerlessness and passivity of the public This form of self consciousness is even evident when citizens react against their alienation from the political system. Such reactions often assume the form of a demand for an apology, compensation, recognition or affirmation. This response often resembles that of a disenchanted customer rather than a public interest oriented citizen.

The consciousness of powerlessness or what sociologists describe as a **loss of agency** is continually fuelled by cultural forces that heighten the sense of fatalism. As noted in our discussion on the freezing of history, a mood prevails that discourages the idea that people can, by interacting with each other and their circumstances, shape their own destinies. Instead of acting as agents of history, humanity has effectively been recast in the role of an object to which things happen by forces that are beyond all control. The assumption of numerous policy documents is that people are not trustworthy and cannot be expected to live their lives responsibly. The tendency to treat adults as children informs the action of the entire political class. Individuals are no longer presented as the 'political man' or even as 'citizens'. Today's political vocabulary emphasises the passivity and powerlessness of the public. We have the excluded, the vulnerable (potential victim), the victim, the bullied, the client, the end user, the consumer or the stakeholder but not people as political animals.

The infantilisation of the electorate is assisted by social processes that have served to disconnect people from one another. The increasing fragmentation of social experience has had a significant impact on people's lives, helping to normalise a more privatised and individuated way of living. Some commentators claim that this more privatised existence has encouraged the development of a thrusting individual consciousness, of the kind they now associate with the "greedy eighties". But they could not be more wrong. Without known points of contact and a reliable system of support, individuation only encourages powerlessness. The sense of being on your own and of having to rely on individual solutions has only led to a heightened consciousness of isolation. It has had the effect of altering the way that people see their relationship with the world, helping to induce an exaggerated sense of weakness and a fatalistic outlook The numerous surveys which claim that people expect that their future will be worse than today is symptomatic of this trend. So is the powerful tendency to continually emphasise the negative side of every new development.

The heightened sense of individual insecurity that prevails today tends to fluctuate between passivity and a sporadic outburst of anxiety of the kind that characterises public reaction to MMR, global warming or the threat of terrorism. The coincidence of social passivity with outbursts of anxiety has helped to endow political action with a peculiarly timid bias. Today's causes tend to be about the politics of survival – global warming, pandemic, save our food from contamination.

The growth of individual insecurity is a by-product of a fundamental alteration in the relation between the individual and society. Individual attitudes are mediated through a complex of institutions and relations; classes and communities have provided an important experience through which individuals make sense of the world. Over the past three centuries people's experience of modernity through these institutions has served to widen people's horizons and helped forge a sense of human agency. The development of individual ambition and of a class or a community based vision of social change often expressed outwardly contradictory aspirations. But their differences notwithstanding, what such responses had in common was a perception of future possibilities, and the belief that human action could make a difference.

Today, this human-centred view of the world has been replaced by one in which the range of possible options has been severely narrowed. This is strikingly expressed in the domain of politics, where even the capacity of the state to give direction to society is increasingly called into question. Politics matters less to people for the very simple reason that what people can do does not appear to matter. The sense of impotence often takes on the form of attacking politics itself. Anti-politics, the cynical dismissal of the elected politician and the obsession with sleaze and corruption, expresses a deeply cynical view of the human experience. This orientation renounces the history-making potential of people on the grounds that trying to do something either makes no difference or makes matters worse. If this was simply a case of saying that that there is no point voting for any of today's parties, it would be fair enough. But the current disparagement of politics goes way beyond that. The conviction that we cannot trust politics is ultimately a roundabout way of saying that we cannot trust anybody – and that includes ourselves.

Pouring scorn on political ambition is not simply motivated by scepticism regarding the efficacy of participation and engagement. It is also informed by the conviction that the pursuit of ambition is likely to end in tears. In the 19th century people were criticised for not knowing their place. Today they are castigated for not knowing their natural limits.

Humanising humanism

It is perverse that 21st society, which relies so much on human ingenuity and science also encourages deference to Fate. At a time of widespread disenchantment with the record of humanity's achievements, it important to restore confidence in the capacity of people to reason and influence the course of events. This is a challenge that confronts everyone – of whatever political, philosophical or religious persuasion – who upholds a human centred orientation towards the world. This task may appear as a modest one compared to the grand visions of the past but in our anti-humanist pre-political era its realisation is a precondition for the restoration of a climate hospitable to politics.

The reconstitution of the sense of agency and of historical thinking is the pre-requisite for the reengagement of the public with political life. That requires that we uphold humanity's past achievements, including standards of excellence and civilised forms of behaviour and values. Far from representing a yearning for the good old days, overcoming our alienation from the legacy of human achievement helps us deal with the issues thrown by change. It is through drawing on the achievements of the past that we can embrace change with enthusiasm.

Promoting a consistent belief in human potential underpins progressive thought. A human-centred view of the world recognises that people can be destructive and that conflicts of interests can lead to devastating outcomes. However, the negative and sometimes horrific experiences of the past two centuries, up to and including the Holocaust, are not the price of progress, but of the lack of it. Contemporary problems are not the result of applying reason, science and knowledge, but of neglecting them and thwarting the human potential.

The humanist intellectual universe needs to be ambitious but open-ended, prepared to countenance the validity of any idea and ready to yield to new experience. Such a perspective must engage in the process of **humanising humanism**. Humanising humanism requires that failure and mistakes are incorporated into the way we regard progress and the exercise of rationality. If human agency is assigned an important role in the making of history than factors like culture, subjective perception, conflict, contingency and limited knowledge all play a role in the way we engage with the world. Such influences can confuse, distract and disorient. Nevertheless, they provide some of the important experiences from which we learn how to move forward. In a sense progress happens through these experiences in the exercise of subjectivity. Humanising humanism requires that we stop treating human development as a foregone conclusion. What we need is a humanism that is not a dogma but a perspective oriented to learning from what humans do.

At a time when the inclination is to wallow in the dark side of humanity, it is worth emphasising that the legacy of the Enlightenment has provided us with a high standard of moral and ethical responsibility. The twentieth century has witnessed appalling atrocities and relapses into barbarism and genocide. Yet though the scale of degradation experienced in modern society may have been greater than in earlier times, it is only in our era that such events would have been popularly regarded with moral opprobrium. Torture, slavery, the slaughter of defeated enemies – before the modern era such activities were generally considered legitimate and went without question. Autocracy, hierarchy, elitism were considered to be features of a natural order vested with divine authority. It is only with the emergence of modern society, with its concepts of democracy and equality that the possibility of progress and of the improvement of humanity is both material and moral sense arises.

It is ironic that sentiments of moral revulsion against the evils of modern society are often accompanied by a tendency to repudiate the framework of rationality and purposeful intervention in nature and society that make a more truly human society possible. What we need is a more balanced assessment of the state of society, one that rejects the gross exaggeration of problems and recognises what we have achieved. But most important of all we need to understand that whatever the mistakes that we have made we can extract from them lessons that can guide us to move forward. The reconstitution of agency does not require the invention of grand philosophies but the humanising of humanism through empowering personhood.

We need to retrace our step to the time before there was a left and right – to recover the progressive legacy of the past. We do this not because we want to escape from politics as we know it but because these are pre-political times that require the recovery of ideas through which a challenge to fatalism can be mounted. This demands that we let go of the categories that helped illuminate political life in the last century, but which have now become emptied of its meaning. Previously we noted that the right has given up on the past and left on the future – we have to re-establish a claim on both. The line of division that matters today is between those who subscribe to the conformist embrace of the present and those who want to mobilise the past achievements of humanity to influence the future. The tendency to freeze the present coincides with a fatalistic perception of change. What we are offered is an interpretation of history that distances men and women from the events that impact on their lives. Human beings are viewed as extraneous to the process of change and therefore are seen to exercise little influence over their destiny. Neither autonomous nor self-determining, individuals are assigned an undistinguished role as are objects of history.

People making choices do not need support from bureaucratic institutions. What they require is the freedom to engage with new experience. What they need is not just the formal right to choose but cultural support for experimentation and individual choice making. Back in the 18th century, the German philosopher Immanuel Kant recognised that it was the emergence of the condition where the individual could pursue such activities unimpeded that constituted the point of departure of the Enlightenment. Experimentation and the pursuit of knowledge are not simply good in and of themselves they give freedom and democracy real content.

Kant claimed that the 'enlightenment is man's emergence from his self-imposed immaturity'. By immaturity he meant 'the inability to use one's understanding without guidance from another'. According to Kant this immaturity was self-imposed and its 'cause lies not in lack of understanding, but in lack of resolve and courage to use it without guidance from another'. And confronting his reader with what he characterised as the motto of the Enlightenment - *Sapere Aude* or Dare to Know – he challenged them to use their understanding. Today, when the Precautionary Principle constantly communicates the prejudice science threatens to run ahead of society and that those mounting experiments are 'playing God', daring to know is often represented as an act of irresponsibility. Kant would have been perplexed by contemporary society's uneasy relation with science and knowledge.

Of course, our ambiguous relationship with knowledge and reason is not due to the failure of individual character but the outcome of a more deep-seated process of cultural disorientation. Unfortunately, Kant's diagnosis of self-imposed immaturity is more pertinent to contemporary times than to the circumstances he faced. At a time when the claims of knowledge and science are regarded with mistrust and cynicism the motto *Sapere Aude* goes against the grain of contemporary cultural sensibility. Yet fortunately many of us sense that daring to know is what makes us human.

Human action often results in unexpected outcomes some of which are uncomfortable to live with. For example, the genetics revolution provides us with important new insights into our constitution, but it may also give us information about ourselves that we would rather not know. Nevertheless, the pursuit of the ideal of autonomy offers people the promise of choices and frequently results in progress. It is precisely because some individuals have taken this ideal seriously that they successfully challenged repressive institutions and the use of arbitrary powers that sought to thwart their ambition. We have also learned that the aspiration for autonomy often goes hand in hand with the display of altruism and social solidarity. An enlightened society needs to harness the ideal of individual autonomy to create the optimum conditions for human development. Societies that fail to valorise this ideal end up dominated by a culture of fatalism and risk collapsing into a state of stasis.

The enlightenment ideal of individual autonomy insist that society and the state must recognise the independence of each individual. As Bronner argues 'autonomy originally implied the right for each to have his or her faith'.[17] Such a perspective puts to question the right of the state to promote a particular faith – be it in the form of a traditional religion or the lifestyle crusades associated with the current policy of behaviour modification. Recognition of the ideal of individual autonomy -an important component of the legacy of the Enlightenment – represents the foundation for choice making, moral and political decision making and social engagement.

Popular suspicion towards the exercise of human agency means that the ideal of individual autonomy is frequently dismissed as an illusion fostered by

17   Stephen Eric Bronner, *Reclaiming The Enlightenment: Towards a Politics of Radical Engagement, Columbia* University Press, 2004, p.136.

apologists for the free market. It is argued that in a society which is dominated by the media, big corporations and forces unleashed by globalisation, individuals lack the capacity for autonomous action. Moreover, as diminished or vulnerable subjects, people do not so much choose their faith as have it foisted on them. That is why the Enlightenment model of the autonomous and responsible citizen is displaced by a more passive disoriented individual who requires the 'support' of public institutions. What we are left with is a regression to the condition of the immature self of the pre-Enlightenment era.

The mood of cultural pessimism does not leave society untouched. It has a profound impact on how people see themselves. It is difficult to *Dare to Know* when our culture continually transmits the signal that risk taking is irresponsible and that caution and safety are the principal virtues of our time. Such signals serve as an invitation to people to constrain their aspirations and limit their actions. If people are repeatedly told that not much is expected of them and that indeed they are vulnerable individuals in need of support – they will frequently begin to play the part that is assigned to them. Today the promise of individual autonomy is contradicted by the reality of a culture that is uncomfortable with its exercise. As a result, individual existence is experienced not so much through the prism of autonomy but of isolation.

The lack of validation accorded to the ideal of autonomy goes hand in hand with a lack of respect for democracy. Public policy is frequently inspired by the belief that the electorate cannot be relied on to figure out what is in its best interest. The politics of fear provides one instrument for 'raising the awareness' of people about what's good for them.

Humanising Personhood

The version of personhood that is most consistent with the ideals of autonomy, the exercise of choice and history making is that given by the legacy of the Enlightenment. Risk taking, experimentation, the exercise of critical judgement and reason are some of the important attributes of historical thinking and agency. The exercise of these attributes is the pre-condition for the reconstitution of public life. Through such human activities people develop an understanding of how purposeful public activity may lead to positive results in the future. Without a sense of agency personhood lacks the imagination one associates with political engagement. Humanising personhood requires challenging the prevailing paradigm of vulnerability and gaining acceptance for the humanist concept of personhood.

Humanist Paradigm	Vulnerability Paradigm
Valorises autonomy	Valorises help-seeking
Orientation Towards Reasoning	Scepticism towards the efficacy of knowledge
Search for universal values	
Positive attitude towards risk taking	Affirmation of identity
	Strongly risk-averse
Valuation of experimentation	Celebration of caution and safety
Belief in capacity to change and alter circumstance	Change is perceived as precursor of negative outcome
Oriented towards the future and upholds achievement of the past	Frozen in the present and estranged from the past
Expectation that community possesses coping skills	Anticipation that individuals/ communities are unlikely to cope
Believes that humanity possesses capacity to overcome adversity	Believes that people are defined by their state of vulnerability

The humanist and vulnerability paradigms of personhood never exist in a pure form. Since the rise of the modern era every culture has internalised elements of both. But nevertheless, cultures discriminate when they communicate stories about which forms of behaviour they value and which ones they don't. For example, throughout most of the nineteenth and twentieth century the ideals of self-help and self-sufficiency enjoyed cultural affirmation. Today, it is help-seeking that benefits from cultural validation. In contrast to the celebration of the risk taking in former times, society today has turned safety into a veritable religion. The ideal of experimentation has been displaced by the conformist embrace of caution, which has been institutionalised through the precautionary principle. The values associated with the humanist paradigm of personhood are not entirely absent, but they have become subordinate to ones that promote the sensibility of vulnerability.

Conflicting ideas about the paradigm of personhood are today the equivalent of past clashes of ideologies and political alternatives.[18] They touch upon such fundamental questions as what it means to be human, the meaning of human nature and the relationship between the individual and public institutions.

---

18   These conflicts underpin some of the clashes of the so-called Culture Wars.

Ideas about the paradigm of personhood constitute the point of departure for the formulation of policy and the creation of norms –informal and formal – that regulate people's relationship and individual behaviour. The meaning of personhood has important implications for how we view the relationship of people to history and the potential for changing and altering circumstances. Our attitude towards personhood informs how we make sense of the exercise of choice and of individual responsibility, our capacity to know, to reason and gain insights into the truth. Ultimately different ideas about personhood lead to conflicting ideas about public life. Whether people are perceived as the problem or as the solver of problems depends on which paradigm one subscribes to.

Progress or Fear

The politics of fear thrives on the terrain of misanthropy and cynicism towards the endeavour of people to alter and improve their circumstances. From this perspective the instinctive response to such efforts – be it an invention, a new product, or an institutional reform – is an expansive sense of suspicion that readily gives way to anxiety and fear. Such attitudes stand ready to write off claims of human progress both in the present and in the past. Indeed, there is a widespread conviction that it is the development of human civilisation, particularly the advance of science and technology, and the resulting subordination of the natural order to the demands of human society, that is the source of many of today's problems of environmental destruction and social disintegration. Further developments in the sphere of science and technology tend to be greeted with apprehension rather than celebration. So recent advance in genetics or nanotechnology, for example, are regarded as creating more problems than benefits for society.

Suspicion towards the possibility of progress means that significant advances in the human condition are regularly reinterpreted as bad news. The very fact that Western society has become concerned about its ageing population reflects the huge progress that has been made in recent years in humanity's struggle against disease. Since 1950 there has been a 17 per cent increase in life expectancy worldwide: this increase has been most spectacular in the poorer nations of Asia where it has reached 20 per cent. Yet time and again we are told that the struggle to contain disease has been a failure and that we now face new species of plagues and super bugs. Increasingly we are made to feel as if the risk to our health is greater than before.

Despite the prevailing sense of disappointment with the human subject, individuals possess an unprecedented potential for influencing the way they live their lives. It is only now that the promise of choice and control has acquired meaning for a significant section of the public. Autonomy and self-determination are still little more than ideals that can inspire. But we have moved away from the Stone Age of ideologies to a time where the transformative potential of people has acquired a remarkable force. We have also learnt that history does not issue any guarantees. Purposeful change is indeed a risky enterprise. But whether we like it or not, the taking of risks in order to transform our lives and to transform ourselves is one of our most distinct human qualities. The making of history, too, is one of those transformative experiments that helps us to realise and define our humanity.

In these conditions we have two choices. We could renounce the distinct human qualities that have helped to transform and humanise the world and resign ourselves to the culture of fatalism that prevails today. Or we could do the opposite. Instead of celebrating passivity and vulnerability we can set about humanising our existence. Instead of acting as the audience for yet another performance of the politics of fear we can try to alter the conditions that give rise to it.

References

Ashton, Jennifer, The New Normal, [edition missing], HarperCollins, 2021. Available at: https://www.perlego.com/book/2100434/the-new-normal-pdf

Bauman, Zygmunt, *Liquid Modernity,* Polity Press, Cambridge, 2000.

Bronner, Stephen Eric, *Reclaiming The Enlightenment: Towards a Politics of Radical Engagement,* Columbia University Press, 2004.

Gamble, Andrew, *Politics and Fate,* 1st edn., Wiley, 2013. Available at: https://www.perlego.com/book/1535657/politics-and-fate-pdf (last accessed on 25 September 2021).

https://blogs.worldbank.org/psd/long-road-new-normal-economy

https://www.weforum.org/focus/the-great-reset

https://www.pewresearch.org/internet/2021/02/18/experts-say-the-new-normal-in-2025-will-be-far-more-tech-driven-presenting-more-big-challenges/

https://reliefweb.int/report/world/creating-new-normal-new-global-public-health-system

https://www.foreignaffairs.com/articles/united-states/2016-12-09/end-globalism .

https://www.theatlantic.com/magazine/archive/1994/09/the-end-of-the-book/376361/

https://www.amazon.com/End-Science-Knowledge-Twilight-Scientific/dp/0465065929/

https://www.livescience.com/65633-climate-change-dooms-humans-by-2050.html

https://www.amazon.co.uk/s?k=The+End+of+the+Future%3A+The+Waning+of+the+High-Tech+World&i=stripbooks&crid=2L6MK1Q8Z54I2&sprefix=the+end+of+the+future+the+waning+of+the+high-tech+world%2Cstripbooks%2C61&ref=nb_sb_noss

https://www.amazon.com/New-Dark-Age-Technology-Future/dp/178663547X

COVID-19 and the Ecophobic Reflex[1]

Simon C. Estok

Among the lessons that we have learned on our journey through the COVID-19 pandemic is that the depth of the relationship between ecophobia and the disease has become stronger as we moved through the pandemic. To understand this requires an understanding of the nature of "ecophobia." In *The Ecophobia Hypothesis*, I write about ecophobia as a spectrum condition that can manifest in several different forms–ranging from fear to lack of mindfulness, from outright contempt to blasé indifference. On the other end of the spectrum is the idea of biophilia, which Erich Fromm defines as a "passionate love of all that is alive"[2]. It is a term that E.O. Wilson further developed in his influential *Biophilia Hypothesis*, to which my book was a direct response. The problem with the idea that we are biophilic and "love nature" is that it just doesn't explain the bad things that we do to the environment, bad things that have resulted both in our current climate crisis and in our current pandemic. Obviously, it is necessary here to address this second matter—the pandemic as an environmental issue—before moving on.

The early focus on the sources of the disease clearly revealed that our chronically exploitative relationships with animals need immediate attention. The disease is, after all, zoonotic. "Zoonosis" is the term for the transcorporeal pathogenic leap of disease from one species to another. History is clear on the matter of zoonosis. Jared Diamond succinctly explains that "questions of the animal origins of human disease lie behind the broadest pattern of human history, and behind some of the most important issues in human health today"[3]. For Diamond, disease is one of the prime movers of human society, along with war and industrialization—with which disease is intimately linked.

---

1   Parts of this chapter appear in different form in "The Global Poltergeist," "Merchandizing Veganism," "Painful Material Realities," and "Ecophobia and Covid-19."

2   Erich Fromm, *The Anatomy of Human Destructiveness*, Toronto, Holt, Rinehart and Winston, 1973, p.365.

3   Jared Diamond, *Guns, Germs, and Steel: the Fate of Human Societies*, New York, Norton, 1997, p.197.

Diamond reminds us that "the major killers of humanity throughout our recent history—smallpox, flu, tuberculosis, malaria, plague, measles, and cholera—are infectious diseases that evolved from diseases of animals"[4]. But there are several others Diamond does not mention (some of which post-date his book): bird flu (in 2013), SARS (in 2002), Swine Flu (in 2009), mad cow disease (in 1996), Ebola (in 1976), and so on. Our chronically exploitative relationship with animals is based in ecophobia no less than patriarchal exploitation of women is based in misogyny or than Nazism is based in anti-Semitism—and I will loop back to zoonosis later in this chapter, but would like, for a brief moment, to explore a bit more about ecophobia and *why* the need for the term. When men are prejudiced against women and fearful of their agency, this is called sexism. When people are prejudiced against other races and fearful of their agency, this is called racism. When straight people are prejudiced against LGBTQI people and are fearful of their agency, this is called homophobia. And when people discriminate on the basis of species and are fearful of the agency of other animals, this is called speciesism. Discrimination against the environment has, until recently, lacked a term—hence the work on ecophobia. For simplicity, we might argue that when people are prejudiced against nature and fearful of its agency, this is called ecophobia. It manifests in such phrases as Mother Nature and in ideas about nature being our enemy.

The aspect of ecophobia that concerns us most immediately with pandemics is what I am calling our chronically exploitative relationship with animals. Rather than attend to our chronically exploitative relationship with animals, the real root of the problem, the world's most powerful "leader" at the time instead seized on the pandemic as an opportunity to conceptualize the disease along nationalist lines—with phrases such as "Kung Flu" and "the Chinese Virus." Trump is certainly not alone in doing this, and there is a long history of such behavior. Indeed, as Priscilla Wald explains in her remarkable and prescient 2008 book entitled *Contagious: Cultures, Carriers, and the Outbreak Narrative*, "surfacing routinely in outbreak accounts, [pandemic discourse] establishe[s] disease outbreaks as 'foreign' or 'alien' agents that pose a national threat"[5]. But whatever the political configurations of a given nation with China, we need to be pellucidly clear that the disease did NOT come from the Chinese;

---

4   İbid. p.196-197.
5   Priscilla Wald, *Contagious: Cultures, Carriers, and T\the Outbreak Narrative*, Durham, Duke UP, 2008, p.27.

it came from animals. As with 75% of the other diseases we suffer, animals (and the flesh that we eat from them) are the core origin of the COVID-19 pandemic, the *sine qua non* of human vulnerability to the death and unprecedented changes that the pathogen offers.

COVID-19, like the Black Death before it, is, we must be clear, an environmental event. In his *Environmental History of Medieval Europe*, Richard Hoffmann explains that the Black Death was "the largest ecological and demographic event in pre-modern European history"[6]. Citing Hoffmann, medievalist Shawn Normandin argues that the social effects of the pandemic—the disappearance of villages, the collapse of economies, changes in agricultural practices, and so on—had profound effects that we can, to some degree, chart in the literature of the time (see Normandin, esp. 1-50). The COVID-19 pandemic is an environmental catastrophe, too, with its own winners and losers.

Pandemics turn caution into fear and fear into phobias, and COVID-19 shows this well with the whole matter of sanitizing—and this is not on any level a criticism of the need to sanitize but rather the necessity for understanding the fundamentality of microbial worlds to our very existence, worlds that compulsive sanitizing threatens. We need to teach our children well. It is very likely that our efforts, combined with the limits of the virus itself, will spell the end of COVID-19—or, at the very least, its taming. But that is not the end of the story, and at some point, we really do need to think about what all of the sanitizing has done and how the effects of it will come back to haunt us. I am not referring to Trump's idea that we drink disinfectant but am concerned rather with the microbial worlds inside our bodies, about which more below.

First, however, it bears remarking that a lot of what we are going through is *not* new and that novelists have already written about such experiences that have seemed recently so singular in our history. Albert Camus, for instance, stated decades ago in his novel *The Plague* something that may seem a much more contemporary *popular* recognition: that "what is natural is the microbe" [7]. Microbes are a fundamental part of nature indeed, but this is a recognition that has been and remains fiercely—and it is challenging to find the right word here—*resented*. The worlds microbes create, without question, are the imagined enemies in pandemics. They are the agential enemy, and in many important

---

6   Richard C. Hoffmann, *An Environmental History of Medieval Europe*, Cambridge, Cambridge UP, 2014, p.289.

7   Albert Camus, *The Plague,* (trans.) Robin Buss, Tony Judt, Penguin, 2013, p.195.

ways, the COVID-19 pandemic capitalizes on our fears, firstly highlighting how a confluence of adaptive strategies can really work *against* our best long-term interests and secondly raising vital questions about just *how* to respond to mortal threats—that is, how to respond when under siege, when we are terrified. The response of George W. Bush to the 9/11 terror attacks was a reflex response—to hit back, to create an enemy (terror) and wage war on it (the War on Terror). It was a nationalistic and inherently racist response. If there is one thing that characterizes the COVID-19 pandemic more than the actual virus itself, it would have to be fear, and the (in this case) ecophobic reflex is to demonize the source of that fear.

In her famous book *Illness as Metaphor*, Susan Sontag points out how "feelings about evil are projected onto a disease. And the disease (so enriched by meanings) is projected onto the world"[8]. This remark implies complex relationships between the subject and the object world, between the imagined and the real, and between our abilities to grasp the emotional and the indifferent. And Nature, to be sure, is utterly indifferent. Priscilla Wald reminds us that "Nature is far from benign; at least it has no special sentiment for the welfare of the human versus other species"[9]. Neither, however, is Nature evil; yet among researchers, as Wald continues, "the microbes are not only sinister; outbreak accounts manifest researchers' respect for and even awe of their foe"[10]. Even so, it bears repeating that Nature is indifferent, and this is a concept that we simply find difficult to digest. The microbe and the virus don't think or feel, any more than a rock falling would think, "hey, I'm going to fall." It just falls. Jared Diamond is of course being a bit tongue-in-cheek in characterizing microbes as "damned clever" in how they modify "our bodies or our behavior such that we become enlisted to spread microbes"[11]. But he knows and we know that it is not cleverness; it is the logic of genetic mutation in a huge population with a short generation. It is pure chance, not cleverness, and, for all of our cleverness, genetic chance does not rule in our favor—not with our long wait for "gene frequencies from generation to generation"[12]. While microbes have a genetic advantage over us, however, our cleverness is a potent response. I write today with genetically modified material (the mRNA vaccine)

8   Susan Sontag, *AIDS and Its Metaphors*, New York, Farrar, Straus and Giroux, 1989, p.58.
9   Wald, 2008. p.40.
10   Ibid, p.43.
11   Diamond, 1997, p.198.
12   Ibid, p.201.

coursing through my system. Even so, viruses can mutate quicker than we can develop responses, and they do it by chance (and they have lots of chances) in order to perpetuate themselves, wherever and whenever possible and without emotion. It is the power that these infinitesimally small and unintelligent life forms have over us that evokes the ecophobic reflex.

It is utterly disempowering—"ego-deflating," to use Diamond's phrase (197)—to think that a brainless and infinitesimally small thing can take us down. Perhaps nowhere is this more eloquently or succinctly put than by the character Sam Daniels in the film *Outbreak*: "You've have to love its simplicity. It's one billionth our size, and it's beating us." Because this is unfathomable, incomprehensible, and, in so many ways, unacceptable, we project notions of the sort Sontag describes. Who or what can unravel our carefully crafted tapestry, our intricate global web of production and distribution, our delicate financial networks and chains? We are reluctant to see Nature as indifferent. Wald argues that "nothing better illustrates the reluctance to accept Nature's indifference toward human beings and the turn from the ecological analysis in accounts of emerging infections of all varieties than the seemingly irresistible tendency to animate a microbial foe"[13]. Isn't it better, after all, to imagine a vindictive and evil microbe moving like a suave devil with the best laid plans—rather than a brainless and virtually invisible thing—undoing everything? And that fact that we just can't make them go away is all the more taunting to our powerfully exceptionalist mentalities. It is nothing short of haunting when Camus ends his novel promising that "the plague bacillus never dies or vanishes entirely"[14].

Yet, to come back to the matter of winners and losers, microbes are the long-term biological losers of our current sanitizing regimes. Efforts to wipe out dangerous microbes, we need to remember, will have long-term consequences. Viruses, the smallest of all of the microbes, provoke retaliatory responses from us that can produce worse results than the virus itself. The questions about social responsibilities versus individual liberties aside, serious as they are, pale before what are clearly more important biological questions—none of which are currently being addressed in mainstream media or popular scientific peer reviewed research. These questions need immediate attention.

---

13 Wald, 2008, p.42.
14 Camus, 2013, p.237.

In 2019, not long before the COVID-19 pandemic, I wrote in *ISLE* as follows (and I have received some hostile responses about it):

Today, as Michael Pollan notes in a discussion about fermentation, "the microbial world is regarded foremost as a mortal threat"[15]. The legacy of Louis Pasteur, he explains,

is a century-long war on bacteria, a war in which most of us have volunteered or been enlisted. We deploy our antibiotics and hand sanitizers and deodorants and boiling water and 'pasteurization' and federal regulations to hold off the rot and molds and bacteria and so, we hope, hold off disease and death.[16]

Pollan calls it "germophobia"[17], but it is also known as "microbiophobia," "Mysophobia," "verminophobia," "bacillophobia," and "bacteriophobia"—all of them clearly falling under the rubric of ecophobia, which, as I have suggested elsewhere, plays out in many spheres, including the personal hygiene and cosmetics industries.[18]

These words are as true now as they were before the pandemic, notwithstanding hostile responses. Compulsive use of hand sanitizers in public venues is a recent example of our obsessive fear of dirt and bacteria. The reality, however, is that the human body is comprised of more nonhuman than human DNA, and *obsessive* hand sanitizing is more harmful in the long-run than it is beneficial in that we are killing microorganisms that are beneficial to our own survival. For instance, we need intestinal flora in order to digest our food, regulate our immune system, and reduce inflammation. These gut flora (the bacteria) produce antimicrobial substances that outnumber the total count of cells in the human body by 1000%–ten to one, in other words. The biological questions about what we are doing to future generations with our compulsive sanitizing needs our attention. No less does our sense of being besieged, outnumbered, and under attack by our microscopic companions need attention; imagining war rather than cohabitation with the microbes will not help us in the long-run, and the fact remains that "we are more microbe than human"[19]. There will be blood for tearing into microbial ecosystems.

---

15 Michael Pollan, *Cooked: A Natural History of Transformation*, New York, Penguin, 2013, p.296.

16 Ibid.

17 Ibid, p.297.

18 Simon C. Estok, "Ecophobia, the Agony of Water, and Misogyny." *ISLE: Interdisciplinary Studies in Literature and Environment,* Vol. 26, No. 2, Spring 2019, p.473-474.

19 Margaret McFall-Ngai, "Noticing microbial worlds: the postmodern synthesis in biology",

We are facing a serious loss—one that has nothing to do with personal liberties or social freedoms: before COVID-19, with the growth of the Anthropocene, we had already begun to face "the loss," Margaret McFall-Ngai explains, "of the complex microbial worlds both within and beyond organismal bodies— worlds that make nearly all life possible"[20]. These microbial worlds are absolutely essential for us, yet we are tearing into them willy-nilly with our sanitizing regimes. Again, to be clear, this is not to argue on any level against the need for good hygiene in the COVID-19 era, but we need to know that there will be blood for this. Summarizing the work of Carl Woese, McFall-Ngai describes how, by the early 1990s, it had become clear that "the earth's biological diversity is far more microbial than ever imagined"[21] and that "microbes don't just 'rule' the world: they make every life form possible, and they have been doing so since the beginning of evolutionary time"[22]. McFall-Ngai summarizes important arguments about how "bacteria matter not only in themselves but also in relation to other living beings, who depend on them for processes as basic as bodily development"[23]. She spells it out so that even the most non-scientific of readers can clearly understand:

Bacteria are not only changing the way our guts behave; their metabolic products interact with our entire bodies in complicated ways that we are just beginning to explore. For example, we are finding out that gut bacteria have significant impacts on our brains, affecting the ways we think and feel.[24]

Citing the work of Yang Wang and Lloyd H. Kaspar, McFall-Ngai contends that "there is growing evidence that the presence or absence of certain microbial strains is linked to depression, anxiety, and autism"[25] (ibid). So why in the world is there no media attention to the possible harm that our anti-septic, anti-biotic, compulsive sanitizing might be doing to our future? At least part of the answer is quite simply that we do indeed suffer from that branch of ecophobia called Pollan called "germophobia." In the middle of the COVID-19 pandemic, his words could not be timelier.

Arts of Living on a Damaged Planet, (eds.) Elaine Gan, Anna Tsing, Heather Swanson, and Nils Bubandt. Minneapolis, U of Minnesota P, 2017, M52.

20 Ibid, M51.
21 Ibid, M54.
22 Ibid, M59.
23 Ibid.
24 Ibid, M64.
25 Ibid.

We should make no mistake about it that our reactions have been more phobic than rational. And we should be equally clear that these often phobic reactions have saved countless lives. This may seem contradictory, since survival responses are not in and of themselves ecophobia, but there is a very important qualifier needed here: we need to understand that even survival responses *are* ecophobic when they are simply *reflexes*, responses based on no material or empirical facts, just fear with no rational or reasonable basis. When animals flee from people, it is often because we have shown ourselves to be dangerous, and they have learned to fear us. We too have learned to fear much in our evolutionary history. Much of what we had had to be fearful about in our evolutionary history, however, is now just a part of history. When children are young, they are scared of the dark. Adults tell them that there is nothing to be scared of. It is a lesson we all learned as children (namely, that it's okay to turn the lights off and go to sleep), and the fear of the dark that many of us felt as children is dormant in most of us as adults. The reality, however, is that dark places have, in fact, been dangerous for diurnal animals in their evolutionary history, including us. Dormant fears can always be awoken. What the COVID-19 pandemic has done is to awaken a lot of dormant fear—primarily about microbes but also, as I will explain a bit later, about animals.

As we all know, the pandemic has brought to the fore questions about the security of our freedom, our agency, and our deeply personal lives. Personal liberties—and secrets—dissolve as much in the narratives microbes tell as in the outbreak narratives humans create:

microbes tell the often hidden story of who has been where and when, and of what they did there. Contagion, that is, charts social interactions that are often not otherwise visible, and the manifestations of those contacts and connections is another important feature of outbreak narratives.[26]

In what we perceive through an ecophobic reflexive understanding as a threat to our individuality is a chance to re-envision ourselves and our relationships with the world. To come back to the work of Margaret McFall-Ngai, we might do well to listen to the argument for the need to see "bacteria [less] as disease-causing invaders . . . than [as] potential symbiotic partners"[27], something that is *not* happening in microbiology circles: "Human bodies can no longer be seen as fortresses to defend against microbial onslaught but must be

---

26   Wald, 2008, p.37.
27   McFall-Ngai, 2017, M65.

re-envisioned as nested ecosystems"[28]. Moreover, given that "individuals are ecosystems," it becomes clear "that the loss of a single species probably entails the loss of many kinds, not just one. Attention to microbial life raises the specter that our extinction crisis may be even more serious than we thought".[29] McFall-Ngai concludes powerfully that "in the era of the Anthropocene, noticing microbial worlds seems more important than ever".[30] A sense of embeddedness must replace our sense of individual privilege and exceptionalism—and I will return to the topic of exceptionalism shortly.

To return to the matter of how pandemics turn caution into fear and fear into phobias, a dynamic that COVID-19 shows well, compulsive sanitizing is troubling not only for its ecophobic overtones but because it treats a symptom and not a cause. It is a reflexive action that simply fails to reach beyond the surface. It is like a Band-Aid for cancer. The stress in COVID-19 media about sanitizing similarly addresses the symptom (the disease) but not the cause (our chronically ecophobic relationship with animals). The pandemic hits us at our most ecophobic weak spot: our fear of animals themselves. Pandemics in some ways level the field, reminding us that we are not so different from the rest of the animal world.

One of the interesting things about COVID-19 is how it has revealed our "animalistic" responses and thus called into question our sense of our own exceptionalism—and our responses to danger *are* natural. When danger appears, a flock of birds takes flight, a school of fish flees, a colony of mudskippers retreat to their holes, and people stay at home—we are not all that different from other animals. Our vulnerabilities reveal our affinities. Like other animals, we are susceptible to disease—even extinction. A large part of this whole issue has to do with our inflated sense of the supremacy of our own individuality.

Indeed, many of the crises we currently face are the dangerous ecological effects of our notions about own individuality, and part of the horror the COVID-19 pandemic presents is precisely a challenge to such notions. Ed Yong has put the case well: "No matter how we squint at the problem, it is clear that microbes subvert our notions of individuality".[31] And these microbes are zoo-

28   Ibid.
29   Ibid, M66.
30   Ibid, M66-M67.
31   Ed Yong, *I Contain Multitudes: the Microbes Within us and a Grander View of Life,* Harper Collins, New York, 2016, p.24.

notic. Not recognizing zoonotic origins of disease means ignoring human/non-human entanglements, ignoring, to borrow from Nicole Shukin, the "liberal *longing* for interspecies intimacy [that] circulates concurrently[,] . . . longing for posthuman kinship"[32]; but it can also result, as Shukin has noted, in extraordinary speciesism and ecophobia. Keith Thomas once famously commented that "it is impossible to disentangle what people of the past thought about plants and animals from what they thought about themselves".[33] These entanglements have been *hierarchical* in Western thinking. Eastern philosophies and religions (Hinduism, Janism, Buddhism, Taoism, and others) are a different story, not the topic of this chapter. Indeed, it is ironic that while "Western society has fostered a culture of caring for animals . . . it has maintained humanity's right to kill and eat them".[34] I am reminded here of Michael Pollan's comment that "Half the dogs in America will receive Christmas presents each year, yet few of us pause to consider the miserable life of the pig–an animal easily as intelligent as a dog–that becomes the Christmas ham" (Pollan "An Animal's Place"). What enables this paradox is the sense of authority from an imagined divinity that gives men dominion over animals and women. The use of animals for labor, entertainment, clothing, and food clearly presents something contradictory. It is not just the pigs and dogs Michael Pollan mentions: our relationships with animals, understood as a god-given right in Western cultural history, go against the commandment (from the same god) to not cause suffering to animals: in Hebrew Tza'ar ba'alei Chayim (צער ילעב ח"יים), which literally refers to *not causing "suffering to the owners of life"*—the Talmudic tradition generally understands "owners of life" (ba'alei, ח"יים ילעב) to refer to animals. Notwithstanding the long contradictory behaviors with animals within Judeo-Christian thinking, human and nonhuman lives have been, are, and always will be interwoven, and history will repeat and haunt humanity until we learn its lessons.

Nicole Shukin worries about failures to recognize these entanglements and states that "abandonment of the hope of a mutually benefitting material coexistence with other species is possibly the most terrifying prospect of all".[35]

---

32 Nicole Shukin, *Animal Capital: Rendering Life in Biopolitical Terms,* Minneapolis, U of Minnesota P, 2009, p.188.

33 Keith Thomas, *Man and the Natural World: Changing Attitudes in England, 1500–1800,* Allen Lane, New York, 1983, p.16.

34 Tristram Stuart, *The Bloodless Revolution: A Cultural History of Vegetarianism from 1600 to the Present*, Norton, New York, 2006, p.8.

35 Shukin, 2009, p.220.

A failure to recognize the ongoing material intercourse between human and nonhuman animals (the movement of material in and through bodies that Stacy Alaimo has called "transcorporeality"), tacitly reaffirms the exceptionality of the human, casting the nonhuman into a negligible space. Such a reaffirmation virtually guarantees a skewed understanding of human/nonhuman animal relations in which the nonhuman becomes the antagonist, the demonized agent of harm to the human. In Shukin's words, while biomobility is suggestive of a radical ontological breakdown of species distinctions and distance under present conditions of global capitalism, it also brings into view new discourses and technologies seeking to secure human health through the segregation of human and animal life and finding in the specter of pandemic a universal rationale for institutionalizing speciesism on a hitherto unprecedented scale. [36]

Ignoring or downplaying human/nonhuman entanglements and transfers of genetic materials among species has complex causes and implications.

There are several issues that require comment here. Firstly, genes (like microbes) obviously don't have motives in an emotional or psychological sense, but we should make no mistake about it that they are motivated to reproduce—an idea that we find very troubling, in large part because it threatens our sense of individuality. But Richard Dawkins explains that:

Individuals are not stable things, they are fleeting. Chromosomes too are shuffled into oblivion, like hands of cards soon after they are dealt. But the cards themselves survive the shuffling. The cards are the genes. The genes are not destroyed by crossing-over, they merely change partners and march on. Of course they march on. That is their business. They are the replicators and we are their survival machines. When we have served our purpose we are cast aside. But genes are denizens of geological time: genes are forever.[37]

The genes that run the microbes, then, do have motives that truly haunt humanity. The other issue (and we have seen it in Diamond's remark about "damned clever" microbes and in the demonizing of microbes that Wald and Sontag discuss) is the whole question of antagonism often embedded in comments about understanding and beating a virus imagined as an "enemy." Part of what guarantees fear during a pandemic is the perception of danger in the agency of genomic material. Columbia University Assistant Professor of Medicine Siddhartha Mukherjee writes that "one of the most powerful and dangerous

---

36   Shukin, 2009, p.183-184.
37   Richard Dawkins, *The Selfish Gene- 40th Anniversary Edition*, Oxford, 2016, p.44.

ideas in the history of science [is] the 'gene,' the fundamental unit of heredity, and the basic unit of all biological information".[38] He identifies two other dangerous ideas: the atom and the byte, arguing that "each represents the irreducible unit—the building block, the basic organizational unit of a larger whole: the atom, of matter; the byte (or bit), of digitized information; the gene, of heredity and biological information".[39] He goes on to state what we know cerebrally but not viscerally: "it is impossible to understand organismal and cellular biology or evolution—or human pathology, behavior, temperament, illness, race, and identity or fate—without first reckoning with the concept of the gene".[40] This of course begs the question of agency outside of genes: do we have any free will or individuality?

Famed entomologist E.O. Wilson—whom we've already met today as the father of *The Biophilia Hypothesis*—speaks directly to the question about relationships between genes and agency:

[...] genes hold culture on a leash. The leash is very long, but inevitably values will be constrained in accordance with their effects on the human gene pool. The brain is a product of evolution. Human behavior—like the deepest capacities for emotional response which drive and guide it—is the circuitous technique by which human genetic material has been and will be kept intact. Morality has no other demonstrable ultimate function.[41]

Haruki Murakami puts it more forcefully in his epic novel *1Q84*: "*Human beings are ultimately nothing but carriers—passageways—for genes. They ride us into the ground like racehorses from generation to generation. Genes don't think about what constitutes good or evil. They don't care whether we're happy or unhappy. We're just means to an end for them. The only thing they think about is what is most efficient for them.*"[42]

Dawkins rhymes in yet more succinctly: "they go by the name of genes, and we are their survival machines".[43] However we word it, the thought is terrifying: our sense of agency is overblown. This is perhaps the single, most important insight of New Materialist thinking, and it has profound implications for how

38   Siddhartha Mukherjee, *The Gene: An Intimate History*, Scribner, 2017, New York, p.9.
39   Ibid, p.9-10.
40   Ibid, p.11.
41   Edward O. Wilson, "Biophilia and the Conservation Ethic", *The Biophilia Hypothesis,* (ed.) Stephen R. Kellert and Edward O. Wilson, Island Press, Washington, DC, 1993, p.167.
42   Haruki Murakami, *1Q84: a novel,* Alfred Knopf, New York, 2011, p.269.
43   Dawkins, 2016, p.25.

we think about materials and how they matter. The development of interest in the gene over the past hundred years is very encouraging because it may very well help to dislodge us from our destructive sense of exceptionalism, call into question our hubris in our agency, and overcome biases against less sophisticated organisms—including things that haunt us and cause deadly pandemics.

One of the matters that is critical here is precisely about *how* bias against less complicated organisms is dangerous. To what degree do cultural matters such as class and hierarchical thinking prevent us from addressing the agency of pathogens (at least until a pandemic begins) with the same vim and vigor that we address perceived threats to national security? What do we make of the resonances between terrorism and pandemics, since these clearly do not translate into equal funding: military spending far outweighs health care spending globally. One of the ways to come at these issues is to recognize that there are common misconceptions about evolution and how it works, a point that Norwegian Professor of Molecular Biology Andreas Hejnol has made well. Hejnol argues that misconceptions that evolution proceeds from simple to complex and that less complex animal groups are eventually superseded remain not only in textbooks but also among zoologists. They deserve our attention because they matter: they shape our thinking about the biology of life and have consequences for what we find important to investigate.[44]

The top/bottom metaphors (humans are at the top of the tree or ladder while bacteria and viruses are at the very bottom), Hejnol shows, "have proved particularly discouraging" to some forms of investigation.[45] More than this, however, such metaphors predispose us to underestimating pathogens, and given that one of the metaphors for comprehending human/pathogen relations is a military one (we are in a war against them), such a predisposition is particularly dangerous. No one would under-estimate the deadly potentials of a hammer in the hands of a psychopathic serial killer, even though hammers are utter unsophisticated and are among the most ancient of human tools. A hammer is no magnetic flux generator that fires projectiles without any kind of chemical explosive, but it can kill—and dead is dead.[46] We are incredibly sophisti-

---

44   Andreas Hejnol, "Ladders, Trees, Complexity, and Other Metaphors in Evolutionary Thinking", *Arts of Living on a Damaged Planet, (*ed.) Elaine Gan, Anna Tsing, Heather Swanson, and Nils Bubandt. Minneapolis, U of Minnesota P, 2017, G97.

45   Ibid, G100.

46   This example, however, is problematical, obviously because while magnetic flux generator weapons are the result of an evolution that has proceeded from simplicity to complexity, biological evolution doesn't quite work that way.

cated organisms and imagine, therefore, that we are *above* the far *less* sophisticated pathogens that threaten us and haunt our existence. We will win the war because we are better—or so the thinking goes. The reality, however, is that our survival has never been guaranteed. Because of our misconceptions about evolution and our ecophobia and sense of our own exceptionalism, we willingly forget our vulnerabilities when each pandemic or plague passes, and we think we have won. We do well to heed the ominous warning Camus offers about the plague never disappearing.

Our refusal to reckon with pathogens as permanent co-inhabitants in the world is in part a result of our utilitarian ethics, our understanding of the rest of the world not as partners but as commodities for our use. It is a worldview that has led to a spiralling out of control. One of the implications of global corporate capitalism is that biomobility has all sorts of possibilities unique to our point in history. Indeed, Shukin explains that "[b]ecause globalization unwittingly supplies the conditions for disease to travel rapidly and because a future pandemic will by all accounts be zoonotic (animal) in origin, the species line emerges as a prominent material stress line in neoliberal culture".[47] Written in 2009, those words today are haunting. Shukin also explains that "pandemic discourse speculates in the coming of an event that threatens to precipitate the collapse of the global economy and a hard reckoning with materiality"[48] and that "interspecies exchanges that were once local or 'place-specific' are experienced as global in their potential effects".[49] We are currently making those hard reckonings and finding that the global effects of COVID-19 are simply too big to conceptualize. As pandemics and disease have haunted our steps, so too have the representational problems that they offer—solutions to which may, in fact, make things worse.

There are some very unsavory implications to how we imagine "beating" the pandemic "enemy." One of these has to do with violent metaphors of control. Another has to do with violent actions of control. Both require attention.

Pandemics and plagues defy control or predictability, and it is this that makes them so frightening and urgent. There are other diseases out there that are very deadly: cancer and heart disease, for instance, but these do not arouse the sense of urgency that COVID-19 does. Among the reasons that COVID-19

47   Shukin, 2009, p.184.
48   Ibid, p.185.
49   Ibid, p.183.

does so are its novelty, which paradoxically both engenders a more visceral sense of unpredictability than cancer or heart disease while also evoking a sense that it can be "beaten," while both cancer and heart disease have consistently proven unbeatable. COVID-19, like terror, produces reflexive responses. Isomorphically similar to terror attacks and, indeed, to climate change, pandemics (so we imagine) corner us and throw down the gauntlet, and this evokes fiery responses laced with military metaphors that drip machismo. Shukin notes the "chilling resonances between a discourse of pandemic preparedness and the imperial rhetoric and machinery of the war against terrorism"[50], and presciently observes that "pandemic discourse prepares us . . . for a new imperial war against nature".[51] But the similarities don't stop there. Indeed, war and disease both have been with humanity for time immemorial, and yet they continue to surprise us. This is one of the key themes of Camus in *The Plague*. Despite our long history with pandemics and plagues, as with wars and social unrest, we are never really prepared for them when they come: "Pestilence is in fact very common, but we find it hard to believe in a pestilence when it descends upon us. There have been as many plagues in the world as there have been wars, yet plagues and wars always find people equally unprepared".[52] Pandemics, like war, moreover, offer an opportunity to imagine a demonized enemy, an opportunity we invariably seize. Demonizing people is often racist, and demonizing the environment, ecophobic. Pandemics encourage ecophobia.

Another implication in the metaphor about beating the enemy is far more material than metaphorical. We have all heard about the wholesale slaughter of chickens and pigs and cows, euphemistically described as "culling." The ethical indifference here (by definition, ecophobia) to the lives of animals is disturbing and destructive in the long run. Post COVID-19 life will require us to revisit nature-denying behaviours that right now are helping us. One of the lessons COVID-19 is teaching us is that what is ecophobia in one time and place is survival in another. Context is all. Survival responses are not ecophobia (a comment I qualified earlier), but it bears repeating that what is a survival response in one context is raw ecophobia in another. After a hike on a hot summer's day, I will immerse my entire head in the icy waters of Lynn Valley Stream in North Vancouver, open my mouth, and drink until I get brain

50   Ibid, p.219.
51   Ibid.
52   Camus, 2013, p.30.

freeze. I don't think I'd do such a thing at the Han River in Seoul, the Tamshui River in Taipei, or the Ganges River that runs through India and Bangladesh. When the survival response at the Han, the Tamshui, or the Ganges, however, becomes a fear of any and all free flowing water in the world, then we have ecophobia. Ecophobia is the survival instinct gone mad. It is easy to see how this can happen, surrounded as we are by threats. The fact is that we are *immersed* in germs, viruses, bacteria, and bugs. And while it is perhaps true that we "cannot overestimate the evil that flies do," as Philip Roth explains in *Nemesis*, a novel about polio[53], neither can we live in fear of every bug that comes our way, every dirty surface that we touch, and every smell that is not quite right.

Yet, the previous sentence feels a bit disingenuous—at least as a blanket statement. The responses of city and country people toward the environment obviously differ. If there is a bug in my house in Vancouver, I may wonder how it got in before ushering it back outside. If I have a bug in my penthouse flat in Seoul, my first thought is that it may be nesting somewhere. Context is all. Bugs in Mumbai and bugs in Saskatoon are not the same. Different city, different climate, different culture, different responses. Again, what is survival in one place is ecophobia in another.

Entangled with our ecophobic reflex toward COVID-19, too, are a number of other things: sexism, individualism, and racism. Detractors and not-so-well-meaning scholars who feel threatened by the notion of ecophobia have asked for a template (and not getting one have dismissed ecophobia)—we all know that desire for a one- or two-sentence summary of ecophobia. Perhaps this may suffice:

The ecophobic condition exists on a spectrum and can embody fear, contempt, indifference, or lack of mindfulness (or some combination of these) toward the natural environment. While its genetic origins have functioned, in part, to preserve our species (for instance, the fight or flight response), the ecophobic condition has also greatly serviced growth economies and ideological interests. Often a product of behaviours serviceable in the past but destructive in the present, it is also sometimes a product of the perceived requirements of our seemingly exponential growth. . . . Ecophobia exists globally on both macro

53 Philip Roth, *Nemesis*, Vintage, Toronto, 2010, p.92.

and micro levels, and its manifestation is at times directly apparent and obvious but is also often deeply obscured by the clutter of habit and ignorance.[54]

It is a viable definition, if we keep in mind that context is everything.

As with ecophobia, so too with COVID-19—responses have been far from uniform globally, but the ecophobic reflex has been irrepressible. Globally, pandemic discourse sells as entertainment because it is a topic that we can relate with, a topic full of matters that haunt and threaten, matters that require a response. Pandemic discourse covers matters we really do not want to think about too much—for instance, our material entanglements with animals. Or genetic materialism. The past. A widespread amnesia haunts humanity. From century to century, amnesia is in full play, and today we seem to have forgotten everything that happened in 1918 with masks, and quarantines, and individuality, and social welfare, and pandemic fatigue, and so on. I had certainly not been taught in school about the 1918 flu, though it has come back into history with the current pandemic. But where was it until now? Where? Forgotten.

We have forgotten other things too. At the very moment that it announces an environmental crises, COVID-19 silences discussion of the very environmental crises that brought it into being. Media coverage of climate change (at least until COP26) has been all but absent. CNN remarked once about how 9/11 trumped climate change in the news: "After 9/11, the world's attention shifted to fighting international terrorism. Climate issues took a back seat. And all the while greenhouse gas emissions continued to soar" (Dewan et al, video clip). We witness the same thing with COVID-19, at least before COP26, with most of the world's attention shifting to fighting the virus, while environmental issues took a back seat. People have made much about our clear skies and about how greenhouse emissions plummeted during the pandemic, but these will not make much difference: "Think about it this way," says renowned Canadian climate scientist Katharine Hayhoe. "We've been putting a brick on a pile every month since the beginning of the industrial revolution. Last year we put 20 per cent smaller-sized bricks on that pile that has thousands and thousands of bricks already on it. Those 12 or 24 slightly smaller bricks are not going to make a big difference" (English). "'Even at a seven per cent reduction, emissions for 2020 will be roughly the same as 2011,' says Corinne Le Quéré, one of the authors of a study in *Nature* last year".[55]Clearly, we need to

54   Simon Estok, *The Ecophobia Hypothesis,* Routledge, New York, 2018, p.1.
55   Ibid.

be circumspect with the news about how great our lockdowns have been for the environment.

COVID-19 has, however, shown us that we *can* make immediate changes, that we *can* shut off fossil fuel taps virtually overnight, and that we make delays—really—only in the interests of preventing financial problems. Short-term financial consequences (because so immediate) seem more horrifying than long-term environmental ones. Mindfulness. Circumspection. Perhaps we just need to suck it up and take the pain now. The problem is that so very much of how we see the world is mediated through other voices, narratives that are in the service of interests that are perhaps not the interests of the planet. And let's make no mistake about it: we're a very credulous species. We are gullible. If it is on the internet or in the news, even "alternative facts" pass as real. It is hard to forget Mr. Trump and his sleazy, lying Counselor—the one who said that lies are "alternative facts"? And trumped up claims about the eco-virtues of digital media need circumspection too. Zoom meetings are certainly better than everyone flying everywhere, but cloud storage? While it is best to be circumspect with the news, the problem is that news is all that most of us have, since we are not MIT emissions researchers. We really do need to be mindful about what we consume—I mean, not only food, but narratives too.

How we know what to and what not to fear is often the product of the narratives we consume. How media narrate the material is obviously important, as it determines both the imagined contours and the possible trajectories that ecophobia—and viruses—can take. Ecomedia often acts as a transmitter of ecophobia through its enmeshment with other rights-denying behaviors. The enmeshment of ecomedia with ideologies that have a proven record of marketability and consumption is indeed problematical. We know, for instance, that sexism sells well, and it sells whatever it is attached with—hence, the prevalence of the phrase "Mother Nature," even in sources that are evidently trying to address the problem (albeit reiterating and reinforcing it). Much of pandemic discourse is filmic, and much of this filmic material is science fiction (*28 Days Later, World War Z, I am Legend*, and so on), and one has to wonder just how effective this *entertainment* is in moving minds and hearts. Like entertainment, news indulges in the very things it seems to be critiquing. I've written before but would like to repeat here that sexist, anthropomorphic, and clearly ecophobic metaphors of a malevolent nature are counterproductive and are simply not going to help make our environmental crises any better; on the contrary, such sentiments (although they may sell well) are simply perpetuating the idea that nature (and women) should be controlled. This is the very kind of sexist ecophobia that has produced the kinds of troubles we currently face. But it sells well, and there is receptivity to endorsements of attitudes that deprive others of liberty; after all, these very attitudes have allowed slave owners, sexists, and colonialists (the founders of the United States) to thrive. It is telling that the most commercially successful film about veganism to date is the Schwarzenegger *et al* flick entitled *The Game Changers*, a shocking example of a post-truth, alternative fact world. It is a Netflix film with a host of luminaries behind it (Martin Scorsese, James Cameron, Arnold Schwarzenegger, Jackie Chan, and a host of professional athletes, actors, famous directors, and doctors) who claim to have discovered veganism as a "new" healthful diet. But this is just dishonesty. Ecofeminists were onto it long, long before these guys were on the scene. The problem is that lay people swallow this shit thinking it is real just as they do with lies about COVID-19.

Mainstream media seems to enjoy pretending that all of this was unpredictable, unimaginable, and inevitable. "Unimaginable." That's the word CNN's Nic Robertson used to describe the streets of London on the 23rd of March 2020, following British Prime Minister Boris Johnson's "stay at home" order. But it *was* imagined. Danny Boyle's 2002 post-virus-apocalypse horror film *28 Days Later* shot scenes of desolate streets and thoroughfares in London— one of them Piccadilly Circus, precisely the spot Nic Robertson was surveying when he said that the images of desolation were unimaginable. Did I mention that we are a credulous species? To say that it is unimaginable is simply dishonest. To neglect meat-eating as the cause of this desolation is similarly dishonest. How we consume narratives (and food) will determine how we act in the world—indeed, how we are able to act.

Eco-media is a huge and growing topic, and its importance to how the ecophobic reflex is generated is not to be underestimated. Many people find scientific discourse utterly boring, and such discourse, if it is to reach people, needs to be mediated—that means, carried through mainstream media outlets—and one of the ways these media make the material more accessible is through commonly accepted and understood metaphors, metaphors that have relied for their purchase on sexism and ecophobia. Outbreak narratives and apocalypticism appearing in film are also appearing in print media (books, magazines, newspapers), in academic papers and discussions in the Humanities and hard sciences, on television, in video games, in music, through cell phones, in various kinds of software, in social media, through the Internet—in short, it is an intermedial apocalypticism we are witnessing, and the affect of each media is different. Moving forward means understanding that there is no foolproof template and that the medium and the context are vital for understanding how the ecophobic reflex comes into play. If nothing else, one thing is certain: it does come into play. That's a universal. How? That's not a universal.

As I write, almost 600 million have been infected with COVID-19, and 6.4 million have died. To see the effects of the scale of responses to COVID-19— the empty airports and hazmat flight attendants, the empty playgrounds and eerie schoolyards, the bankruptcies and the proximity of social turbulence and chaos—is soul-numbing and staggering. It is easy to look back and say "Oh, we should have done better." COVID-19 requires us to look at our behaviors *en voyage, in media res*, as it were, to look at our behaviors as we perform them, to be mindful of the ecophobic reflex as it happens because the stakes are high, and we really do not have time for a "plan B" anymore. Seeing those ecophobic reflexes to the COVID-19 pandemic and hopefully to changing some of our behaviors— or at least to being mindful of their effects—is really our best hope for a better future than the one currently in our trajectory.

References

Camus, Albert, *The Plague,* (trans.) Robin Buss, Tony Judt. Penguin, 2013.

Dawkins, Richard, *The Selfish Gene, 40th Anniversary Edition*, Oxford, 2016.

Dewan, Angela, Ivana Kottasová, Amy Cassidy, and Ingrid Formanek, "Reality check: Here's what the COP26 deals actually mean for our future climate." *CNN.* November 7, 2021. https://edition.cnn.com/2021/11/07/world/cop26-climate-agreements-reality-check-intl/index.html

Diamond, Jared, *Guns, Germs, and Steel: the Fate of Human Societies,* Norton, New York, 1997.

English, Jill, "Why your reduced carbon footprint from lockdown won't slow climate change." *CBC News.* May 23, 2020. https://www.cbc.ca/news/science/pandemic-climate-change-covid-emissions-1.5579232

Estok, Simon C., *The Ecophobia Hypothesis,* Routledge, New York, 2018.

Estok, Simon C., "Ecophobia, the Agony of Water, and Misogyny.", *ISLE: Interdisciplinary Studies in Literature and Environment,* vol. 26, no. 2, Spring 2019, pp. 473-85.

Estok, Simon C., "Ecophobia and Covid-19.", *International Journal of Fear Studies,* vol. 3, no. 2, 2021, pp. 90–99.

Estok, Simon C., "Merchandizing veganism.", *The Routledge Handbook of Vegan Studies,* (ed.) Laura Wright, Routledge, New York, 2021, pp. 333–342.

Estok, Simon C., "The Global Poltergeist: Covid-19 Hauntings.", *Haunted Nature: Entanglements of the Human and the Nonhuman,* (ed.) Sladja Blazan, Palgrave Macmillan, New York, 2021, pp. 181-195.

Estok, Simon C., "Painful Material Realities, Tragedy, Ecophobia", *Material Ecocriticism,* (ed.) Serpil Opperman and Serenella Iovino, Bloomington, Indiana UP, 2014, pp. 130-40.

Fromm, Erich, *The Anatomy of Human Destructiveness*, Rinehart and Winston, Holt, Toronto, 1973.

Hejnol, Andreas, "Ladders, Trees, Complexity, and Other Metaphors in Evolutionary Thinking.", *Arts of Living on a Damaged Planet,* (ed.) Elaine Gan, Anna Tsing, Heather Swanson, and Nils Bubandt. Minneapolis: U of Minnesota P, 2017, G87-G102.

Hoffmann, Richard C., *An Environmental History of Medieval Europe,* Cambridge, Cambridge UP, 2014.

McFall-Ngai, Margaret, "Noticing microbial worlds: the postmodern synthesis in biology.", *Arts of Living on a Damaged Planet,* (ed.) Elaine Gan, Anna Tsing, Heather Swanson, and Nils Bubandt, Minneapolis, U of Minnesota P, 2017, M51–M69.

Mukherjee, Siddhartha, *The Gene: An Intimate History*, Scribner, New York, 2017.

Murakami, Haruki, *1Q84: a novel,* Alfred Knopf, New York, 2011.

Normandin, Shawn, *Chaucerian Ecopoetics: Deconstructing Anthropocentrism in the Canterbury Tales*, Palgrave Macmillan, 2018.

Outbreak, Directed by Wolfgang Petersen, Warner Bros, 1995.

Pollan, Michael, *Cooked: a Natural History of Transformation*, Penguin, New York, 2013.

Pollan, Michael, "An Animal's Place." New York Times Magazine. November 10, 2002. https://michaelpollan.com/articles-archive/an-animals-place/

Roth, Philip, *Nemesis, Vintage,* Toronto, 2010.

Shukin, Nicole, *Animal Capital: Rendering Life in Biopolitical Terms,* Minneapolis: U of Minnesota P, 2009.

Sontag, Susan, *AIDS and Its Metaphors, Farrar, Straus and Giroux*, New York, 1989.

Stuart, Tristram, *The Bloodless Revolution: A Cultural History of Vegetarianism from 1600 to the Present*, Norton, New York, 2006.

Thomas, Keith, *Man and the Natural World: Changing Attitudes in England, 1500–1800*, Allen Lane, New York,1983.

Wald, Priscilla, *Contagious: Cultures, Carriers, and T\the Outbreak Narrative,* Durham, Duke UP, 2008.

Wang, Yan, and Kaspar, Lloyd H., "The role of the microbiome in central nervous system disorders", *Brain, Behavior, and Immunity*, vol. 38, May 2014, pp. 1–12. https://doi.org/10.1016/j.bbi.2013.12.015

Wilson, Edward O., "Biophilia and the Conservation Ethic." *The Biophilia Hypothesis,* (ed.) Stephen R. Kellert and Edward O. Wilson, Island Press, Washington, DC, 1993, pp.32–41.

Wilson, Edward O., *On Human Nature*, Harvard UP, Cambridge, 1978.

Yong, Ed., *I Contain Multitudes: the Microbes Within us and a Grander View of Life,* Harper Collins, New York, 2016.

Limits, Scarcity and the Malthusian Justification of Economic Growth

Giorgos Kallis

Introduction: Malthus and the naturalness of unlimited expansion

> *Malthus's "An Essay on the Principle of Population" claimed that population growth would eventually reduce the world's ability to feed itself. He based his conclusion on the theory that populations tend to increase more quickly than can food production. His predictions did not come to pass because he failed to predict the agricultural and industrial revolutions that would substantially increase yields and enable larger amounts of people to be fed. However, today, issues such as continuing population growth, rising per capita consumption, depletion of natural resources and climate change suggest that Malthus might have been on the right track after all.*

'Why Malthus is still relevant today', from Population Matters (2016)[1]

The figure of Malthus looms large in any discussion about limits to growth and hence sustainability and the future of the human species. Reverend Thomas Malthus (1766-1834) was an English cleric and scholar, most remembered for his influential Essay on the Principle of Population[2]. Friends and foes may disagree on whether his supposed predictions about population growth will eventually turn out to be right or wrong; but they agree on what Malthus said, and his place in intellectual history. Malthus is the supposed apostle of limits to growth, a prophet of doom who put a question mark on the promise of unlimited progress.

---

1   Quotes are not always endorsements. They are arguments that I engage with or criticize in the section that follows.

2   Thomas Malthus, An Essay on the Principles of Population, London, 1978.

In this chapter, I follow the footsteps of Dale[3] and elaborate an alternative reading of Malthus. Malthus' long-standing intellectual contribution, I argue, is not the discovery of natural limits, but the assumption of unlimited expansion as the natural and desirable, if always unattainable, state of human affairs. In fact, Malthus was not an apostle of limits, but an apostle of growth, an early contributor to the ideology of the 'growth paradigm'[4], the idea that is, that an unlimited expansion of the means of production is desirable and constitutes the natural call of humanity. Malthus was not a prophet of doom; he did not 'predict' anything, nor was he concerned with resource shortages or overpopulation.[5] Pre-figuring modern economics, he established a natural law of universal scarcity,[6] and used it like other economists after him, to legitimate and naturalize inequality and the relentless pursuit of growth.

I start this chapter by proposing to read Malthus as a social theorist and not as the Malthus of the Malthusians and their critics.[7] I show that for Malthus population growth was not a problem, but a goal: a happy nation for Malthus is one that its numbers are increasing as much as possible. Following that, I dissect the anatomy of Malthus' thesis in the Essay on Population and show how the assumption of a natural and desired state of population growth creates a universal scarcity that militates against redistribution. Malthus is a prototype economist, one of the early inventors of scarcity[8] and an apologist of endless accumulation[9].

My interest in Malthus is not historiographical. The point here is not to 'correct' an academic misreading of his oeuvre and revise the history of ideas. I am interested in Malthus because the way he framed limits and scarcity is still with us. Understanding what he did and why, opens a window to understand how and why capitalism perceives and produces limits the way that it

---

3   Gareth Dale, "Adam Smith's Green Thumb and Malthus's Three Horsemen: Cautionary Tales from Classical Political Economy", *Journal of Economic Issues,* Vol. 46, No. 4, 2012.
4   Ibid.
5   Frank W. Elwell, *A Commentary on Malthus' 1798 Essay on Population as Social Theory,* Edwin Mellen Press, New York, 2001.
     Malthus' Social Theory, Retrieved May 12, 2016, http://www.faculty.rsu.edu/~felwell/Theorists/Malthus/Index.htm (excerpt from Elwell, F. W. 2001.)
6   Nicholas Xenos, *Scarcity and Modernity*, Routledge, 1989.
7   Elwell, 2001.
8   Xenos, 1989.
9   Dale, 2012.

does. Following Dale[10], I show how neo-classical economics refined Malthus' theory of scarcity, and made it the cornerstone of the discipline, always putting it in use of limiting redistribution and equality.

In this respect, it is important to revisit the question of why Malthus was wrong. I argue that Malthus was not wrong because he did not foresee agricultural and industrial growth. He was wrong because he refused to see that collectives and societies may limit themselves; and he refused to see this, because if he did, he would have to accept the possibility of a classless society. Nonetheless, against Malthus' intention, elements from his work can, and have been reworked for a very different politics than what he had in mind. Paradoxically I will argue, Malthus offers analytical ammunition to those who want to question capitalism's promise of progress and its pursuit of relentless expansion, and a basis for rethinking limits as revolutionary praxis.

Rereading Malthus

Malthus has been buried many times, and Malthusian scarcity with him. But as Garrett Hardin remarked, anyone who has to be reburied so often cannot be entirely dead. [11]

Malthus is very much alive and with us, but this is no testament to the veracity of his views on population and scarcity, as Daly or Hardin suggest. It is a testament to his influence upon the subsequent development of liberal economics and government.[12] Plagiarism of Burke[13] or not[14], Malthus' Essay had an enormous immediate success[15] and its enduring influence cannot be taken lightly.

It is difficult to read Malthus dispassionately, ignoring the political consequences of the Essay. Not only did he sway public opinion against the Poor Laws, a proto-welfare system of poverty relief of his time. Malthus was also the first British chair in political economy in the Hailebury College established

10 Dale, 2012.

11 Herman E. Daly, *Steady-State Economics: With New Essays,* Island Press, 1991, p.43.

12 Mitchell Dean, "The Malthus Effect: Population and the Liberal Government of Life", *Economy and Society*, vol. 44, no. 1, 2015, p.22.

13 Edmund Burke, *Thoughts and Details on Scarcity (1795),* The Works, London, 1826, p.7.

14 Paul R. Ehrlich, L. Bilderback and A.H. Ehrlich, *The Golden Door: International Migration Mexico and the United States*, Ballantine Books, New York, 1979, p.40.

15 Ibid.

by the British East India company to train colonial administrators[16] His 'law of population' and his rejection of charity were behind the *'laissez faire'* food policies of British authorities in their colonies contributing to devastating famines and millions of avoidable deaths in Ireland and India.[17] Perelman[18] and Lohman[19] argue that the enduring success of the Essay is not because of its merits, but because of the narrative it offered in the service of the ruling class absolving it from a responsibility to do much about poverty.[20]

It would be a mistake though to reach on this basis the content of the essay as 'nonsense'.[21] Of course, as all political theses it has logical jumps and circular reasoning[22], but its argumentative, theoretical, and political power can be underestimated only at one's peril. Marx engaged with Malthus (as with all his intellectual adversaries) with passion but also with rigour confronting substantive and logical claims and not only the – appalling at places - rhetoric. This spirit of antagonistic, but reasoned engagement guides me here.

Lohman argues that Malthus combines - and complements - a 'darkness and terror' rhetoric of 'Us' versus 'Them' (Westerners versus the Barbarians, Rich versus the Poor) with a cold-factual economic reasoning[23]. I have my doubts whether the dark narrative would appear so dark to its contemporaries as it appears to us: diseases, loss of children and wars were not uncommon experiences for Malthus' readers as they are for Europeans or North-Americans today. In my reading, it is the (pseudo)rational and commonsensical economic reasoning that holds sway in the Essay. Malthus' rejection of poor relief for example is not grounded on apocalyptic images of poverty or a moral scorn of the poor.[24] As any good economist (sic) after him would do, Malthus rejects welfare support on the basis of the greatest good for the greatest number

16 Dean, 2015, p.25.
17 Dale, 2012; Mike Davis, *Late Victorian Holocausts: El Niño Famines and the Making of the Third World,* Verso, London, 2002, p. 529.
18 Perelman, 1979.
19 Larry Lohmann, "Malthusianism and the Terror of Scarcity", *Making Threats: Biofears and Environmental Anxieties,* (eds). B. Hartmann, B. Subramaniam, and C. Zerner, Rowman&Littlefield, 2005.
20 David Harvey, "Population, Resources, and the Ideology of Science", *Philosophy in Geography,* Springer Netherlands, 1979, p.160.
21 Lohman, 2005.
22 Lohman, 2005.
23 Lohman, 2005.
24 Elwell, 2001.

of people [25]: redistribution to the poor will supposedly harm them more than it will help them.

Following anthropologist Frank Elwell, I propose then to take Malthus seriously and read him as a social theorist. Elwell is a fan of Malthus (I am not), and he is concerned with those who, starting with a positive or negative political reaction to his work subsequently misread and misinterpret him (or, do not even read him). As aptly puts it, 'while there are self-styled neo-Malthusians and anti-Malthusians in the popular literature of the day, the debate tends to focus on the modern ecological situation rather than Malthus' theory'.[26] When Malthus is directly addressed, as by Population Matters in the opening quote of the introductory section to this chapter, then this tends to be what Malthus is supposed to have written, rather than *The Principle of Population* itself. As Agnes Heller suggested referring to Marx (but this applies equally to Malthus), when we read a historical thinker, the point is not to start from a contemporary argument and then find a quotation in his oeuvre that supports or contradicts it, but to discern 'the main tendency (or tendencies) of his thought'.[27]

What is then the main tendency of Malthus' thought? What is the centre of gravity in The Population Essay?

Malthus' essay was not a 'prediction' of a population overshoot and collapse. It was not about 'overpopulation'; he never actually uses this term! And it was not even about explaining poverty, at least not primarily. Such arguments were tangential to its core. The essay was doggedly single-minded in its purpose to 'prove the necessity of a class of proprietors, and a class of labourers'.[28] The 'view that permeates the essay is that no form of social organization can possibly create or preserve a just and equitable society'.[29] To prove the natural (and logical) impossibility of a classless society and the futility of redistribution, Malthus posits a natural law, what he calls the 'principle of population'. Put simply, this states that 'our ability to produce children will always outstrip our ability to provide energy for their survival'[30].

Humankind, Malthus argues, has two basic needs: food and sex. One leads to the production of food and the other to the reproduction of children. But

25   Elwell, 2001.
26   Elwell, 2001, p.3.
27   Agnes Heller, *The Theory of Need in Marx (No. 5)*, Allison & Busby, London, 1976, p.22.
28   Malthus, 1798, p.92.
29   Elwell, 2011, p.2
30   Elwell, 2001, p.1.

the power of reproduction is 'indefinitely greater' than the power of production[31]. Based on these two premises - that humans will always want food and sex, and that the ability to have children supersedes the ability to provide for them - Malthus concludes logically that there is not, and there will never be 'enough for all to have a decent share'[32]. This is what I call Malthus' principle of universal scarcity, which follows from the principle of population. That portion of the population that cannot be supported by existing production is 'the poor'[33]. And given that one person's food is another's hunger, there is a need for private property, to protect what people produce.

This is Malthus' commonsensical, and for this reason compelling to our days, logic. Before going deeper into the thrust and logical fallacies of the argument, let me clarify first some misunderstandings concerning Malthus' views on population.

Population for Malthus

Perelman notes how unlike contemporary environmental Malthusians, Malthus never accepted the limitation of population as an end.[34] Not only that: for Malthus population growth was a principal social end *in and of itself*. He couldn't say this more clearly:

> *'The happiness of a country does not depend, absolutely, upon its poverty or its riches, upon its youth or its age, upon its being thinly or fully inhabited, but upon the rapidity with which it is increasing, upon the degree in which the yearly increase of food approaches to the yearly increase of an unrestricted population'.[35]*

Happiness in other words is the degree to which the population of a country approximates a geometric rate of growth, which for Malthus is the natural rate of growth. Chapters 16 and 17 of the Essay offer a friendly critique to Adam Smith for conflating industrial ('commercial') growth with welfare growth. Industrial growth does not bring progress, Malthus argues, unless it increases also the quantity of food produced, which often was not the case. Only a growth in food subsistence would improve the conditions and numbers of

31 Malthus, 1798, p.4.
32 Ibid, p.24.
33 Elwell, 2001, p.6.
34 Perelman, 1979.
35 Malthus, 1798, p.43.

the lower classes, Malthus points.[36] The produce of the land is the true wealth of nations, since this and only this, can allow population to grow (chapter 17).

This should not surprise us as Malthus was not alone at his time in equating the greatness of a nation to the size of its population. Prominent theologist and reformer William Palley would write in 1790, eight years before Malthus, that 'the decay of population is the greatest evil the state can suffer and the improvement of it the objective which ought to … be aimed at in preference to every other political purpose whatsoever'[37]. How did Malthus square this with his principle of population?

As Elwell points, unlike common-held interpretations, Malthus did not offer a prophecy of overshoot and collapse.[38] For Malthus the constraint of food subsistence upon the growth of population applies constantly. It is *now*, not some time in the future, that food puts a limit on the number of kids we can have. Engels (1844) joked that if that were the case, then 'the earth was already overpopulated when only one man existed'[39]. Adam and Eve were two too many, since they would have more kids than they could provide for. However, this was precisely Malthus' point, only with a twist. As he claimed, 'the world would not have been peopled but for the superiority of the power of population to the means of subsistence'[40]. What Malthus meant is that it is precisely the food constraint that made Adam and Eve (so to speak) industrious and allowed them to produce a surplus above their own needs, populating the earth. 'The reason that the greater part of Europe is more populous now than it was in former times', Malthus writes, 'is that the industry of the inhabitants has made these countries produce a greater quantity of human subsistence'[41]. It is 'the constancy of the laws of nature that is the foundation of the industry'[42]. For Malthus, people work hard to increase the produce of the land and hence increase their numbers. A civilized part of the world like Europe is civilized because it is industrious and as a result populous. The labour however that

---

36   Malthus, 1798, p. 96-102.

37   Robert. L. Heilbroner, *The Worldly Philosophers: The Lives, Times and Ideas of the Great Economic Thinkers,* Simon and Schuster, 1999.

38   Elwell, 2001, p.7.

39   Friedrich Engels, "The myth of overpopulation from Outlines of a critique of political economy", *Deutsch-Französische Jahrbücher,* no. 1, 1844.

40   Meek, 1953, p.114.

41   Malthus, 1798, p.17.

42   Malthus, 1798, p.114.

allows to populate the earth and 'procure subsistence for an extended population [would] not be performed without the goad of necessity', that is without the constant pressure from the principle of population.[43]

Growth of food and population might be a happy outcome but is one rife with suffering from the misery that keeps the growth of population within the limits of food growth. Suffering, Malthus argues, comes from the inevitable positive and preventive checks that control population.[44] 'Positive checks' are those that 'repress an increase which is already begun'[45] and they include hunger and famine, infanticide and premature death, war and disease; anything that reduces the life-span. 'Preventive checks' are those where reason intervenes and involve sexual abstinence and birth control; anything that reduces the number of off-spring. Abstinence creates misery and suffering too, since the sexual passion is a natural human need. Sex without procreation is a 'vice' in the lexicon of Malthus: it degrades morals and might also lead to misery by sexually transmitted disease. Malthus goes at lengths in chapters 18 and 19 to explain why all this suffering is part of God's providence. Without it, human mind would not awaken. It would never become creative, industrious and capable to respond to the difficulties of life. Suffering, in other words, is a pre-requisite for civilization.

Misery and growth proceed in cycles. Malthus suggests an oscillating, cyclical pattern of population growth and collapse, within an overall trajectory of population growing on average at the rate of growth of food production. Once food productivity and production increase, people have more kids. At some point the number of people exceeds the available food supplies, and then positive checks take hold, falling primarily upon the poor who are by Malthus' definition those who are in excess. High prices for food however, and lower wages for the overpopulous poor restore equilibrium, incentivizing productivity growth, more food, and a new cycle of expansion.

Two paradoxes can already be noted. First, in Malthus' model there is no space for abundance. As he puts it: 'man cannot live in the midst of plenty'[46]. A happy state of a stable (or declining) population living with its food supplies is *a priori* inconceivable for Malthus, and not only because it is the natural

---

43 Malthus, 1798, p.47.
44 Malthus, 1789.
45 Malthus, 1798, p.23.
46 Malthus, 1798, p.57.

call of people to have as many kids as possible. It is inconceivable, because it is undesirable: only a growing population is sign of (periodical) happiness and health. A stable, or worse declining, population can only be the result of intense suffering, the reign of misery and vice: there can be nothing 'abundant' about it from Malthus' gaze. I will return to this value-laden premise of Malthus in section 2.6.

Second, Malthus could only be proven wrong if his standard of happiness were to be met. What do I mean by this? In defence of Malthus, Elwell argues that the fact that food productivity and population are growing since Malthus' time is no proof that he was wrong.[47] Malthus postulated that population is bound to grow at the rate of growth of food production, or less. As others have noted, the 'prediction' that population cannot grow faster than its subsistence is a truism, a non-falsifiable proposition[48]. Elwell however argues that Malthus *does* offer a falsifiable proposition. The proposition is that population is unlikely to ever grow for a prolonged period of time at its *natural* rate. If Malthus were wrong, then assuming 'one billion people at the time of the Essay, and a 25 year doubling time for unchecked population, today's population would be up to 256 billion'[49]. As it is not nearly so high, there *must have* been severe checks on population. Malthus was therefore right, Elwell concludes.

Of course, no one in their right mind, even the staunchest advocates of progress, would claim that an indefinite geometric growth of population is desirable or possible. The only one who claimed this and equated it to the wealth and happiness of nations was Malthus himself. If happiness, i.e. the 'natural' rate of population growth were to be realized, Malthus would turn out to be wrong and his thesis of eternal scarcity and periodic suffering proved wrong; but everyone would be happy, at least happy in Malthus' peculiar terms of having as many kids as naturally possible.

Growth, Not Redistribution: The Thrust of Malthus' Argument

There is not at present enough for all to have a decent share... Increase the demand for agricultural labour by promoting cultivation, and with it consequently increase the produce of the country, and ameliorate the condition of the labourer, and no apprehensions whatever need be entertained of the

---

47 Elwell, 2001.
48 Dale, 2012; Harvey, 1974.
49 Elwell, 2001, p.7.

proportional increase of population. An attempt to effect this purpose in any other way is vicious, cruel, and tyrannical, and in any state of tolerable freedom cannot therefore succeed.[50]

We have now the ingredients to reconstruct Malthus' causal argument. First there is the principle of population: it is easier to have kids than provide for them. This for Malthus is a fact of nature and there isn't much that can be done about it. Then, follows the principle of universal scarcity: there is not enough for everyone. Finally, this scarcity causes all social ills, such as hunger, disease, violence and war. Trying to overcome this natural scarcity with reason produces more suffering: the misery of abstinence or the vice of non-reproductive sex. What is then to be done?

Malthus wrote the Essay not as an exercise in philosophy, but as a manifesto against what was being done at his time, which was the Poor Laws, a scheme of poor relief where Parishes secured the basic food needs of those without work. Malthus' goal was to undo the theoretical justification for the Poor Laws[51]. Malthus wrote his fierce pamphlet in reaction to the egalitarian spirit of the French revolution expressed in the then popular books of Godwin and Condorcet. He was inspired after an argument he had with his father (the 'friend' mentioned in the first sentence of the Essay), an acquaintance of Hume and Rousseau and favourable of progressive intellectuals like Godwin, against whom Malthus wrote his essay. People like Godwin were arguing that poverty was the result of human institutions, and it could be alleviated with redistribution. In a society of equals, no one will be poor, Godwin argued. Malthus purported to prove the opposite. Poverty was natural and inevitable. Human institutions are imperfect, but their improvement cannot eradicate poverty. In a society of equals everyone will be poor. Misery will spread equally upon everyone, instead of falling only upon the unlucky few who ended up poor.

In principle, there is nothing wrong with spreading food (or even misery) equally upon everyone, rather than having a small minority with excess food and riches, while many have none. To justify his defence of a class society, Malthus develops a complex argument against redistribution and equality. His argument is that redistribution will make things worse *for everyone*. Remember he argued that an increase in population can only be sustained if there is a growth in the means of subsistence. Redistribution however, Malthus claims,

50   Malthus, 1798, p. 24, 42.
51   Perelman, 1979; Harvey, 1974.

hampers this growth. Redistributive institutions like the Poor Laws that guarantee a basic income for the poor provide an incentive for leisure and against the spirit of industry[52], diminish the will of the poor to save and accumulate, since their needs are covered[53] and are inflationary, since they increase incomes without increasing food supplies, hence increasing the real cost of food for the poor and for the rest[54]. If the poor get access to more food without producing more, this 'larger share [they] cannot receive without diminishing the shares of others'[55], hence making society as a whole worse off.

Furthermore, the artificial security that the Poor Laws provide 'operates to prevent the price of labour from rising' when population falls, keeping people poorer than necessary while also 'keeps it down some time longer', when population grows, hampering a growth in food production[56]. Malthus' proposals are then 'an attempt to tie population growth itself to increases in the produce of the land'[57]. First and foremost, he proposes a 'total abolition of all the present parish-laws' ... to 'give liberty and freedom of action to the peasantry of England ... to be able to settle without interruption, wherever there was a prospect of a greater plenty of work and a higher price for labour'. Poor relief kept people tied to the parishes that provided it, and diminished the incentives to move around and search for jobs. 'The market of labour would then be free, and those obstacles removed which, as things are now, often for a considerable time prevent the price from rising according to the demand'[58]. Malthus' Essay might well be the first rejection of redistribution and welfare support on the basis of the growth benefits of the free market.

Malthus develops also a second line of reasoning, purporting to show the natural and logical impossibility of a society of equals. He invites his readers to a thought experiment where Godwin's utopia has come to be realized: there is no property and everyone has their needs met with an equal share of food secured. With subsistence secured for themselves and for their descendants, people will have as many kids as naturally possible. As the rate of population will exceed the rate of food growth, the total share available to each

---

52 Malthus, 1798, p.25-27.
53 Malthus, 1798, p.27.
54 Malthus, 1798, p.25.
55 Ibid.
56 Malthus, 1798, p.11.
57 Elwell, 2001, p.14.
58 Malthus, 1798, p.30.

will gradually diminish: someone will then have to live with less. Those luckier in their harvest will want to protect their food against those less lucky; private property will have to be invented to protect their crop against intruders. And once there is a propertied class with sufficient food and a propertyless and hungry lot with nothing to sell but their labour, it would be inhuman to prohibit the latter from doing work for the former. Anything else would be tyranny. 'An administration of property, not very different from that which prevails in civilized states at present, would be established'[59]. Godwin's society of equals 'in a very short period [will] degenerate into a society constructed upon a plan not essentially different from that ... at present; ... a society divided into a class of proprietors, and a class of labourers'[60]. This is nature's outcome and there is nothing that can be done about it.

Inequality is inevitable, but fortunately is not so bad, Malthus argues, because it is the motor of growth. The whole society could never become a middle class since: 'in society the extreme parts could not be diminished beyond a certain degree without lessening that animated exertion throughout the middle parts ... If no man could hope to rise or fear to fall, in society, if industry did not bring with it its reward and idleness its punishment, the middle parts would not certainly be what they now are'[61]. 'Self-love', what today economists call self-interest[62] demands that under conditions of inequality and unprotected competition, everyone has to work as hard as possible to keep up with the one above and beat the one below. The end result, for Malthus and economists after Malthus, is everyone rising up together. Malthus I conclude is an early apostle or apologist if you prefer of the ideology of growth.

As Dale notes, it is a paradox then that Malthus and his Essay are seen by scholars like Herman Daly as precursors of ecological economics and the 'limits to growth' thesis.[63] Malthus is adamant that natural resources are unlimited. 'There is an essential difference', he claims, 'between food and ... commodities, the raw materials of which are in great plenty. A demand for these

---

59   Malthus, 1798, p.62.

60   Malthus, 1798, p.64-65.

61   Malthus, 1798, p.116.

62   David Nally, "Imagine All the People: Rockefeller Philanthropy, Malthusian Thinking and the "Peasant Problem" in Asia", *New Perspectives on Malthus: 250th Anniversary Essays*, (ed.) R. Mayhew, Cambridge University Press, 2016.

63   Dale, 2012.

last will not fail to create them in as great a quantity as they are wanted'[64]. For food too 'no limits whatever are placed to the productions of the earth; they may increase for ever and be greater than any assignable quantity'[65]. As Elwell defends, the Essay 'was not of a dour writer, unremitting its pessimism ... it is actually quite lively, and generally upbeat regarding the future of human societies[66]... [since Malthus had a] healthy respect for the powers of technology'[67]. Indeed in the second edition of the Essay Malthus goes as far as claiming that a nation could 'go on increasing in riches and population for hundreds, nay, almost thousands of years'[68]

On the other hand, it is true that Malthus claimed that food growth can at best be arithmetic. This was an *ad hoc* assumption, not only based on dubious empirical evidence, but also logically indefensible and contradicting the rest of his Essay. Not only because more people can clear and cultivate more land, but also because if food growth at some point had become arithmetic, then by Malthus' time it should have reached a stationary state of nearly 0% growth. This definitely was not the case and also was not what Malthus had in mind, since unlike his arithmetic example, there are various passages where he clearly foresees continuous, albeit limited, growth in food production.

It was Ricardo who developed Malthus' arithmetic growth into the more solid hypothesis of diminishing returns in agriculture, on the basis that the most productive lands are developed first and returns from already developed lands tend to diminish with effort.[69] Ricardo's theory however highlighted only a theoretical possibility, not an inevitable empirical fact. Ricardo allowed the counter-dynamic of capital making land more productive. Ecologists in the 1970s reclaimed from classical economists the idea of resource limits and diminishing returns to growth. Some of them were proud to call themselves (environmental) Malthusians[70]. The problem is not that they erroneously traced the idea of limits to growth back to Malthus, when Malthus himself did not believe in limits and was concerned with how to grow production so as to

---

64 Dale, 2012, p.28.

65 Dale, 2012, p.8.

66 Elwell, 2001, p.2.

67 Elwell, 2001, p.6.

68 Dale, 2012, p.870.

69 David Ricardo, *Principles of Political Economy and Taxation*, G. Bell and Sons, 1891.

70 Thomas Robertson, *The Malthusian Moment: Global Population Growth and the Birth of American Environmentalism*, Rutgers University Press, 2012.

people the Earth. The problem is that they framed their critique of growth in the terms set up by Malthus, and refined by economists after him, terms designed to justify the need for eternal accumulation and growth, precisely what was destroying the planet and many of them were up against.

Why Malthus Was Wrong

The common argument goes that Malthus was wrong because he didn't predict the agricultural and industrial revolutions; his technological pessimism fooled him. However, as I argued, and as Elwell is at pains to show, Malthus was positive about the prospects of technological change, expected unlimited strides in industrial growth and resource extraction, and was concerned with - but supportive of - efforts to increase food production.[71] Neoclassical economists are right that he did not foresee an increase in food availability and consumption per capita, thinking that food production would be taken up by higher numbers of people. But this does not make Malthus a pessimist who thought the trap of stagnation could not be escaped. This is reading Malthus from the vantage point of the present, as if he was a neoclassical economist concerned with stagnant income per capita. For Malthus welfare meant population growth, and he was optimistic that welfare can grow, modestly and with the right amount of discipline.

The claim that Malthus was wrong because he did not predict production growth risks reproducing Malthus' own framework. Mill and Keynes, or even Marx, have responded, explicitly or implicitly, to Malthusian concerns with the prediction that there will be enough for everyone, if only we wait until tomorrow. Concerned that if Malthus were right, socialism could not abolish poverty but only generalize it, Engels contended that "too little is produced, that is the cause of the whole thing", but that's because of the limits capitalist production puts on the productive forces, limits that will be superseded in the future under socialism.[72] Mill's stationary state[73], Marx and Engel's unfettered development of the forces of production, or Keynes' post-industrial future - where decades of productivity growth will allow his grandchildren enjoy leisure working only a few hours each week - share a vision of overcoming scarcity by

---

71 Elwell, 2001.
72 Engels, 1844.
73 John Stuart Mill, "Of the stationary state", *Principles of Political Economy Book IV: Influence of the Progress of Society*, London, 1848.

increasing production, distributing the bounty so that everyone has enough[74]. They all accept Malthus' diagnosis of scarcity, but unlike him, believe that re-distribution will be good for growth.

But as Xenos perfectly puts it "by relying on economic forces to transcend themselves, Keynes, and Marx and Mill before him, are waiting for Godot".[75] The economic forces that promise to transcend scarcity are also the ones that increase needs together with production, ensuring that there is not, and there will never be enough for everyone. To live a dignified life and die a dignified death, the average person today needs to mobilize resources unthinkable even to royals of bygone eras. Focussing on the question of production accepts the myth of scarcity, a legitimating meta-narrative for the institutions of capitalism and modernity, which position themselves as the only ones that can confront scarcity[76]. Criticism of these institutions is possible "but only on the basis of a point in time that is always in the future, due to the functioning of social need, and so the criticism oddly winds up endorsing the institutions of scarcity while positing a different future because those institutions make that future possible"[77]

Marx and Engels cannot be put in the same basket with Mill and Keynes, but I think the unintended acceptance by the first two of the rules of the game set by Malthus, might go a long way into explaining their tolerance, at least to an extent, of certain institutions and techniques of modernity (if not capitalism) on the grounds that they unleash the forces of production that will supersede scarcity.

One can challenge a fable not only by proposing alternative deductions, but by revealing the non-sense, rather than common-sense, of its premises[78], while revealing how the final deduction depends crucially upon these nonsensical premises. The core assumption in Malthus and the basis for the principle of universal scarcity is the premise of an unlimited human nature confronting

74   John Maynard Keynes, *Economic Possibilities For Our Grandchildren (Essays in Persuasion)*, W.W.Norton & Co., New York, 1963.

75   Nicholas Xenos, "IV. Liberalism and the Postulate of Scarcity", *Political Theory*, vol.15, no. 2, 1987, p.239.

76   Xenos, 1987, p.239.

77   Ibid.

78   Larry Lohmann, "Malthusianism and the Terror of Scarcity", *Making Threats: Biofears and Environmental Anxieties,* (eds). B. Hartmann, B. Subramaniam, and C. Zerner, Rowman&Littlefield, 2005.

the limits of a limited life. Life is surely limited by death, but it is questionable if the natural state of human beings is to be obsessed with doing as much as possible within every millisecond before they die. Malthus' edifice for example rests on the peculiar assumption that human nature dictates that we need to have as many kids as physically possible. "Nature" here refers to the sexual instinct and the insatiable demands it generates. This flies though in the face of evidence that humans more often than not control how many kids they have anticipating the consequences. If humans are beings of nature then this anticipatory self-limitation is natural too; but for Malthus these were "unnatural acts"[79].

An interesting historical fact is that at the time before Malthus' essay, the main concern was depopulation, not population growth[80]. This depopulation was not the outcome only of epidemics, wars and disease, but also of women silently asserting control over their own bodies and lives and resisting men and the Church[81]. Low population growth however placed a limit on early capitalism, keeping the costs of labour high. As Federici shows, natalist state policies and the "witch hunt" of childless women were part of the counter-offensive of capital accumulation to dispossess women from the control of their own bodies and to appropriate their reproductive labour.[82]

Malthus was surely aware of the possibility, and the actual practices that could limit reproduction. He himself recognizes early in the Essay, that his fellow bourgeois calculated how many kids they would have in order to prevent undesirable outcomes such as a lowering of their rank, or a life full of hard toil and labour[83]. And in addition to delaying marriage and abstention, he refers to "promiscuous corcubinage". If it was possible to have sex without having children, as of course it was, how did Malthus hold his story together?

One possible answer is that he didn't; he was simply classist in a way that resonated with his bourgeois audience[84]. As Harvey notes, Malthus has one law of population for the poor and another law for the rich. Whereas the numbers of the poor are controlled mostly by positive checks, the rich can exercise

79   Malthus, 1798, p.48.
80   Heilbroner, 1999.
81   Silvia Federici, "The Devaluation of Women's Labor", *Eco-sufficiency And Global Justice: Women Write Political Ecology*, (ed). Ariel Salleh, Pluto Press, 2009.
82   Federici, 2009.
83   Malthus, 1798, p.8-9.
84   Lohman, 2005.

reason and check their numbers preventatively[85]. Selby and Hoffman note a broader classist and racist pattern in Malthusian and neo-Malthusian thought, where the Europeans and the rich are civilized and apply reason to their actions, whereas the poor and the "barbarians" are like animals at the mercy of instincts and forces of nature.[86]

In the Essay Malthus makes the casual observation that this is how things are, and that it is the poor that tend to die of hunger or lose their kids to disease. But he doesn't go as far as basing his story in this distinction. His logical claim is that if you secure the survival of the poor and their kids independent of the efforts that they make, then you give them the wrong incentive to have as many kids as they like, and work as little as they wish[87]. The difference of the law of population among classes is economic, not genetic or hereditary (there is nothing indeed in Malthus to suggest that he was making a sociobiological argument against the poor.)[88] The rich control their procreation because they suffer the financial consequences, while those on welfare do not. The logical problem with this (that Malthus could not accept since it would go against the interests of his own class) is that then neither the rich should be left to be wealthy and secure, since this would make them lazy and procreative; and if they are to feel secure, as no doubt the wealthiest of them felt, how come and they didn't procreate at the "natural" rate? And if they did, wouldn't this be enough - given the geometric, exponential rate of increase of their numbers - to deplete the food for all the rest?

Malthus did not need to go there, because he posited that the preventative checks of the rich were only marginally less painful than the positive checks falling upon the poor. Delaying marriage and the satisfaction of the instinct of sex was painful, Malthus argued, quite daringly for a member of the clergy. Perhaps he was talking here from direct experience, since he practiced celibacy until his marriage, at the age of 38. Why not non-procreative, recreational sex though? Obviously because he was a priest. The interesting question though is always how Malthus makes the *logical* case in defence of his priest and classist views, not the fact that they are such. Criticizing Condorcet, he responds that yes, at some point in the future people could limit their numbers and satisfy

---

85   Elwell, 2001.
86   Jan Selby, Clemens Hoffman, *Divided Environments: Water wars and Climate Conflict revisited*, I B Tauris, London, 2016.
87   Malthus, 1798, p.62.
88   Elwell, 2001.

their sexual instincts, but only by recourse "to a promiscuous concubinage, which would prevent breeding, or to something else as unnatural"[89]. The operational word here is "unnatural". If God makes the natural world, then unnatural is to go against His wish; and His wish is for people to populate the earth, not sit idle and enjoy its fruits. This sacredness of work is the very core of the protestant ethic and at the origins of capital accumulation.[90] Malthus gives also other more instrumental arguments against the "vice" of non-procreative sex such that it degrades morals or it causes disease, increasing the sum of unhappiness.[91] But his main point is that it goes against nature and God. Religion is dressed as natural science; and ideology provides the backbone for a circular logic.

Only from this perspective one can make sense of Malthus' vehement opposition to birth control. If he was indeed concerned with the risk of overpopulation, he would advocate or at least sanction the use of contraception and other ways of having sex without kids. He didn't and ignored the pleas of his contemporaries to do so.[92] In the 5th edition of the Essay he goes as far as condemning 'artificial and unnatural modes of checking population', because of 'their tendency to remove a necessary stimulus to industry'.[93] Precisely: Malthus wanted unchecked population growth, because this is what God wanted, and this is what his class needed: cheap and industrious workers.

I do not argue here that Malthus was wrong because he failed to *predict* birth control. Malthus was wrong because he tactically chose not to see the capacity of humans to limit their numbers, a capacity that was apparent all around him. The evidence from the Essay that I provided proves that he was acutely aware of the possibility, but that he refused to allow for it, presumably because it would leave his whole argument in shambles and disprove his ideology and moral convictions. Remember, Malthus was not a demographer: he was a philosopher arguing for the impossibility of a classless society. Allow in the capacity of humans to limit their numbers, and then there is no natural scarcity; and worse, there might even already be enough for everyone to have

---

89 Malthus, 1798, p. 48.

90 Max Weber, *The Protestant Ethic and the Spirit of Capitalism: And Other Writings,* Penguin, 2002.

91 Malthus, 1798, p. 48.

92 Donald Winch, *Malthus (Past Masters Series),* Oxford University Press, Oxford, 1987.

93 Thomas Malthus, *Essay on Population,* 5th Edition, Johnson, London, 1817, p.393; Perelman, 1979.

a decent share. The common-sensical observation that humans can, and often do, individually and collectively limit their procreative or recreational instincts in the face of the consequences of not doing so, is precisely the one that destroys his "myth of scarcity".[94]

Malthus therefore *is* a short-sighted pessimist, but not because he didn't foresee technological progress; he is so because he *didn't want to* see social innovation and change. Malthus did not want to imagine a future where women have free sexual relations without having kids, without being prostitutes and without anyone suffering as a result. Malthus could not imagine a feminist or an LGBT movement. He could not imagine government incentives to limit population growth. And he would definitely freak out if he was ever to know that a bunch of feminists, anarchists and socialists would gather in 1900, 66 years after his death, uniting under his own name in the first International Neo-Malthusian conference to claim the right of women for birth control, and all this as part of a revolutionary strategy to overthrow the ruling class that Malthus catered for.[95] What Malthus could not imagine was that social science changes the world that it purports to describe, and fortunately not always in the ways that it intends to.

94 Xenos, 1987.
95 Joan Martinez-Alier, "Neo-Malthusians", *Degrowth. A vocabulary for a new paradigm,* (eds.) G. D'Alisa, G. Demaria, F. and G. Kallis, Routledge-Earthscan, 2015.

References

Bookchin, Murray, *Post-scarcity anarchism*, Ramparts Press, San Francisco, 1971.

Burke, Edmund, *Thoughts and Details on Scarcity (1795)*, The Works, London, 1826.

Costanza, Robert; Cumberland, John H.; Daly, Herman; Goodland, Robert; Norgaard, Richard B.; Kubiszewski, Ida and Franco, Carol, *An introduction to ecological economics*, CRC Press, 2014.

D'Alisa, G.; Demaria, F. and G. Kallis (eds), *Degrowth, "A vocabulary for a new paradigm"*, Routledge-Earthscan, 2015.

Dale, Gareth, "Adam Smith's Green Thumb and Malthus's Three Horsemen: Cautionary Tales from Classical Political Economy," *Journal of Economic Issues*, vol. 46, no. 4, 2012, pp.859-880.

Daly, Herman E., "Mass migration and border policy," *Real-world economics review*, 2015.

Daly, Herman E., "A Marxian-Malthusian view of poverty and development", *Population Studies*, Vol. 25, No. 1, 1971, pp.25-37.

Daly, Herman E., *Steady-state economics: with new essays*, Island Press, 1991.

Daoud, Adel, "Robbins and Malthus on scarcity, abundance, and sufficiency", *American Journal of Economics and Sociology*, Vol.69, No. 4, 2010, pp.1206-1229.

Davis, Mike, "Late Victorian holocausts: El Niño famines and the making of the third world", Verso, London, 2002.

Dean, Mitchell, "The Malthus effect: Population and the liberal government of life", *Economy and Society*, Vol. 44, No. 1, 2015, pp.18-39.

Ehrlich, Paul, R., *The population bomb*, Ballantine, New York, 1968.

Ehrlich, Paul R., Bilderback, L. and Ehrlich, A.H., The golden door: international migration Mexico and the United States, 1979.

Ehrlich, Paul R., Ehrlich, A.H. and Holdren, J.P., Ecoscience: population resources environment, 1977.

Elwell, Frank W., Malthus' Social Theory, Retrieved May 12, 2016, http://www.faculty.rsu.edu/~felwell/Theorists/Malthus/Index.htm (excerpt from Elwell, F. W. 2001. A Commentary on Malthus' 1798 Essay on Population as Social Theory. Lewiston, NY: Edwin Mellen Press, 2001.)

Engels, Friedrich, *The myth of overpopulation, from Outlines of a critique of political economy*, 1844.

Federici, Silvia, The devaluation of women's labor, In Salleh, A (ed), Eco-sufficiency and global justice. Women write political ecology, Pluto Press, 2009.

Foucault, Micheal, *The order of things: An archaeology of the human sciences*, Psychology Press, 1970.

Frank, Robert H., Luxury fever: Money and happiness in an era of excess, Princeton University Press, 1999.

Galbraith, John K., *The affluent society*, Houghton Mifflin Harcourt, 1998.

Galor, Oded and Weil, David N., "From Malthusian stagnation to modern growth", *The American Economic Review*, Vol. 89, No. 2, 1999, pp.150-154.

Glassgold, Peter, *Anarchy!: An Anthology of Emma Goldman's Mother Earth*, Counterpoint Press, 2012.

Goldman, Emma, *The Social Aspects of Birth Control*, Mother Earth, XI (2), 1916. Reprinted In Glassgold, P., 2012. Anarchy!: An Anthology of Emma Goldman's Mother Earth. Counterpoint Press.

Gordon, Scott, "The economics of the afterlife", *Journal of Political Economy*, Vol. 88, No. 1, 1980, pp.213-214.

Gramsci, Antonio, *Selections from the Prison Notebooks, (ed. and trans.) Quintin Hoare and Geoffrey Nowell Smith*, International, New York, 1971.

Hardin, Garrett, "The tragedy of the commons", *Science,* 162(3859), (1968), pp.1243-1248.

Hardin, Garrett, "The survival of nations and civilization," *Science,* 172(3990), (1971), p.1297.

Harris, Marvin, *Cows, pigs, wars, & witches: the riddles of culture*, Vintage, 1989.

Hartmann, Betsy, "Converging on disaster: Climate security and the Malthusian anticipatory regime for Africa," *Geopolitics,* Vol. 19, No. 4, 2014, pp.757-783.

Harvey, David, *Population, resources, and the ideology of science*, Springer, Netherlands, 1979, (pp. 155-185).

Heilbroner, Robert L., *The worldly philosophers: The lives, times and ideas of the great economic thinkers*, Simon and Schuster, 1999.

Heller, Agnes, *The theory of need in Marx (No. 5),* Allison & Busby, 1976.

Hirsh, Fred, Social limits to growth, Routledge and Kegan Paul, 1976.

Hodgson, Geoffrey M., Economics and evolution: bringing life back into economics, University of Michigan Press, 1993.

Homer-Dixon, Thomas F., *Environment, scarcity, and violence*, Princeton University Press, 2010.

Kallis, Giorgos and March H., "Imaginaries of Hope: the dialectical utopianism of degrowth", *Annals of the Association of the American Geographers*,Vol. 105, No. 2, 2015, pp.360-368.

Kallis, Giorgos, "Social limits of growth", *A vocabulary for a new paradigm,* (eds). D'Alisa, G. Demaria, F. and G. Kallis Degrowth., Routledge-Earthscan, 2015.

Kaplan, Robert D., *The coming anarchy. Globalization and the Challenges of a New Century: A Reader,* Indiana University Press, Bloomington, 2000, pp.34-60.

Keynes, John M., *Economic possibilities for our grandchildren, Essays in persuasion,* 1933, pp.358-73.

Krugman, Paul, *Malthus was right! The conscience of a Liberal*, New York Times, March 25 2008.

Lohmann, Larry, "Malthusianism and the Terror of Scarcity", *Making threats: Biofears and environmental anxieties,* 2005, pp.81-98.

Malthus, Thomas, Thomas Malthus, *An Essay on the Principle of Population*, London, 1798.

Malthus, Thomas, An Essay on the Principle of Population, as it affects the future improvement of society with remarks on the speculations of Mr. Godwin, M. Condorcet and other writers, printed for J. Johnson, in St Paul's Church-yard, St. Paul's Church-yard, London.

Martinez-Alier, Joan, "Neo-Malthusians", *Degrowth. A vocabulary for a new paradigm,* (eds), D'Alisa, G. Demaria, F. and G. Kallis, Routledge-Earthscan, 2015, pp. 125-128.

Martinez-Alier, Joan and Masjuan, Eduard, "Neomalthusianism in the early 20th Century", *Encyclopedia of Ecological Economics, 2005,* Available at Isecoeco.org

Meadows, Dennis H.; Meadows, Donella L.; Randers, Jorgen and Behrens, William W., *The limits to growth*, New York, 1972.

Meek, Ronald L., *Marx and Engels on Malthus, Lawrence and Wishart*, London, 1953.

Mill, John Stuart., "Of the stationary state", *Principles of political economy Book IV: Influence of the progress of society*, 1848.

Mitchell, Timothy, *Carbon democracy: Political power in the age of oil*, Verso Books, 2011.

Nally, David, *Imagine all the people: Rockefeller philanthropy, Malthusian thinking and the "peasant problem" in Asia*, In citation missing, 2016.

Nelson, Richard R., "Recent evolutionary theorizing about economic change", *Journal of economic literature*, Vol. 33, No.1, 1995, pp.48-90.

Paley, William, *The principles of moral and political philosophy*, B. and S. Collins, 1790.

Phillips, Leigh, *Austerity ecology and the collapse-porn addicts*, Zero Books, 2015.

"Population Matters Why Malthus", (2016), available at http://populationmatters.org/documents/why_malthus_is_still_relevant_today.pdf (Accessed 12 May 2016)

Ricardo, David, *Principles of political economy and taxation*, G. Bell and sons, 1891.

Robbins, Lionel, *Essay on the nature and significance of economic science*, Springer, 2016.

Robertson, Thomas, *The Malthusian moment: global population growth and the birth of American environmentalism*, Rutgers University Press, 2012.

Rockström, Johan, Steffen, Will, Noone, Kevin, Persson, Å., Chapin, F. Stuart, Lambin, Eric F., Lenton, Timothy M., Scheffer, Marten, Folke, Carl, Schellnhuber, Hans J. and Nykvist, Björn, "A safe operating space for humanity", *Nature*, Vol. 461, No. 7263, 2009, pp.472-475.

Ronsin, Francis, *La grève des ventres- Propagande neo-malthusienne et baisse de la natalite en France 19-20 siècles*, Aubier-Montaigne, Paris, 1980.

Sassower, Raphael, "Scarcity and setting the boundaries of political economy," *Social epistemology: a journal of knowledge, culture and policy*, Vol. 4, No. 1, 1990, pp.75-91.

Sayre, Nathan F., "The genesis, history, and limits of carrying capacity", *Annals of the Association of American Geographers*, Vol. 98, No. 1, 2008, pp.120-134.

Selby, Jan and Hoffman, Clemens, *Divided Environments: Water wars and Climate conflict revisited*, 2016.

Skidelsky, Robert J.A. and Skidelsky, Edward, *How Much is Enough?: The Love of Money and the Case for the Good Life*, Penguin, UK, 2012.

Vogt, William, *Road to survival*, 1948.

Weber, Max, *The Protestant Ethic and the Spirit of Capitalism: and other writings*, Penguin, 2002.

Weisskopf, Walter A., *Alienation and economics*, Dutton, New York, 1971.

Winch, Donald, Malthus, *Past Masters Series*, Oxford University Press, Oxford, 1987.

Xenos, Nicholas, "IV. Liberalism and the Postulate of Scarcity", *Political theory*, Vol. 15, No. 2, 1987, pp.225-243.

Xenos, Nicholas, *Scarcity and modernity*, Routledge, 1989.

Contemporary Global Economic Crisis:
A World-System Approach

Ruslan Dzarasov

The current world economic crisis continues for the last 15 years. After the great global financial meltdown of 2008-2010 - the age of diminished expectations - as some economists say, the age of the so-called "Great Stagnation" started, and we are still living in it. However, the current problems of the world economy are usually related to the effect of the pandemic measures caused by COVID-19, and the Russian-Ukrainian military conflict. Of course, both events created great disturbances and had hurt the global economy. However, in fact the Great Stagnation started long before the 2020s. I would like to emphasize that in the last years, the share of economies embraced by recession was the highest for the last 150 years.[1] Thus, in 2020-2021, i.e. on the eve of the pandemic crisis and a few years prior to the eruption of the Ukrainian crisis, even more countries suffered from recession than in course of the Great Depression of the 1930s. The data on the weighted average of the rate of profit in the global corporate sector demonstrate steady decline in 2000s and sharp drop in 2017-2020.[2] This means that preconditions for a new second wave of the global slump reappeared in the world economy long before the current turmoil just as it happened earlier in 2008-2010. From this, in turn, follows that the world economy is haunted by some deep disease. It is the subject of the current chapter.

The World-System Approach

This problem can be addressed in the framework of the so-called World-System analysis, which develops after the Second World War by such famous intellectuals as Immanuel Wallerstein (2004), Samir Amin (2010), André Gunder Frank (1978), Giovanni Arrighi (2010) and a number of other excellent

---

1   World Bank Group, "Global Economic Prospects: A World Bank Group Flagship Report- June 2020", p. 5.
2   Michael Roberts, "More on the World Rate of Profit", Michael Roberts Blog, 20 September 2020, https://thenextrecession.wordpress.com/2020/09/20/more-on-a-world-rate-of-profit/, (last accessed on 14 January 2023.)

researchers. They are focused, despite other differences, on unequal exchange between the core of the world economy, which is represented by the developed capitalist countries, and the periphery, which is represented by developing countries. Researchers like Wallerstein are also focused on so-called semi-peripheral countries, which are situated somewhere in between the core and periphery, to which I believe both Türkiye and Russia belong. These are the systemic factors that characterize the world capitalism from the very beginning. Historians, think that capitalism appeared somewhere about around 1500 in Mediterranean. From the very start, from the very ascendance of Italian trade city-states, capitalist economies accumulated capital on a global level through unequal relations between the core and periphery. And a number of ways were developed by world capitalism how to control the periphery and how to extract additional income from the periphery.

A brilliant Latin American economist Raúl Prebisch (1901-1986) suggested the idea of the 'dependent development'.[3] Explaining this phenomenon he was focused on so-called price disparity. Under this term he meant the fact that index of prices of raw materials and agricultural products in the world economy on average systematically falls behind the index of prices of manufacturing products. He believed that this means that developing countries every year have to sell more and more of their products in order to buy the same amount of products suggested by transnational corporations from the core countries every year. Of course, this causes dependent development of nations. However, he thought that this is just a technical problem, which can be solved by so-called 'input substitution'. This strategy in Latin America, in fact, failed. Reasons of this had been revealed by further development of World-System analysis. The latter embraced the idea of price disparity but suggested a number of other important insights into the unequal relations between the core and periphery on which the global accumulation is based.

It is worthy to single out the concept of 'development of underdevelopment' suggested by the brilliant American intellectual of German origin Andre Gunder Frank (1929-2005), who was an economist, historian, and sociologist deeply understanding the problems of development, especially of Latin America, and Asian countries as well. In a number of works he described the global accumulation of capital especially focusing on the fate of Latin America,

---

3   Edgar J. Dosman, *The Life and Times of Raul Prebish, 1901-1986,* Montreal & Kingston, Mc-Gill-Queen's University Press, London, 2008.

China, India and Africa[4] (see, for instance, Frank, 1978, 1966). He arrived at the conclusion that developed capitalist countries expanding capitalism to developing countries of the world periphery, initially in the form of colonization, and there, by means of neocolonial policy, transformed both production in these countries and their social relations. Transformation of production of the dependent societies led to a reduction of their relatively diversified economies to monocultures. This means that such countries are more focused now on supply of a few products demanded by manufacturing of the developed countries. Simultaneously transformation of their social structures follows, depriving peasantry access to land, which turns it into a pool of cheap labor available for exploitation by the nascent bourgeoisie. The latter is recruited from the former landowners. This new elite assumes specific character. In Latin America it was dubbed 'Comprador bourgeoisie', which means that it operates as a proxy of the transnational capital of the developed countries and intermediates the exploitation of the population and natural resources of the dependent countries for the sake of accumulation of capital by transnational corporations. On such a basis, colonialism in China, India, Latin America and a number of other countries, operates.

It is interesting to note that these problems were anticipated by controversies between the Populists and Marxists in 19th century Russia, where discussion of the perspectives of capitalist development was the focus of debates. Populists argued that capitalism could not develop in Russia because the world market has been already captured by the developed countries, while the national domestic market was too narrow to provide a space for decent accumulation of capital. On this basis, Populists argued that Russia should avoid capitalism moving to socialism without the capitalist stage of development. Initially, Marxists criticized them and argued that capitalism was developing in Russia, just as in the Western countries, although with a certain delay. However, at the turn of the 20th century Marxists had split in Mensheviks and Bolsheviks. The former insisted on two stages of the future Russian revolution, believing that capitalist development should work out itself up to the full capacity before the socialist revolution can take place. Unlike them Lenin developed his famous theory of "overgrowth of the bourgeois-democratic revolution into the socialist one". It assumes that Russian capitalism is deficient - the weak chain of imperialism - and that is why Russian bourgeoisie, too dependent on

---

4   Andre Frank, *Dependent Accumulation and Underdevelopment*, The Macmillan Press ltd, London, 1978.; A. Frank, "The Development of Underdevelopment", *Monthly Review,* Vol. 18, No. 4, 1966, p.21.

Tsarism and too reactionary, will be unable to lead the democratic revolution. In the absence of leadership on the part of the bourgeois-democratic circles, revolution will inevitably move to socialist transformation. This was anticipation of the idea of 'backward capitalism', crippled by unequal core-periphery relations. And in fact, the current studies of how capitalism developed in Tsarist times in Russia (see, for instance, Kagarlitsky, 2008) puts emphasis on the fact that Russian Tsarism invited Western capital on the basis of export of grain to Europe. Russian peasantry paid a high price for this. Accumulation of gold and foreign currency reserves was achieved at the expense of degradation of Russian agriculture, which created preconditions for the participation of the Russian peasantry in the Russian Revolution. So Russian development fits very well into the world picture suggested by the World-System analysis.

The current World-System

At this historical backdrop the current global capitalism should be considered and evaluated. Let us consider the Figure 1. It reflects the structure of export from the developing countries in 1980-2003,

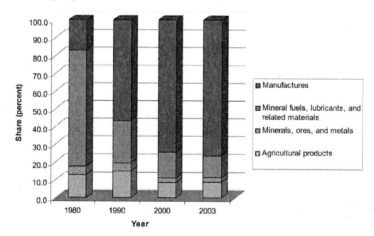

Table 1. Composition of merchandise exports from developing countries by major product group, 1980-2003.[5]

The above figure shows how relations between the core and periphery changed in the last decades of the 20th century. The diagrams reflect the structure of the exports of the countries with low and medium incomes to the countries with

---

5   Razmi Arslan and Robert, Blecker, "Developing Country Exports of Manufactures: Moving Up the Ladder to Escape the Fallacy of Composition?", *The Journal of Development Studies*, Vol.44, No.1, 2006, p.44.

high incomes. If we take the data from 1980, then we see that only 20% of this export was represented by manufacturing, while 80% was represented by such groups as raw materials, minerals and agricultural products. If one moves from the 1980s to the data for the 2003, one sees the opposite picture. Now, 80% of exports are represented by manufacturing groups, while only 20% represent core materials and agricultural products. This is an enormous shift. If one thinks that this means that the problems of development were successfully solved and that at last the developing countries had reached the aim of high industrial development, then such an optimistic picture would be premature. The above change is the result of enormous global shift of production from the global North to the global South in the recent 3-4 decades starting, from the 1980s.

This was response of the world capitalism to the so-called 'Stagflation' crisis of the early 1970s, which put an end to the Golden Age of capitalism after the Second World War. In the 1950s and 1960s, Western countries enjoyed higher rates of economic growth and social welfare states, high rates of technical progress, and some people argued in the Soviet Union (not officially, but in informal conversations, of course) that capitalism solved all social problems which socialism tried to solve. However, Stagflation contradicted this optimistic understanding, and corporate profits went down. Capital of the core found response to this crisis shifting the burden of production to the periphery[6], in an attempt to benefit from local cheap labor. Let us consider the Figure 2.

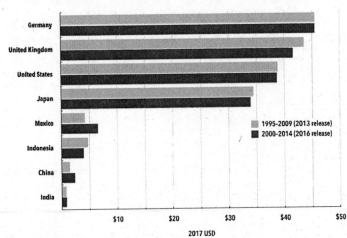

Table 2. Average Hourly Compensation in Manufacturing, 2017 USD[7]

6   Peter Dicken, *Global Shift: Reshaping the Global Economic Map in the 21-st Century*, SAGE Publications Inc, London, 2003.
7   Suwandi *et al.*, 2019.

The figure presents certain data on the relation between wage rates in the core countries and in the periphery. One can see that the difference is enormous. If we take China and the average real wage rate in industry in this country, now, even now after wages started growing in China, still it is only a fraction of the average real wage rate in American industry. And probably this is the reason why Donald Trump fails to fulfill his pledge to return production to America. And of course, this cheap labor was the prime source of growth of incomes of Western transnational corporations in the last decades. In the end, it has enormous consequences for the global economy. First of all, the global economy experienced shock expansion of the global workforce. In the 1980s, the global workforce amounted to nearly 1.5 billion workers. In two decades, on the eve of the new millennium, and now it is greater than 3.32 billion.[8] For the first time in history the number of workers in the global population exceeds the share of peasantry operating on the basis of manual power. This shock expansion of the global workforce took place not on the basis of technical progress and greater productivity, but mainly on the basis of labor-intensive production processes.

The global capital/labor ratio decreased in 1990s-2000s by 55-60%[9], which means that the world followed the way opposite to technical progress, and this resulted in a number of very important consequences. The effect of this global shift of production on real GDP growth rates depends on deficiency of aggregate demand at the world scale in relation to aggregate supply in the last 30 years. Industrialization of China, India, Mexico and many other countries led to enormous growth of production capacities. However, the world aggregate demand falls behind and this led to growth of idle productive capacities worldwide.[10] In turn, this conditioned decline of productivity in the real sector economy, which generated decline of real GDP growth rates before the world financial meltdown.

8   David Clark, "Number of Employees Worldwide 1991-2022", Statista Internet-resource, 7 December 2022, https://www.statista.com/statistics/1258612/global-employment-figures/ (last accessed on 15 January 2023)

9   Richard Freeman, "What really ails Europe (and America): the doubling of the global workforce", The Globalist, 5 March 2010, https://www.theglobalist.com/what-really-ails-europe-and-america-the-doubling-of-the-global-workforce/ (last accessed on 17 January 2023)

10   This was obvious as early as in 1990s. For instance, in 1985 only one-fourth of the world car industry productive capacities were idle. In 1995 this figure had grown to 30%, and to 36% in the end of the decade. The same was peculiar to the global aviation, chemistry, steel and semi-conductor producing industries, Greider, 1998, p. 111, 112.

The global investments and savings as the share of world GDP in the last 50 years declined considerably again following this global shift of production from the global north to the global south. This led to a financial meltdown. For decades, the American domestic market, for example, was growing due to the growth of consumer debt and in a situation of stagnant wages and stagnant real incomes of hired labor. This led to the famous mortgage crisis of 2007, which precipitated this global slump. Currently, these problems still affect the world economy. This inadequate aggregate demand, which is a result of low real wages in the world economy, is the main reason why the world suffers the Great Stagnation.

The unprecedented growth of financial speculations, which became one of the most salient features of modern capitalism, can also be traced to the global shift of production from the core to the periphery. In response to dramatic decline of corporate profits in the 1970s the US corporate sector was restructured. A wave of redistribution of property rights in result of hostile takeovers rolled through it. Corporations were downsized and stripped of allegedly non-core assets, which allowed to cut circular capital and investment funds to increase dividend payments.[11] This was done with one aim – to increase share prices. This process, dubbed 'Revolution of shareholders', had led to maximization of shareholder value replacing long-term growth as the main aim of US corporations.[12] In such conditions Wall Street (financial capital) took over the Main Street (industrial capital), imposing on the latter its intrinsic short-termism.[13] This process of so-called financialization facilitated outsourcing of production to the partners in the periphery.

Essentially, modern capitalism shifted its emphasis from production to financial activities, which were increasingly assuming speculative nature. On the eve of the global meltdown in 2007 sum of capitalization of shares, debt obligations and bank assets exceeded the world GDP by 4,4 times, while the shadow market of infamous derivatives amounted to $600 trillion (!), which is eleven times greater than the world GDP[14]

11   Margaret Blair, "Financial Restructuring and the Debate about Corporate Governance", *The Deal Decade, What Takeovers and Leveraged Buyouts Mean for the Corporate Governance*, (ed.) M. Blair, The Brookings Institution, Washington D.C., 1993.

12   William Lazonick and Mary O'Sullivan, "Maximizing Shareholder Value: A New Ideology for Corporate Governance", *Economy and Society*, Vol. 29, No. 1, 2000.

13   Karen Ho, *Liquidated: An Ethnography of Wall Street*, Duke University Press, Durham and London, 2009.

14   Kean Birch and Vlad Mykhnenko, "Introduction", *The Rise and Fall of Neoliberalism. The Collapse of an Economic Order?*, (eds.) K. Birch and V. Mykhnenko, Zed Books, London-New York, 2010, p.13.

Since the deepest cause of the current Great Stagnation is inadequate wage rates in the periphery, the most important condition for starting the real growth of world GDP and development is increasing the wage rate globally. It is impossible to achieve this in the current system of relationships because the countries that increase real wage rates will lose international competitiveness, which is what happens with China nowadays. There is evidence that competitors are able to replace China at the world markets following the growth of wage rates in this country (see, for instance, BS, 2022). However, if the wage rates grow worldwide, then this will eliminate the most important dimension of the world economic crisis - this inadequate global aggregate demand. However, it is very painful for the ruling elites, which control the world economy today because, at the first place, the domination of financial speculative capital in the modern global economy should be overcome in favor of industrial capital. But if this will be implemented, then immediately the world capitalism will find that production shifted from Western countries to Asia, at least largely shifted. And in conditions of domination of industrial capital, the world domination will shift to Asian countries. So, this is very damaging for the ruling elites and national states which dominate the current world system. That is the most important problem. However, without such a growth of global wage rates, it is impossible to find a long-term solution to the current global economic crisis.

Short-termism of Russian Capitalism and Its Position in the World-System[15]

Short-termism of Russian big capital became one of the most telling features of the current Russian capitalism, and it is related to the position of Russia in the world economy. The most lucrative sectors of the Russian economy are those, which export products and earn hard currency in the world market, the world reserve currency, the US dollar. And these sectors produce raw materials, natural resources, metals, fertilizers, or some other products with a low level of processing raw materials. They are much more lucrative than Russian manufacturing. Such a situation leads to a decline of manufacturing in the Russian economy, and has made it much more vulnerable to external shocks, which are quite often very damaging in the age of global stagnation. Another institutional problem is that Russian big capital is based on a highly authoritarian model of corporate governance, which relates to two major sources.

---

15 This section of the paper is based on the book: Ruslan Dzarasov, *The Conundrum of Russian Capitalism. Russian Economy in the World System,* Pluto Press, London, 2014.

Firstly, to degeneration of the Soviet bureaucracy, which controlled all economic resources in the Soviet Union. In the late stages of the Soviet history, bureaucracy increasingly enjoyed greater and greater informal control over economic resources and used this informal control for private enrichment. This created preconditions to shift to capitalism in Soviet society. Secondly, the roots of the current Russian model of corporate governance can be traced to the influence of the modern financialized global capitalism. In the early 1990s, when the Soviet system collapsed and radical market reforms were introduced in Russia, the world capitalism, especially the American ruling elite, enjoyed enormous influence on the course of market reforms, and the principles of the famous Washington consensus were introduced. And they were at the foundation of Russian market reforms, just as in the very foundation of market reforms in all former Soviet republics as well. This strengthened the informal control of the degenerated Soviet bureaucracy over the most lucrative assets of the former state enterprises. This determined the social essence of privatization, for instance, which was in fact, appropriation of the best assets, the most lucrative assets by people close to the power. Such measures of Yeltsin's reforms as, for instance, the liberalization of prices, in fact, represented a shift of national income in favor of nascent big business in Russia. So, all this led to the enormous growth of social inequality in Russian society. As a result of all that, the informal control of assets was strengthened in Russian big business and determined the Russian mode of corporate governance.

The problem is that the position in the world economy affects very much the development of corporate governance, and if you follow export-led growth, then from these certain problems emerge. If big business is interested in investing money abroad in the world financial markets more than in manufacturing in your own country, then you deal with redistributive capitalism. And if we take Russian big business, then the great part of its incomes can be called not industrial profit, but rent, which is earned due to control over the financial flows of enterprises. And this is the result of this highly authoritarian model of corporate governance. It is based on a set of formal and largely informal institutions, which can be called *an infrastructure of control*. It includes external and internal elements. The former assumes informal protection on the part of the state functionaries, lobbying structures, private security firms and organized crime groups. Internal elements of infrastructure of control include direct control of strategic owners over the top management, highly developed procedures of monitoring and auditing all activities of the personnel, extended departments of internal security. These institutions are created to protect control of the dominating groups over enterprises from their outside rivals and from embezzlement of money on the part of their own personnel.

The main feature of infrastructure of control – is its largely informal character. This means that it is impossible to legally fix it and bequeath it to inheritors. At the same time, it can always be challenged. And waves of redistribution of the property rights and control over enterprises regularly roll over the Russian industry. In the 1990s this process was predominantly based on criminal violence. Nowadays the role of criminal structures significantly diminished (although, by no means, it disappeared). However, new forms of redistribution of control were introduced. Now it is often carried out by the state apparatus. For instance, introduction of so-called 'State corporations' essentially meant change of ownership rights. All this means that control over enterprises, based on infrastructure of control, is intrinsically unstable. This instability leads to preference of short-term incomes over long-term profits on the part of Russian big business.

Of course, infrastructure of control is used to enrich the dominant group. The income appropriated by strategic owners of enterprises most often does not assume the form of entrepreneurial profit depicted in the mainstream economics textbooks. The latter amounts to the difference between returns and costs of production and depends on efficiency of technologies and corporate management. Groups, dominating Russian enterprises, appropriate a kind of rent. It is based not on entrepreneurial skills as such, but rather on their power of control over assets. Widespread practice of Russian big business assumes that dominant groups sell their products at the domestic market not directly, but through intermediation of some trade houses registered in offshore jurisdictions. These trade structures are ostensibly independent, but only by appearance. In fact, they are established by the same individuals who control enterprises. Such system allows to supply products domestically by prices lower than the market level to the intermediaries, which further sell them on market prices. As a result, profit is concentrated on offshore accounts of intermediaries and later are transferred to private offshore accounts of the members of the dominating groups.

This infrastructure is very costly, and it in itself cuts investment funds, cuts the wage fund and leads to opportunistic behavior of rank-and-file managers and workers. At the same time, as was already mentioned, it leads to the short-term orientation of investors.

This instability of informal control is a very important institutional pre-condition for the short-term orientation of Russian capitalists. They set certain norms of payback period of investment projects which are, for instance, they say we will consider only investment projects with payback period that is no greater than three or four years. Very often, most important investment projects, which introduce the best technologies, exceed this period, and are abandoned and not considered. Money is most often invested in the medium-term or short-term investment projects. You see, so this is another reason, institutional reason, which is a result of history and of the influence of global capitalist elite on Russian reforms which resulted in such types of institutions. And as a result, we have very high rates of capital flight and net outflows of private capital from Russia that amounts to hundreds of billions of dollars every year, which means that Russian economy is bleeding. If you take the structure of Russian GDP, 42% of Russian GDP is represented by private profit, and only 21% of GDP is the share of investment in productive capacities. The other half of the GDP share of the private profit is lost by Russia through a net outflow of capital. According to Russian Central Bank, while in 2021 the net outflow of private capital from Russia amounted to $74 billion, in 2022 it reached the unimaginable $251 billion.[16]

This infrastructure of informal control over assets should be overcome due to joint efforts of governments, increasing playing and greater participation of hired labor in management. And in such a situation, when a financial transparency will increase and more collegial bodies, such as investment councils, for instance, will be introduced, then embezzlement of money due to control over financial flows will diminish. This should be the result of action from the above and from the below.

The principal way to reform the corporate governance in Russia is the involvement of some, or the development of some kind of indicative planning which will combine the regulative and planning force of government and market relations on the one hand, but on the other hand it is very important to

---

16   Alexandre Zlobin, "CB Povysil Prognoz po Ottoku Kapitala iz Rossii (CB Increased its Forecast of the Capital Outflow from Russia)", Forbes, Internet-Rsource, 28 October 2022. https://www.forbes.ru/finansy/480414-cb-povysil-prognoz-po-ottoku-kapitala-iz-rossii (last accessed on 26 January 2023)

increase the rights of higher labor. And here, not the American mode of corporate governance, but the German mode of corporate governance, based on the so-called participation system. These are very good examples, and on such a basis, it is possible, I believe, to diminish this informal aspect of corporate governance, because currently these informal institutions of corporate governance assume very developed infrastructures of control. For instance, relations with the functionaries of the state, on the one hand, on the other hand, a very developed system of control over hired labor.

Financialization and production

Financialization is one of the most crucial problems of the current world economy, affecting periphery and semi-periphery including Russia. Under this term economists usually mean outflow of capital from production into financial-speculative sector of economy. The latter started systematically growing in conditions when material production in the economies of the core decreased dramatically. This problem is again related to the global shift of production from North to South. In the current situation, the world financial markets became an additional and a very important mechanism of redistribution of a part of incomes created by the labor of the periphery in favor of transnational capital of the core.

This can be illustrated by the so-called 'new fixed exchange rate regime'. We live in the world of floating currencies. However, semi-peripheral countries like China, Russia, Brazil and a number of others, which follow export-led growth models, cannot allow the forex market to determine the exchange rate according to free interplay of supply of currencies and demand for them. This happens because if you have a positive international trade balance, then you experience systematic inflow of additional foreign currency to your national forex market. In such conditions your national currency inevitably appreciates. Due to this competitiveness of your exports goes down because exporters increase prices in order to overcome their losses due to the appreciation of the national currency. In response, national governments that follow export-led growth models, are compelled to print national money to buy this 'excessive' foreign currency and remove it from the national market. Then they have to invest it somewhere beyond their countries, somewhere in the world financial markets, and the most reliable financial assets in the world financial markets are the assets of Western countries, especially of the United States. Such countries as China, Russia, Mexico, India are earning foreign reserves at the expense of hard labor of their population, exporting mainly cheap products to American and Western markets, and creating savings on this basis. They reinvest enormous shares of these savings back in Western economies. That is why in the late XXth-early XXI centuries negative values of current accounts and decline of savings and investments of the core countries coincided with positive values of the same variables for the periphery and semi-periphery. Russian big capital benefited enormously from high oil and energy prices on the world market.[17] However, if one takes into account enormous outflow of private capital from Russia, one realizes that these high profits of energy-exporting firms are lost for investment in Russian economy. These riches do not trickle down, as one famous saying argues, to the common people. No, they are reinvested in the world financial markets, and of course, the owners of these firms enrich themselves. Largely the same is done by the Chinese. China replaced Japan as the prime foreign creditor of the United States, despite the fact that these savings in US dollars are created due to the hard labor and low wages of Chinese workers. Chinese money largely helped to inflate the US mortgage market.[18]

This enormous inflow of finances from the periphery and semi-periphery to the core created new investment opportunities at the financial markets of the developed countries. Thus, preconditions for financialization of the Western economies are created by the current development of the World-System, when production is largely shifted from the core to the periphery and semi-periphery (excluding Russia).

Conclusion

The principal way for producers in semi-peripheral and peripheral countries to overcome the predicament of the current globalization is to develop their own production networks with all chains of production, starting from labor intensive processes to capital intensive processes as well. And I think that core countries, really have advantages, but disadvantages as well. The main problem of the core countries is that they shifted production abroad, largely in Asia, and focus on financial speculative operations, and earn additional income through

17 IMF, "World Economic Outlook April 2005 Globalization and External Imbalances," International Monetary Fund, Washington, DC, 2005, pp. 109-156
18 Ravi Jagannathan, Mudit Kapoor and Ernst Schaumburg, "Why are We in a Recession? The Financial Crisis is a Symptom, not the Disease!," 2009, NBER WP 15404

that. However, if they want to return industrial production back, they have to increase savings to finance investment, and consequently they have to decrease consumption. Both problems are very painful and very difficult to solve because they lead to a certain decrease in the level of consumption to which no population agrees easily. For the semi-peripheral countries, the problem is that export-led growth from a historical standpoint has ended because in conditions of the Great Stagnation, the world market is stagnant and they should focus on the domestic market and domestic demand, which depends on the wage fund - on the national wage fund. If these countries want to survive the times of global economic crisis, they have to increase wages and expand domestic demand on this basis, increasing profitability of investment in the real sector domestically on this basis. This can be achieved only if government and firms operate together. Governments should invest not at the world financial markets but in fundamental and applied research, creating pre-conditions for developing better technologies. All countries in certain areas have such pre-conditions, even poor countries can achieve something in terms of technical progress. And if they create consistent production networks inside their countries, and encourage domestic demand, they can at least partially compensate for the external shocks which come from the other nations and find their way out from the crisis. The reform of corporate governance is part of this policy and introduction of such reforms is part of the solution.

References

Amin, Samir, *The Law of Worldwide Value*, Monthly Review Press, New York, 2010.

Arrighi, Giovanni, *The Long Twentieth Century. Money, Power and the Origins of our Times*, Verso, London, New York, 2010.

Birch, Kean and Mykhnenko, Vald, "Introduction", *The Rise and Fall of Neoliberalism. The Collapse of an Economic Order?*, (eds.) Birch K. and V. Mykhnenko, Zed Books, London, New York, 2010.

Blair, Margaret, "Financial Restructuring and the Debate about Corporate Governance", *The Deal Decade. What Takeovers and Leveraged Buyouts Mean for the Corporate Governance*, ed. M. Blair, The Brookings Institution, Washington, D.C., 1993.

Brenner, Robert, "What is good for Goldman Sachs is good for America. The origins of the present crisis", *Center for Social Theory and Comparative History UCLA,* WP, Los Angeles, 2009.

https://escholarship.org/uc/item/0sg0782h (last accessed on 17 January 2023)

Clark, David, *Number of Employees Worldwide 1991-2022*, Statista, Internet-resource, December 7, 2022.

https://www.statista.com/statistics/1258612/global-employment-figures/ (last accessed on 15 January 2023)

Dicken, Peter, *Global Shift: Reshaping the Global Economic Map in the 21-st Century*, SAGE Publications Inc., London, 2003.

Dosman, Edgar, *The Life and Times of Raul Prebish, 1901-1986*, McGill-Queen's University Press, Montreal, 2008.

Dzarasov, Ruslan, *The Conundrum of Russian Capitalism. Russian Economy in the World System*, Pluto Press, London, 2014,

Frank, Andre, *Dependent Accumulation and Underdevelopment*, The Macmillan Press, London 1978.

Frank, Andre, "The Development of Underdevelopment", *Monthly Review,* Vol. 18, No. 4, 1966, pp. 17-31.

Freeman, Richard, "What really ails Europe (and America): the doubling of the global workforce", *The Globalist*, 5 March, 2010.

https://www.theglobalist.com/what-really-ails-europe-and-america-the-doubling-of-the-global-workforce/ (last accessed on 17 January 2023)

Greider, William, *One World, Ready or not: the Manic Logic of Global Capitalism*, Simon & Schuster, N.Y.,1998.

Ho, Karen, *Liquidated: An Ethnography of Wall Street*, Duke University Press, Durham and London, 2009.

IMF, 2005, "World Economic Outlook April 2005 Globalization and External Imbalances," International Monetary Fund, Washington, DC, pp. 109-156.

Jagannathan, Ravi, Kapoor, Mudit and Schaumburg, Ernst, "Why are We in a Recession? The Financial Crisis is a Symptom, not the Disease!," 2009, NBER WP 15404.

Kagarlitsky, Boris, *The Empire of the Periphery: Russia and the World System,* Pluto Press, London, 2008.

Lazonick, William and O'Sullivan, Mary, "Maximizing Shareholder Value: a New Ideology for Corporate Governance," *Economy and Society*, Vol. 29, No. 1, 2000, pp. 13-35.

Razmi, Arslan and Blecker, Robert, "Developing Country Exports of Manufactures: Moving Up the Ladder to Escape the Fallacy of Composition? American University", Department of Economics, 2006, WP 2006-06. pp.21-48.

Roberts, Michael, "More on the World Rate of Profit", Michael Roberts Blog, 20 September, 2020.

https://thenextrecession.wordpress.com/2020/09/20/more-on-a-world-rate-of-profit/ (last accessed on 14 January 2023)

World Bank Group, "Global Economic Prospects. A World Bank Group Flagship Report June 2020", The World Bank Washington-DC, 2020.

Zlobin, Alexandre, CB Povysil Prognoz po Ottoku Kapitala iz Rossii (CB Increased its Forecast of the Capital Outflow from Russia), *Forbes*, Internet-Rsource, October 28, 2022.

https://www.forbes.ru/finansy/480414-cb-povysil-prognoz-po-ottoku-kapitala-iz-rossii (last accessed on 26.01.2023)

Global Change, Science and Society

H. Nüzhet Dalfes

Introduction

Our planet is 4.5 billion years old, and since 3.5 billion years there has been a physicochemical system on this planet that we call life. Regarding these, we have not encountered anything like it at this time on other planets in the Solar System. That does not mean that they will not happen on other planets, in other solar systems. It is essential not to think in a geocentric way. But on other planets there are currently no signs of this type of system. In this respect, our planet is a very special one and here the physical, chemical conditions, the chemistry of the atmosphere, the chemistry of the seas, the water, the formation of soil on the land are ideal conditions. Ozone layer is also a crucial part of this system. The evolution of these things, the changes in them, and the evolution of what we call *life* are actually things that go together. So, none of them is something that evolved in response to the other. They co-evolved, and we are trying to grasp this co-evolution. We, as scientists, are trying to understand a 3.5-billion-year-old story here.

On the other hand, we are concerned with an issue that is a little more anthropogenic, and especially in the last 200 years. It brings us about the beginnings of 1800's and to the beginning of a period in which the Industrial Revolution was developing very fervently, and people started to use fossil fuels as a new energy source. There have been some changes that have taken place since then, that is, over the last 200 years which are of primary interest to us.

The geological term used as a standard for the period after the end of the last Ice Age, up to the present day, was the Holocene. However, the term "Anthropocene" is now widely used. The Anthropocene is such a concept that you actually see a trace of humans on all the systems and environments of the earth which has been changed by humans. First of all, there is no escape from human influences on the planet and there are human traces everywhere. 5 or 10 million years later, when people look around, if some accumulations have formed, traces of humans will be found here in various layers, as in geological times. Throughout our period, this human trace will always be found in the corresponding layers. Of course, I would like to say that perhaps the most unpleasant trace will be these microplastics. I always see microplastics and plastic pollution as one of the biggest problems faced by humanity.

Three issues have emerged crucial concerning the climate crisis which I prefer to call it as global change. To name something as global change, global can be one of two things. As one of them, we can talk about a change in global-scale systems. For example, the composition of the atmosphere, which is a very well mixed gas layer that covers the earth, has changed and these changes we have made in it are global-scale changes. It means what they call *cihanşümul* in old Turkish terms, that is, the whole world. We geoscientists distinguish between the term *world* and the term *earth*. World is a slightly more popular and human-inclusive term. But when you take the earth, the change you make is in this gas around the earth. On the other hand, there are some changes that may be local when you look at them one by one. But these are the changes that we see almost everywhere and they are also part of global change. For example, there is deforestation, decrease in marine oxygen, which we call eutrophication, due to waste materials in the coastal seas or the extinction of species. It's a global problem. Species go extinct in one place, of course. But at the same time, if this extinction occurs almost everywhere on the earth, almost everywhere on the globe, it becomes a global problem. Likewise, microplastics.

Global Climate Change

The climate of the earth has been changing for the last 4.5 billion years, and there is nothing to argue about. Yes, there are some changes, there are some very distinct periods at the last years which we call "near past", for example. There is a warm period in the Middle Ages, and then there are some periods that we call the Little Ice Age, but now we see the change that we can present in quantitative terms, especially with the global average temperatures. These changes have not occurred in the last thousand years, maybe not even in the last two thousand years. For this reason, this is a very serious change, and this change also occurs very quickly. The important thing here is that the change is not only happening, but also that it is fast at the same time.

The thing that interests us in the first place is a change that is rapid and at the same time contains some uncertainties, that is, it creates some question marks in our minds when we look forward, and a question mark about which direction it will develop. This is a core feature of human-induced climate change, and we're trying to understand it. We are trying to make some predictions on this. Why is the climate changing? Today, everyone, including primary and secondary school students, probably knows the answer to this question in some way, people who have wondered about that subject, read and studied it a little. We are changing the composition of the atmosphere; it is one of the most fundamental things.

There are some gases in the atmosphere, we are increasing the amount of carbon dioxide, which is one of the most basic gases, because we extract fossil fuels from underground. The gas that comes out as a result of combustion is called "*carbon dioxide*". The oceans can absorb some of this carbon dioxide. But almost half, or even a little more than half, remains in the atmosphere, and gradually this accumulates. Today we have exceeded the 400 ppm level and it continues like this.

This change in the composition of the atmosphere did happen before in history and there are times when there is more carbon dioxide in the atmosphere than today, but we are talking about 30-40 million years ago. But when you look at the last 500 thousand years, we reached the level we have reached and surpassed now for the first time in the last several hundred thousand years and we are reaching it very quickly. In the last 500 thousand years, we experience an unprecedented change. It is very difficult to say something about the future by looking at the past because we have seen a different path in various time zones. However, this 500 thousand year is important, because we can collect quite detailed information about it. We obtain this information especially from tiny air bubbles in the ice formed in the ice sheets which has been a very interesting technology and one of the most important scientific developments of the last twenty or thirty years.

There are serious troubles that gases cause. First of all, the most common gases in the atmosphere are nitrogen and oxygen, which have two atoms. They have their place, but they have no role in changing the climate. Water vapor is very important, but water vapor is perhaps the main character of this issue. But water vapor is not something we change like that. It self-balances its concentration in the atmosphere. However, what we're changing first is carbon dioxide, especially because of this fossil fuel use. We increase the amount of carbon dioxide. There is a second gas, methane, a much stronger greenhouse gas than carbon dioxide, but there isn't much in the atmosphere right now. Methane began to take its place in these days in academic and scientific discussions, but it especially came to the fore at the last Conference of the Parties in Glasgow, because methane shows an increase in the atmosphere due to natural resources, animal husbandry, and leakages in natural gas extracted from underground. But there is also another problem. The emission of methane from the frozen soils of the Arctic region, of course, gives us fearful dreams as a disaster scenario. That's why these gases are important, namely carbon dioxide and methane.

Regarding this issue of climate change, the scientific approach to this issue is not something new. It's roughly in the middle of the nineteenth century, and the person who gave the first warning, made the first observations on this issue, and measured them in the laboratory was a lady, a woman named Eunice Newton Foote. In his article titled "On the Influence of Carbonic Acid in the Air upon the Temperature of the Ground" published in 1896[1], Swedish scientist Svante Arrhenius argued that if we double the carbon dioxide in the atmosphere, we increase the surface temperature by 5-6 °C. As a result of the very sophisticated scientific studies, calculations and modeling we have done today, we come to more or less the same conclusion. In other words, since 1896, those words have been said about what it is, what it could be. Of course, what are the details of this, that is, the increase in the average temperature is one thing, but we cannot be satisfied with that alone. A number of numerical models have been developed since the 1960s, and the same results are sought in all of these models. In other words, if the amount of carbon dioxide in the atmosphere increases and other greenhouse gases naturally increase, this will result in serious warming in the climate, warming in terms of the global average and many other components of the climate, not only temperature, but also wind, precipitation, hydrological cycle, i.e. the water cycle. It is thought that there will be some serious changes in these. The organization that carries out the summarization, promotion, 'distillation' and presentation of this science to decision makers and policy makers, is the structure we call the *Intergovernmental Panel on Climate Change* (IPCC). This structure is established in 1988 and produced its first report in 1989. Something very important happens in

---

1   Svante Arrhenius, "On the Influence of Carbonic Acid in the Air upon the Temperature of the Ground", *Philosophical Magazine and Journal of Science Series 5*, Vol. 41, (April 1896), p. 237-276

1992, a very important meeting that we call the Rio Summit in 1992, where issue of climate change is indeed placed on the international agenda, on the agenda of international platforms.

Calculations about the climate change are done with numerical models, which are based on the division of the atmosphere and the oceans into tiny little boxes. Detailed calculations about heat, energy, and momentum and of course conservation of mass play a crucial role in this process which makes climate modelers the most important customers in the civilian domain regarding computers. It is a fact that climate scientists are in a field of science that uses computer technologies very well and intensively.

There is a very important problem here, and this problem actually reveals the uncertainties. It is easy to deal with natural sciences, physics, chemistry, biology if needed. I will not say easy, we are dealing with a difficult, complex system. It is difficult, but at least you are progressing by making improvements. The main problem is about the question, "what will be the amount of these greenhouse gases in the atmosphere in the coming years, at least until the end of the century, what will be the emissions here, what technologies will people use?" Will they be able to give up fossil fuels, how fast will they give up? These are very important questions, and they are not the task of naturalists. These should be dealt by social scientists and economists. When you try to do something about human nature and the dynamics of societies, there are some very serious uncertainties here. Creating scenarios, such as worst or optimistic, is one of the main methods to cope with these uncertainties.

As a result of different scenarios, it is mentioned how the average earth surface temperature will rise compared to the average value in the 1850-1900 range, and the global temperature will easily increase by 4.5-5°C in the worst scenarios. Such conclusions are actually reached using scientific methods and climate models. However, it is worth to mention that due to the differences in emission scenarios, we have some uncertainties there. We have to live with these uncertainties. In the future, the future and uncertainties will come together.

The question of "How will temperatures on Earth change in various situations as a result?" is important. It is certain that there will be places that will warm up more, more than the average, with a feedback mechanism, especially in the northern latitudes. The interesting thing is not only the temperature, but also the precipitation. What we call the water cycle is important. In some places the water cycle will be negative, in some places the water balance will be positive. Especially in Mediterranean countries like ours, we will face some serious water scarcity. As you know, the northern half of Türkiye is another world, the southern half is another world too. But the southern half, i.e. the Mediterranean region, all Mediterranean and Mediterranean type climates will face a precipitation reduction elsewhere in the world too.

Ozone Layer Issue

The second important factor is the ozone layer issue, in other words, the ozone layer depletion issue. Ozone, stratospheric ozone or ozone in the stratosphere, which is about fifteen or twenty kilometers above the ground. Actually, there are two types of ozone. There is ozone in the upper layers of the stratosphere, and there is ozone at the ground level. Ground-level ozone is harmful to human health. It is harmful to the lungs, creates some respiratory problems and is usually something that comes from car emissions. Ozone in this stratosphere, in the upper layers is very important because it protects living things on earth from ultraviolet rays. In other words, historically, let me take you back 3 billion years. At the beginning of these 3 billion years, there is not much oxygen in the atmosphere. But after living things begin to photosynthesize, the oxygen in the atmosphere increases. Some of that oxygen turns into ozone, and only after this ozone conversion, ozone accumulation is in the atmosphere, only after that living things come out of the water and begin to live on land. Because if you don't have ozone protection, you're done on land, ultraviolet rays will kill you. That's why this ozone layer is very important for living things to come to land from the sea, for the development of plants, and for the development of land plants.

It has been a concern since the early 1970s that there might be some problems with the ozone layer. There are works that are important in this regard. In the 1970s, Paul Crutzen stated that, due to nitrogen oxides in the atmosphere, especially nitrogen oxides in the stratosphere, the ozone layer would decrease, i.e. the ozone pressure would decrease. On the other hand, in 1974, Rowland and Molina[2], from the University of California Irvine, argues that some chemicals, which we call chlorofluorocarbons, will also cause us trouble. That has been an ongoing discussion about it and we haven't seen any important step to cope with that.

2   M. Jose Molina and F. Sherwood Rowland, "Stratospheric Sink for Chlorofluoromethanes: Chlorine Atom-Catalysed Destruction of Ozone", *Nature,* Vol. 249, 1974, p. 810-812.

It was only in the mid-1980s that an ozone hole was discovered over the Antarctic. It turns out that the ozone layer there decreases, especially in the spring months. The British have a measuring station there and it dawns on people a little that there is a problem here. These CFCs should be specifically banned. It should be banned, but there are also those who produce them, interest groups are very important in this business. One of the actors of this issue are interest groups. For example, Dupont, one of the giants of the chemical industry, produces them. When they started manufacturing less harmful hydrofluorocarbons instead of these chlorofluorocarbons, then they became a little obedient, less interfering with politicians. As a result, the Montreal Protocol was signed in 1987 and it became the Vienna Convention in 1988. Thus, serious restrictions are placed on the production of these chlorofluorocarbons, which we call CFCs.

The book by Richard Elliot Benedict, an American diplomat, called *Ozone Diplomacy*[3], explains the difficult process on that issue. It's not enough for scientists to just discover a problem. It is necessary for them to explain this and to appear in front of people in that way, in a way that cannot be denied. Various bargains are made here, and as a result of the negotiations, it is decided to deactivate the production of these chlorofluorocarbons.

The ozone hole has gradually decreased, but some years it gets a little bigger, a little smaller. We can now easily observe this from space with a set of satellites. However, the ozone problem has not completely disappeared, but it has lost its importance. Of course, if we could completely eliminate not only these CFCs, but also these hydrofluorocarbons, it would be even better. The ozone hole does not exist only over Antarctica. It also exists in some places in the northern hemisphere. It's not just a Southern problem.

Species Extinction

The third important subject is *species extinction,* where you can see on various TV channels that certain species, certain species that the eye can see, elephants, tigers, lions get into trouble. You can watch and hear interesting things about them if you are a person who is fond of watching documentaries. These are real, it's a fact that some species get in trouble. But there is only one thing, the important thing is that one of the questions to be asked is this: Do we know

---

3   Richard Elliot Benedick, *Ozone Diplomacy: New Directions in Safeguarding the Planet,* Harvard University Press, 1991.

how many species there are on earth? I think we don't know. We are trying to guess, some say there are 8.7 million, they say more or less, they say plus or minus, they say there are 1.3 million. It's not very precise. It's tough and these are about eukaryotic species, but when you get to bacteria and viruses things get more complicated. We don't know about many times more species than the ones we know about now. We don't know 5-6 times more than we know now. We know it can happen, we know it's wealth, but we don't know. Of course, the species is a little bit closer to us, I would say, when there are groups with less diversity, for example, we know that there are roughly 5,500 species of mammals. On the other hand, there is a tremendous variety of flowering plants, for example. There is no number there. We know that there are between 250 thousand and 400 thousand species of flowering plants. There are more than 1 million insect species, we know that it is very important data. Perhaps the most diverse taxonomic group we know now are the insects.

The situation with species extinction is nothing new. There were periods in which there was a decrease in these, there were extinctions. These extinctions are also important because in order to distinguish these geological periods on Earth, they look at which creatures lived there, which creatures disappeared after that period, their fossils are looked at, and some names are given based on findings. It is mentioned that there are 5-6 major extinctions.

It is said that the extinction or decline of human origin is actually a sixth or seventh extinction, depending on how you enumerate it now, and this is of course a very serious matter. There have been many small extinctions and bigger extinctions in the history, and the causes of these 5-6 extinctions in the past are attributed to very different things. You cannot pass them all over with the same mechanism, with the same explanation, they have different reasons. There is only one last extinction that happened 65 million years ago, a very serious extinction. But not all species go, of course, some species do. There is already the disappearance of the dinosaurs, which attracts everyone's attention. That's why what happened in that 65 million years, that is, at the Cretaceous/Tertiary boundary, is something we know very well. There are various hypotheses about it. But what interests us now is what is happening today.

Can we keep track of extinctions? It is difficult, because we do not know the number of species, it is not an easy task to pursue the number of species. The more we search, the more species we find, but we're also destroying some habitats. What's happening to the Amazon jungle today is considered such a classic thing, but seriously, Brazil is a very badly managed country right now. So, we know that the political class and the top politician is a man who makes very bad decisions. And as a result, with the destruction of those forests, if we want to make an analogy here, we often burn libraries in which we do not know the books. We don't know what's in it, but the library is in flames, and we will never know what's in those books again. We live in such a world. Now, besides that, if we look at it from a vertebrate perspective, which are amphibians, reptiles, fish, mammals. And birds, of course. There is a "Living Planet Report[4]" by the World Wide Fund for Nature (WWF) and the Zoological Society of London about the reduction in their diversity. The report shows 1970 as the zero point and then tries to show us, somewhere, the speed of decline on land, sea, and globally. It must be admitted that it is a little easier to keep an account of this work on vertebrates. This account is being held and there is a clear reduction here. This is real.

"Then what's wrong with us?", that is, "why do they disappear?" We just asked the question. We're destroying their habitat, that's for sure. Secondly, the climate is changing, the climate is very important. There are also invasive species. When we look at this global issue, when globalization is mentioned, if you are not in natural sciences, when economists, politicians, political scientists talk about globalization, the term is mostly used to refer to the increase in the correlation between countries. Now it means relatedness, commerce, commuting and people moving around. And as a result, when people settle in new places, they willingly or unwillingly carry certain plant and animal species there. In fact, they bring virus types, they bring viruses, they bring bacteria, as in the event we recently experienced. Now these invasive species also pose a great danger to the creatures there, and they are getting them in trouble. Therefore, this is a concrete issue and one that is very difficult to avoid.

So, why do we worry here, what would happen if species disappeared? You can say things like "species come, species go...", but that's not something to be taken so lightly. Because throughout the history of the world, there have been some balances between the rate of speciation and the rate of extinction. When the extinction rate increased, the number of species decreased, and when the speciation rate increased, the number of species increased, and so on. Now here if your rate of extinction is much greater than that of speciation, if you're going through a period of extinction rather than the emergence of new species, then

4   https://www.wwf.org.uk/our-reports/living-planet-report-2022

we're automatically faced with a reduction in this biodiversity. You will ask a question like this, and you will say, "What would happen if biodiversity decreased?" In fact, biodiversity is important. Think of a building, it has bricks, you go from time to time and pull out some bricks. Now, if I were someone living in that building, I would start to get annoyed, "what will happen to us?" I would start to think.

This is something like that... The functioning and stability of ecosystems is based on biodiversity, and will this wall come down after the bricks we pull? Are people ready for the wall to come down? This turns out to be a serious, fundamental problem. Perhaps the most fundamental question in ecology: diversity, ecological stability, ecosystem stability... So why do we care so much about ecosystems and their stability? Because ecosystems do provide us with a multitude of services, I won't go into details right now, but there are many things we don't realize and sometimes we do realize. We collect timber from the forests, but sometimes it offers some services that we do not realize. To put it mildly, we are in trouble if problems arise with the functioning of ecosystems.

Science

The effects of the production of science and its effects on the dissemination of the results produced by science and on the decision mechanisms is also part of the discussion. Science is produced by scientists, produced by teams. There are scientific organizations at the national and international level. These organizations help these people to discuss with each other, exchange views and come up with common conclusions. However, the question of how this information will actually turn into a policy and how it will be used by decision makers is a problematic issue. There are a lot of actors here. First of all, there is the world of science and there is no problem here. On the other hand, there are interest groups, for example, Dupont company, in the case of ozone. There's also the meat industry... There are industries that are interested in destroying the Amazon forests, raising cows and oxen there, and then providing meat to the meat industry.

There are oil companies that look for oil elsewhere, not thinking it could damage very fragile ecosystems. There are a wide variety of economic interest groups and of course they also have serious sanctions and pressures on decision makers. Besides, there is also a group we call the public, the citizens. This is a somewhat more ambiguous concept. How national, how international is what we call public opinion? And with the recent development of communication technologies, how does this national character transform into an international structure? There are non-governmental organizations among them and all of them have one thing in common. Nowadays, in the twenty-first century, everyone is sharing material on social media somewhere. Any kind of information, correct or false information that you can think of is circulating quite freely in this environment. As a result, it has a serious impact on people's ideas about these issues.

Science of this global environmental change has an international scene. On the international stage, people have pondered these issues for many years. The realization that our planet has finite resources was made in the early 1970s. At the same time, there is another problem: the increasing population. We talk about the population these days, but perhaps not as much as it was in the early 70s. At that time, there was a very interesting book written by Paul and Anne Ehrlich called *Population Bomb.*[5] That book made a huge impact in those years. After that, questions such as "On a planet with finite resources, what will happen if the population keeps increasing?", "What about food security?", "What about environmental quality?" were tried to be modeled in some way from early 70s on.

There was a very important initiative at that time, the "Club of Rome", a group of people from the business and intellectual world who supported and financed this type of work. Here, in 1972, Donatella and Dennis Meadows' famous book is one to always remember: *Limits to Growth.*[6] I think this book is one of the books that left its mark on that period and is always talked about. Other reports like this appeared in those years. While these are going on, on the other hand, there is a very important development that affected our perception. That development is a photograph of the Earth taken by Apollo 17. This photograph was not taken with a digital camera, but on color film with a analog camera. It is very important, for the first time we look at our planet, in other words, this "blue marble" from afar, and it can easily be said that it contributed to the perception of how special it is, how special the planet we live on is. That's why this photo should always be in a special place.

5   Paul R. Ehrlich, Anne Howland Ehrlich, *Population, Control or Race to Oblivion? The Population Bomb,* Sierra Club/Ballantine Books, New York, 1968.
6   Dennis Meadows, Donella Meadows, Jørgen Randers, William W. Behrens III, *Limits to Growth*, A Potomac Books, 1972.

As a result, there are some initiatives. In 1972, for example, there was a meeting of the United Nations on Human Environment. A very famous meeting. Seriously, scientists, very respected scientists, but also some very interesting politicians attended. Indira Gandhi was one of the important politicians who attended the meeting. It is a milestone in terms of the acceptance of the science of global change and the perception of the concerns produced by emerging science, at least by decision makers and politicians.

In the same year, something else happened, the environment program of the United Nations is established. The program we call UN Environment Program (UNEP) was established in 1972, this is a very important program. It is a program that is still active and plays a very important role. However, in 1950, the World Meteorological Organization (WMO) was established as an agency of the United Nations. Together, these two play an important role.

In 1988, UNEP and WMO, together, formed the IPCC which is doing a wide variety of studies. It publishes a report roughly every five or six years. The first, second and finally third part, namely the report on mitigation measures and what needs to be done regarding precautionary measures, has been published so far. These reports are very important and very well prepared. These reports are of the quality that you can easily use as textbooks. It is published in three or five languages, the main languages of the United Nations are probably French, German, Russian, Arabic besides English. These reports are reports with very nice infographics. They have some summaries for decision makers, which is not a very large document. It is a readable document and has very nice illustrations and infographics of high quality.

These reports are important. There is another feature of these reports that I would like to underline, and this is something that I think is very important in terms of the perception of science. Because we expect precise answers from scientists. Unfortunately, as science matures, the contrasts between those answers aren't instantly precise. In that respect, when they say something or use an expression in all the reports of the IPCC, there are some such adjectives in parentheses about how certain it is, whether it is almost certain or most likely, and statements about probability. This is very important. At least 300-400 scientists are working in this business. At least one thousand more people do the editing of these reports. In fact, every sentence of this science product that they have distilled has a certain probability, and it is not black and white here either. Some things say black and white, something like that is absolutely certain, it's 99% there. There is no problem there, but some statements on the other hand say that there is no possibility of this, there is no such possibility. But there are many shades of gray in between, and I think it is very important for 21st century people to learn to live with these shades of gray. Instead of waiting for definite answers from science, some answers given with such probabilities, which are not done in vain, are very serious, as a result of discussions, these probabilities are associated with these statements. Based on these, learning to make decisions with scientific results that contain uncertainties is one of the most important features of the 21st century, which I think we have to do. No other choice. Because we will never get black and white results from science. Even if you want to put a gun to the scientist's head, if the probability is 60% -70%, he will not tell you that it is a definite result, that is, a definite result, negative or positive. He will say to you that, according to the probabilities, I am giving such a probability. For this reason, I think this is a very fundamental point of distinction. The results of science being associated with some probabilities, given with them... I think this is a very important communication issue.

The IPCC is established in 1989 and publishes its first report. After that, there is something very important in 1992, maybe again, as in 1972, one of the milestones. The United Nations Conference on Environment and Development is held in Rio, Brazil. This is a very important conference. Türkiye attended this conference with the then President Özal and Prime Minister Demirel. This is a very important conference.

Conferences usually already have preparations. As a result of these preliminary preparations, some documents are brought and they are discussed at the conference, this conference may last for two weeks. Some of the preliminary preparations are already originating from this Intergovernmental Panel on Climate Change report. The *Rio Declaration on Environment and Development* is published. A document called *Agenda 21* is published. There is a document on forestry principles. There are also three conventions. One is the "*Convention on Biological Diversity*", which is very important. The second is the "*Framework Convention on Climate Change*". This convention is the basis of all those meetings held today. The third convention is the "*United Nations Convention to Combat Desertification*". Türkiye signed and ratified the first and third conventions and the second one in 2000's, but it was a bit late in terms of what needs to be done on these issues.

In sum, this science of global environmental change in the 21st century has some features. One of them is that it is a multidisciplinary and interdisciplinary science, that's for sure. There is a common language requirement that comes with it. Cross-border collaborations and networks play a very, very important role here. Because we are talking about a planet, and it is not possible for everyone to stay in their own corner.

Now the 21st century is the century of collaborative approaches which should be accepted by everyone. Big data and high-performance computing, informatics, open data has a huge role in this. These are not the number of guns. These are the temperature at one place, the precipitation in another, the number of species you find on the other side. No one will hide them from each other. The science cannot develop in an environment where data is stored and only given to people in a controlled manner. Everyone understands this now.

There is also the matter of repeatable science. This also became very important. There is gradual progress there compared to the previous years. One of the reasons why we are in a better situation is the developing information technologies and the internet, which is very important. But this repeatability is actually a matter of discipline and ethics at the same time. So, is open data. You can collect open data, you can manage it in some very sophisticated ways, you put it somewhere, but you don't let anyone reach the data. Then you can't reach your goal anyway. This is a very serious problem. If there are people here who are interested in these matters, one of the most important pressures we have to make as citizens is to put pressure on all government mechanisms within our ability, which have their own radius of influence, and ensure that the data is turned into open data.

We need to think about the actors. Regarding these actors, when it comes to science especially this aspect of probability is very important in this business. It's a matter of perception. Policy makers are a little different, they think a little more about this, and there are not only elected but also appointed bureaucrats among them. It's a matter of how they work. There are scientists and science platforms that raise the environmental issue. One of these platforms is the IPCC. On the other hand, there are those who want answers. At the answer point... It is not easy to create such large, uncertain clouds like the public and decision makers, and to make them more obvious. Because there are many different segments, and they interact very differently. It is clear that they do not all have the same culture. But on the other hand, bespoke science is being done in a very positive way. For example, for the meeting where this Paris Agreement was declared, a report was requested on "What would be the effects of an increase of 1.5 °C" from the IPCC and the IPCC prepared and submitted this report. Sometimes, policy makers may have specific requests and needs from the world of science.

There is a question of citizens and public opinion here. Familiarity with the scientific process is a very heterogeneous subject, in many different cultures, there are different levels. This is a topic that Charles Percy Snow has brought up. There is the 'two cultures problem', on the one hand there are "literary people", on the other there are "scientists", as our older generation would say. These two cultures need to live together, be influenced by each other, and understand each other. What kind of a phenomenon is a knowledgeable citizen who understands the scientific way? How does it appear? How does this culture spread over time? Because ultimately, if we are in democracies, the citizens have to internalize certain things. Scientists find something in their labs, then they go and tell the policy makers. Now, there are citizens who have been left out, and if we are talking about democratic processes, these citizens should also make some decisions as informed as possible.

Here is a situation like this. The component of informing the citizens of scientific projects is now very common in the western world, especially in North America, this concept that we call "outreach" is being implemented and should be applied. In other words, these days when you design a science project, you face more and more questions like, "How will you explain the results you will get here to people who are not experts in this subject and to ordinary citizens?"

There is a very nice method here, it is an area that I am very interested in. It is *citizen science* or *participatory science*, the French prefer the term participatory science, for citizen science. What's included in here? You will get curious citizens to do some work that does not require advanced expertise. These are very important, simple observations, but they are of immense value when made in a very wide geography. Thus, science teams are expanded to cover a large geography and long time spans. Citizens also help a lot as a result of this science production process... Observations made in this context are transferred to databases. I think there is a very important development here. It is undisputed that the internet and smartphones serve as perhaps the cheapest, most common scientific hardware. You take a photo of something, with coordinate form GPS, you upload it to the internet, and people can easily collect them.

Regarding the collection and disseminating data, Alexander von Humboldt, a scientist who lived at the end of the 18th century and the beginning of the 19th century, should be mentioned. At the beginning of the 19th century, he has the reflexes of our 21st century today, attached great importance to the establishment of networks, tried to record details such as altitude and location very precisely when he collected samples/information, and wandered around with specialists, such as Aimé Bonpland, his principal companion. Aimé Bonpland is a very good botanist. His observations and plants they collected constitute a rich database, in today's terminology. He has played a crucial role for the development of science in that area because at the beginning of the 19th century, he introduced people to some reflexes that we tried to acquire and spread in the 21st century.

Some conclusions

The first quarter of this century is about to end, and many serious global environmental issues are lurking on the future of our planet. Only savior is a set of science-based courageous decisions. Unfortunately, producing solid science, with ever diminishing uncertainties, will not be enough to generate the political determination to hasten the implementation of required societal and technological fixes. Based on the issues we discussed above; one can suggests a short (non-exhaustive) list of actions to alleviate some of the barriers toward a much more effective science - society dialog:

- Academics/researchers should be encouraged to allocate time to public outreach; they should be given skills and incentives to consider science communication an integral part of their vocation,

- Efforts should be made to mainstream *'citizen science'* where appropriate as a win-win strategy to improve public understanding of science and scientific process and to strengthen time/space scope for environmental monitoring,

- Secondary and higher education curricula should be redesigned to lessen the 'two cultures' divide; environmental humanities could/should provide the much needed 'bridge' and its perspective should be integrated into literature and social sciences teaching in secondary education.

References

Arrhenius, Svante, "On the Influence of Carbonic Acid in the Air upon the Temperature of the Ground", *Philosophical Magazine and Journal of Science Series 5,* Vol. 41, April 1896, pp. 237-276.

Benedick, Richard Elliot, *Ozone Diplomacy: New Directions in Safeguarding the Planet*, Harvard University Press, 1991.

Ehrlich, Paul R.; Ehrlich H., Anne, Population, *Control or Race to Oblivion? The Population Bomb*, Sierra Club/Ballantine Books, New York, 1968.

https://www.wwf.org.uk/our-reports/living-planet-report-2022

Meadows, Dennis; Meadows, Donella; Randers, Jorgen; Behrens, W.William, *Limits to Growth*, A Potomac Books, 1972.

Molina, M.Jose and Rowland, F.Sherwood, "Stratospheric Sink for Chlorofluoromethanes: Chlorine Atom-Catalysed Destruction of Ozone", *Nature,* Vol. 249, 1974, pp. 810-812.

Free Will and Determinism in Classical Islamic Philosophy: Al-Fārābī, Ibn Sīnā and Ibn Rushd

Catarina Belo

The question of free will and determinism is considered a classical problem in philosophy. It has been expressed in different kinds of ways, and it has received different solutions. Determinism assumes that events and substances in the world have necessary causes such that they cannot be otherwise. It means that events are determined and could not have happened otherwise. There are different types of determinism in accordance with the type of agent or the kind of event in question. Metaphysical determinism implies that everything happens necessarily, following necessarily from its causes. One can think of physical determinism as the theory according to which natural phenomena happen in a necessary way. One can also distinguish, among the different types of determinism, ethical determinism, which states that human acts are determined. Biological determinism means that events among living beings happen in a necessary way. The implication for human beings is that our personalities and actions are determined by biological factors.

The problem is discussed in detail by Aristotle in his works, for instance in *Metaphysics* and *Physics*, and it is always formulated as a question of causality, although the concept of necessity is also central to debates on determinism. In the *Metaphysics*, Aristotle mentions human action as a result of a series of causes, and towards the end of Book II of the *Physics* he asks the question whether chance is a cause and what kind of cause it can be. Related issues concern agency and the power of causes, natural or divine. Aristotle also discusses natural events in terms of necessity and voluntariness, in a metaphysical and an ethical context.

In the Middle Ages the question becomes framed as the power of causes in connection with God's omnipotence. The problem of determinism is significant because of its implications for the conception of human action and the way in which it can detract from human agency and responsibility. If human action is determined by external factors, or even internal natural or biological factors, then we are not the true agents of our actions and cannot be made responsible for them. This creates problems for the discipline of ethics, which assumes that human beings have free will and are the agents of their actions. It is assumed that they can alter the course of their actions, choose between good and evil, and in that way be made responsible for their actions, in relation to other human beings, other animals, and even the environment. Accountability ensures that justice is done, since one of the most common definitions of justice is to give each person his or her due.

The debate concerning determinism is also present in medieval and modern philosophy. Kant discusses the question of determinism as a question of causality in the framework of the antinomies of pure reason in his *Critique of Pure Reason*. He argues that either human action is subsumed under natural causality, which would imply the acceptance of determinism, or human action has its own autonomy, which implies free will.[1]

The question of free will and determinism remains a perennial philosophical problem. On the one hand, the need to find necessary causes for natural phenomena is a necessary aspect of scientific development. On the other hand, if human action is determined by natural factors, instead of having its own autonomy, the very discipline of ethics, with its concepts of good and evil, right and wrong, can be called into question. If human action cannot be altered, there is no merit or blame to be attributed to human agents.

For classical Islamic philosophers the question of free will and determinism concerns primarily the articulation between God's power and human agency. It also concerns more specifically the articulation of God's different attributes, in particular His power and His justice. God is omnipotent, but He is also just, which means that He will not praise or blame, reward or punish human beings who are not responsible for their actions.

The question of free will and agency as well as determinism is present in Islamic religious literature, mainly the Qur'ān and hadith. The Qur'ān stresses God's omnipotence, but also the fact that human beings will be held accountable for their actions by God (for instance, Qur'ān 36:54). Hadith literature, which reports on the deeds and sayings of Prophet Muhammad, stresses not only that God determines events, including what happens to human beings in

---

1   Immanuel Kant, *Critique of Pure Reason*, (eds.) P. Guyer & A. Wood, Cambridge University Press, Cambridge, 1998, p. 484.

their lifetimes, but also that these events are determined even before someone is born and while in the mother's womb.[2]

An important theme in the Qur'ān is the theme of *qadar*, God's predetermination of events, and the notion that God creates everything with a fixed measure through *qadar* (54:49). Hadith literature emphasizes the notion that events are predetermined by God before they happen.[3]

Within Islamic theology, which consists in a reflection on religious literature, particularly on the Qur'ān, in order to elicit a comprehensive view on the nature of God and creation, there are different positions according to the different theological schools. Early schools, such as the Qadarites and the Mu'tazilites, emphasized human free will, in order to defend the notion of God's justice. Stressing the divine attributes of oneness and justice was one of the hallmarks of Mu'tazilite theological doctrine. However, other theologians considered that human free will and free agency could be seen to take away from God's omnipotence. Therefore, they sought to resolve the problem by stressing God's power while seeking to find a way of making human beings responsible for their actions, so as to be justly rewarded or punished for them by God. The Ash'arites developed the theory of *kasb* (acquisition) according to which acts are created by God (according to the Ash'arites a fundamental theory to be found in the Qur'ān, namely that God is the only creator and agent), and then appropriated by human beings in such a way that human beings become responsible for their actions.[4]

Religious and theological debates influenced the medieval Islamic philosophers in their approaches to the issue of human and divine agency and they were also influenced by ancient Greek philosophy.

Three philosophers who discuss the question of free will and determinism in their works are al-Fārābī (d. 950), Ibn Sīnā (d. 1037) and Ibn Rushd (d. 1198).

Al-Fārābī wrote different kinds of works, including introductory works to philosophy, commentaries on Plato's and Aristotle's works, and systematic works of philosophy. He discusses the question of determinism in his commentary on

---

2   William Montgomery Watt, *Free Will and Predestination in Early Islam*, Luzac, London, 1948, p. 18.

3   Watt, 1948, p. 17.

4   Maria De Cillis, *Free Will and Predestination in Islamic Thought: Theoretical Compromises in the Works of Avicenna, al-Ghazālī and Ibn 'Arabī,*, Routledge, London and New York, 2014, p. 229.

Aristotle's *De interpretatione* (*On interpretation*), which constitutes one of Aristotle's logical works. One of the questions addressed by Aristotle is the status of propositions regarding the future.[5] Does a proposition stating that there will be a sea battle tomorrow have a definite truth value? If a proposition regarding future events is definitely true or false now, this means that the future is determined. While a proposition and its status may seem to refer simply to logic, it does bear on the way it describes reality. Logic and metaphysics are closely intertwined for Aristotle, and also for al-Fārābī. The latter discusses this issue in his commentary in detail, and adds concerns that are typically theological, namely the question of God's knowledge in connection with determinism. According to al-Fārābī, statements about future events do not signify that the future is determined now, since statements regarding the future do not have a definite truth value.[6] However, another question must be addressed, namely that of God's knowledge. God is omniscient, and this entails knowledge of the future. If God knows now what will happen, and His knowledge does not fail, then the future is already determined now, and this would leave no room for free will or agency on the part of human beings. However, it is necessary to affirm God's omniscience, since His attributes must denote His perfection. At the same time, if the future is determined, there is no place for human free will and God would not be just in rewarding or punishing human beings for their actions. In the case of human action, God's knowledge does not impose necessity. Al-Fārābī defends a kind of position which allows for God to determine and know future events without taking away from human free will, which is a compatibilist position, between accepting determinism, and in particular God's determination of events, and human free will and responsibility.

In his more systematic works, al-Fārābī describes in detail how the world emanates from the First, the most perfect and unique being, with the most perfect attributes. In his most famous work, *The Principles of the Opinions of the Inhabitants of the Virtuous City* (*Mabādī' Ārā' Ahl al-Madīna al-Fadīla*, translated into English by Richard Walzer as *The Perfect State*), he describes the way in which an intellect issues from the First, namely God, which is pure intellect. After a series of emanations resulting in a total of ten emanated intellects and

---

5   Aristotle "De interpretatione 1928–32", *The Complete Works of Aristotle: The Revised Oxford Translation-Volume 2*, ed. Jonathan Barnes, Princeton University Press, Princeton, 1984, p. 30.

6   Alfarabi, *Al-Farabi's Commentary and Short Treatise on Aristotle's De Interpretatione*, (trans.) F. W. Zimmermann, Oxford: Published for the British Academy by Oxford University Press, 1991 (reprint), p. 88–90.

nine spheres (the last emanation is a simple intellect without a sphere), the terrestrial world comes to be.[7] Al-Fārābī makes a distinction between the celestial and the terrestrial realms, the first being perfect with its eternal intellects and spheres, and the terrestrial realm constituting the world of generation and corruption, where substances come to be and pass away. However, and even if the celestial realm is conceived as perfect by al-Fārābī, this does not exclude the existence of free will in the terrestrial realm, in which human beings live. In the political plane, it is clear that his theory of virtue contemplates the possibility of human beings choosing to be virtuous or otherwise, and the leader sets the tone for central decisions taken at the political level. Both for the citizens and the leader, there is a choice between virtue or vice, good or evil.[8]

In his works, which touch on all aspects of philosophy, Ibn Sīnā discusses many topics which pertain to the question of determinism. One of the central topics bearing on this issue is the question of the possible and the necessary, and the modalities of existence from a metaphysical perspective. For Ibn Sīnā, everything which exists is necessary through its cause; more specifically, it exists necessarily through its cause. Therefore, he states that everything that exists is necessary, and this is due to its cause.[9] Only God is necessary through Himself. This is to say that God necessarily exists and cannot not exist. Ibn Sīnā explicitly states that something does not exist as long as it is not necessary.[10] Only God is uncaused, and does not have a cause. Hence necessity is equated with causality or being caused by Ibn Sīnā, except in the case of God, who is the cause of all causes. His metaphysics indicates that he views everything that actually exists as being necessary through its cause. For Ibn Sīnā, necessity is also identified with existence. It is clear that for him everything that actually exists is necessary and could not have been otherwise. For Aristotle, the necessary is the eternal and also that which cannot be otherwise, but Ibn Sīnā has a different conception of necessity. For Ibn Sīnā, the possible is that which does not actually exist, but may exist if a cause brings

7   Alfarabi, *Al-Farabi on the Perfect State: Abū Naṣr al-Fārābī's Mabādi' Arā' Ahl al-Madīnah al-Faḍīlah,* (ed. and trans.) Richard Walzer, Oxford University Press, New York, 1985, p. 100–105.

8   Janne Mattila, *The Eudaimonist Ethics of Al-Fārābī and Avicenna,* Brill, Leiden, 2022, p. 181–182.

9   Avicenna, *The Metaphysics of The Healing, A Parallel English-Arabic Text,* (trans.) Michael E. Marmura, Brigham Young University Press, Provo, 2005, p. 127.

10   Avicenna/Ibn Sīnā, *Al-Ta'līqāt,* (ed.) Badawī, The General Book Organization, Cairo, 1973, p. 83.

it into existence. In addition, everything exists through a hierarchy of causes. Ibn Sīnā's conception of causality means that every existent is causally and necessarily determined.

Ibn Sīnā's conception of necessary causality is also apparent in his remarks on chance in the *Metaphysics of* The Healing, referring to chance as a result from clashes based on necessary principles, which come from God.[11] In the same work, he also states that everything that comes to be is due to a cause, and does not happen without a cause.[12]

Within the *Physics of* The Healing, Chapters 13 and 14 clearly constitute a broad commentary on the final question of Book II of Aristotle's *Physics*. Towards the end of this book, Aristotle asks whether chance is a cause and how it relates to the other essential causes, the formal, the efficient, the final and the material causes. To illustrate these four causes, in the case of a table, we say that the wood is the material cause, the form or shape is the formal cause, the carpenter is the efficient cause and writing is the final cause or the goal.

Aristotle states that some philosophers argue that chance is not a cause while another opinion states that it is an essential cause. Aristotle also refers to the common belief that chance can be considered a goddess, constituting a certain specific power.[13] Aristotle thinks of chance in connection with the frequency of events, and concludes that chance does not happen in that which is always or for the most part. If something happens always or for the most part, such as rain in the winter, it is not a chance event. This is also related to his view that chance does not have a place in the celestial realm, where everything happens in a regular way and never changes.[14] This is a perfect world where substances are eternal, in contrast to the terrestrial world of generation and corruption.

Initially, Ibn Sīnā associates chance with that which does not happen always or for the most part, such as unusual or rare occurrences, but then he also admits that chance may happen in the case of that which is for the most part. In turn, that which is rare can also be considered to be necessary, on account of its causes.[15] In that sense, chance can be something unusual, but it can

---

11 Avicenna/Ibn Sīnā, *The Metaphysics of The Healing*, p. 362.
12 ibid, p. 31.
13 Aristotle, *Physics, 196b5-7,* (ed.) W. D. Ross, Oxford, Oxford University Press, 1998.
14 Aristotle, *Physics, 196a8-12.*
15 Avicenna/Ibn Sīnā, *Al-Samā' al-ṭabī'ī, (Al-Shifā'),* (ed.) Ja'far Āl Yasīn, Beirut, 1996, p. 120.

also be related to things that happen frequently or are to be expected. In this sense he clearly has a more deterministic conception of chance than does Aristotle, since chance is not fundamentally tied to the low frequency of events. One might wonder how we can speak of chance in a meaningful way, if everything is considered to be necessary, and chance is not essentially associated with rare events. Aristotle considers that chance has to be analyzed within the framework of a causal theory, and this is the way in which he introduces the theme of chance, as we have seen, and in view of the fact that people refer to certain events as happening by chance. Aristotle considers that chance is present in goal-directed events that do not happen always or for the most part, as an accidental cause.[16] In general, Aristotle chooses a middle term between these positions and argues that chance is an accidental cause related to an essential cause. These causes could be the efficient or the final cause. For instance, if a builder produces a house, the fact that he is a musician is accidental to the building of the house. On the other hand, in another example given by Aristotle, if someone goes to the marketplace and finds there someone (for example, a debtor) whom he wanted but was not expecting to see,[17] this can be explained as a chance event. Chance can also be explained as existing on account of the final cause. The real intention was to go to the marketplace, and therefore finding the debtor could have been the aim and is attached to the goal and the real intention as an accidental cause. In this case the chance element is linked to the final cause.

Ibn Sīnā discusses this issue and cites several examples present in Aristotle. He emphasizes the example provided by Aristotle of someone who goes to the marketplace to do business and finds there his debtor. In this case, it is said to be a chance encounter because the agent was not expecting to find his debtor in the marketplace.[18] Therefore chance is related to goal-directed actions when the outcome is other than the one expected. If the goal of the agent had been to find the debtor, this would not have been said to be a chance encounter.

Ibn Sīnā also addresses the issue of God's determination of events, al-qaḍā' wa-l-qadar, in his treatises on qadar. He views qadar from a causal perspective. God's determination consists in the arrangement of causes according

---

16   Aristotle, *Physics*, 197a13-32.
17   Aristotle, *Physics*, 196a1-5.
18   Avicenna/Ibn Sīnā, *Al-Samā' al-ṭabī'ī*, p. 118.

to a certain order produced by God.[19] *Qadar* signifies the details of God's de-cree, while this decree (*qaḍā'*) is His first command, and in that sense *qadar* is more specific than *qaḍā'*. This distinction between the two terms referring to God's determination of events goes back to al-Bukhārī.[20]

If we study Ibn Sīnā's conception of necessity and possibility, it is clear that he holds that all events and substances are necessarily caused in such a way that they could not have been otherwise. His views on chance indicate that he does not believe that this is an essential cause, instead it is a way of speaking of some unexpected event because we were not aware of its causes and circum-stances. Finally, his texts on the theological principle of God's decree and de-termination (*al-qaḍā' wa-l-qadar*) indicate that he believes that all events and substances are causally and necessarily determined by God. In these texts, Ibn Sīnā does not seek to reconcile God's omnipotence with the attribute of God's justice by way of granting free will to human beings.

In his prolific philosophical works, Ibn Rushd takes into account the views of al-Fārābī and Ibn Sīnā. He is greatly inspired by al-Fārābī and is critical of Ibn Sīnā on several philosophical points. However, in his mature works he does not accept the emanation schema designed by al-Fārābī and developed by Ibn Sīnā. Ibn Rushd holds that God produces many effects simultaneously, and not just one emanated effect which goes on to produce further effects. How-ever, like al-Fārābī and Ibn Sīnā, Ibn Rushd holds that there are many types of causes and agents, and that although God is the one true agent, things and human beings have powers and produce causal effects.

A current within Islamic thought, particularly within Islamic theology, known as Islamic occasionalism, held that God is the direct agent and other beings, such as plants, animals and human beings, have no agency and are themselves, in their being and actions, caused by God. Al-Ghāzālī (d. 1111) is a famous proponent of this theory and, inspired by the writings of al-Ashʿarī, he opposes the philosophers' conception of causality in his work *The Incoher-ence of the Philosophers*.

In addition, Ibn Rushd takes issue with Ibn Sīnā's conception of metaphys-ical modalities. While al-Fārābī believes that some actually existing beings are

---

19 Avicenna/ Ibn Sīnā, *Lettre au Vizir Abû Saʿd*, (ed.&trans.) Y. Michot, Albouraq, Beirut, 2000, p. 122.

20 Gy., Káldy-Nagy, "Ḳaḍā", *Encyclopaedia of Islam- Second Edition*, (ed.) P. Bearman, Th. Bi-anquis, C. E. Bosworth, E. van Donzel, W. P. Heinrichs. Consulted online on 15 August 2022.

possible, for Ibn Sīnā the possible is that which has not had a necessary cause and therefore does not yet actually exist. Al-Fārābī and Ibn Rushd follow more closely Aristotle's view of possibility, which associates necessary beings with the celestial realm and possible beings with the terrestrial realm, the world of generation and corruption. Ibn Sīnā conceived of two kinds of beings, those possible in themselves, and necessary through another, which include all beings other than God, and one being necessary by Himself, and that is God. Moreover, Ibn Sīnā does not make a distinctiin between celestial beings and terrestrial beings.

For Ibn Rushd God is also necessary by Himself, but it is the celestial bodies which are possible in themselves and necessary through another, while beings in the earthly realm are possible in themselves.[21] Ibn Sīnā and Ibn Rushd have different views on necessity. While Ibn Sīnā associates necessity with existence, and (except in the case of God), being caused, Ibn Rushd associates necessity with eternity, which is the primary meaning of necessity for Aristotle. Therefore, for Ibn Rushd necessity must be the hallmark of the celestial realm, where beings are eternal.

From his view on modalities, it is not immediately clear that Ibn Rushd endorses determinism, because he does not exclude the existence of possible beings.[22]

Ibn Rushd wrote several commentaries on Aristotle's works. In his *Long Commentary on Aristotle's* Physics, he analyzes Aristotle's conception of chance. He also takes into account Ibn Sīnā's analysis of chance. There is a debate as to whether chance exists in events and substances that happen always or for the most part, and an issue arises concerning actions which are equally possible. Ibn Rushd concludes that chance concerns events which are not in this category but is only to be found in rare events. Ibn Rushd also states that if something does not come to be, this is due to its own failure or lack of capacity, and not due to the absence of an external cause, as stated by Ibn Sīnā.[23] Therefore, Ibn Rushd thinks of causality more in terms of the internal capability of agents instead of putting the emphasis on external causes.

---

21   Averroes, *Tahafut al-tahafut (The Incoherence of the Incoherence vol.I)*, (trans.) Simon van den Bergh, E. J. W. Gibb Memorial Trust, London, 1954, p. 238.

22   Catarina Belo, *Chance and Determinism in Avicenna and Averroes*, Leiden, Brill, 2007, p. 176.

23   Averroes, *Long Commentary on the Physics"*, *Aristotelis de Physico Auditu libri octo cum Averrois Cordubensis variis in eosdem commentariis, vol. 4 of Aristotelis Opera quae extant omnia Venice*, Venetiis apud Junctas, Venice, 1562, 66L–67A.

He also comments on the examples of the musician who happens to build a house, and the chance encounter in the marketplace. He holds that the musician builds the house accidentally, but essentially in his capacity as builder.[24] In this case chance is an accident of the efficient cause, namely the builder. He also comments on the example of the man who finds his debtor in the marketplace, stating that chance attaches to the visit to the marketplace. In this case, Ibn Rushd does not consider so much the question of the intention, and the way in which chance consists in the unexpected, but the connection of chance to the actual action of visiting the marketplace. In this sense, he links chance to the efficient rather than to the final cause.[25]

However, Ibn Rushd does not believe in events that are not caused or are spontaneous. In addition, in analyzing chance, he affirms that it is not a divine cause or something inexplicable but can be explained as an accident of the efficient cause.[26] In spite of this, his conception of natural causality is not as obviously deterministic as that of Ibn Sīnā.

Like Ibn Sīnā, he also holds that God's providence rules over events in the celestial and the terrestrial realms, as al-Fārābī had also stated. However, his understanding of God's causation is different from that of al-Fārābī and Ibn Sīnā, who defended the view that the world was created by God when an intellect issued from God, in this way initiating a process of emanation. For Ibn Rushd, God is the Prime Mover who moves others by being their final cause, their ultimate goal. The celestial spheres move out of love of God, and their movements produce the events in the terrestrial world. In this way, God can produce a variety of effects at the same time, instead of emanating just one effect.[27] God bestows existence by bestowing movement and drawing things from potentiality to actuality, from nonexistence to existence.

Ibn Rushd also devotes a chapter of a work on Islamic theology to the issue of God's decree and determination, namely *Unveiling the Methods of the Proofs concerning the Beliefs of the Religious Community* (*Kashf 'an manāhij al-adilla fi 'aqā'id al-milla*). He analyzes what the religious literature has to say, specifically the Qur'ān and hadith literature, on this question, and what it has to say about God's omnipotence and human agency. He holds that God's

24 Averroes, "Long Commentary on the Physics", 68A-B.
25 Averroes, *Long Commentary on the Physics,* 68B-C.
26 Averroes, *Long Commentary on the Physics,* 66A-B.
27 Catarina Belo, "Chance and Determinism in Avicenna and Averroes", *Islamic Philosophy, Theology and Science Texts and Studies*, vol.69, 2007, p.199.

determination of events, *qadar*, means God's omnipotence. On the other hand, the acquisition of actions is contemplated. These two questions are also analyzed by the schools of theology. He studies in particular the views of the Mu'tazilites, the Ash'arites and the Jabarites. The Mu'tazilites emphasize freedom of action and the acquisition of their own acts by human beings. On the other hand, the Jabarites state that people are compelled in their actions. The Ash'arites, according to Ibn Rushd, purport to hold a middle position in the sense that one's acts are created by God but are acquired by human beings. However, according to Ibn Rushd, this position does not truly differ from that of the Jabarites.[28]

Ibn Rushd accepts that God is the only creator, for this is the consensus among Muslim scholars. He goes on to find a solution which preserves God's omnipotence and also His justice. He accepts that certain powers or faculties belong to human beings which allow them to acquire things that are contraries.[29] One of the characteristics of voluntary action, according to the Muslim philosophers, is to choose between opposites, whereas natural action tends to follow one set pattern. For instance, if we are hungry we can choose to eat or not to eat, such as for religious reasons. However, fire does not choose to burn or not to burn a piece of cotton with which it comes into contact. If there is no obstacle, such as humidity, it will burn the piece of cotton. Ibn Rushd accepts that nature follows its natural course in the absence of obstacles.[30]

By stating that human beings have certain powers, Ibn Rushd chooses not to follow the Ash'arite line of thought on this issue, which is also defended by al-Ghazālī in the *Incoherence of the Philosophers*, to the effect that human actions are to be attributed to God and denying that human beings have any power over their actions. Al-Ghazālī's position in *The Incoherence of the Philosophers* is meant to preserve the possibility of miracles, which represent a break with the normal course of events in nature.[31]

In describing the mechanism of human action, Ibn Rushd holds that human beings have certain powers which pertain to our actions and relate to external substances and events. These external causes are made subject to us by

28   Averroes/Ibn Rushd, Al-Kashf 'an-manāhij al-adilla fī 'aqā'id al-milla Kashf, ed. by Muṣṭafā Ḥanafī with Introduction and Comments by Muḥammad 'Ābid al-Jābirī, Center for Arab Unity Studies, Beirut, 1998, p. 187.

29   Ibn Rushd, *Kashf,* p. 188.

30   Averroes/Ibn Rushd, "Long Commentary on the Metaphysics", *Tafsīr mā ba'd al-ṭabī'a,* (ed.) M. Bouyges, Imprimerie Catholique, Beirut, 1938, p. 1152.

31   L. E., Goodman, "Did al-Ghazālī Deny Causality?", *Studia Islamica*, No.47, 1978, p. 112.

God. On the one hand, God makes certain things subject to us; on the other hand, He removes any obstacles between us and those causes.[32] Naturally, Ibn Rushd takes into account human will in order to accomplish certain actions, those actions that are up to us. However, he also states that our will in choosing between two contraries is caused by God through external causes.[33]

In this work, *Unveiling of the Proofs*, Ibn Rushd states that we assent to something after imagining it. If that which we imagine is desirable, then we wish to have it necessarily, which means that Ibn Rushd leaves little room for the kind of action that issues from within us without the necessitating influence of external causes. There are similarities with the position held by the Ash'arites, since Ibn Rushd also states that only God is truly agent, and even with the Jabarites. What does distinguish his position is the acceptance of secondary causality, namely the notion that other beings are causes, and not just God. He holds that the efficient causes that we observe in sensible things are true and real, and that every act must needs have an agent.[34] Nevertheless, he goes so far as to state that the causes which are made available to us by God are only efficient in a metaphorical way.[35] The time in which something happens is also determined, and God's omniscience also ensures that the future is predetermined.[36]

Ibn Rushd views human action as being determined by external factors in a process that includes imagining and assenting, leading to choice and decision over a course of action. Moreover, our power to act depends on external factors, which are ultimately determined by God. His commitment to God's omnipotence is clear and his explanation of the process of human action means that human action is determined and not truly autonomous.

Conclusion

The problem of determinism has attracted the attention of philosophers since ancient Greece. In medieval Islamic theology and philosophy, which examine what the religious texts have to say about divine omnipotence and human responsibility, the problem is expressed in theological terms as the articulation between divine and human agency as well as the harmonious combination of

---

32 Ibn Rushd, *Kashf,* p. 188.
33 Ibn Rushd, *Kashf,* p. 189.
34 Ibn Rushd, *Tahāfut,* p. 318.
35 Ibn Rushd, *Kashf,* p. 190.
36 Ibn Rushd, *Kashf,* p. 190.

divine attributes, in particular power and justice. Classical Islamic schools of theology lean towards the affirmation of human freedom (such as the Mu'tazilites) or divine omnipotence (such as the Jabarites), while the Ash'arites focus on the doctrine of the acquisition of acts by human beings in order to justify divine justice while stressing God's omnipotence and creation of human acts.

In Islamic philosophy we find a variety of positions. Al-Fārābī has a similar conception of possibility to that of Aristotle, which means that events in the terrestrial world are not necessarily determined, a position which allows for human freedom of action. While Ibn Sīnā adopts for the most part al-Fārābī's cosmological views and conception of emanation, he has a different conception of necessity and possibility. For Ibn Sīnā, everything that exists is actually necessary, through its cause. His views on chance mean that it is only the result of subjective expectations on the part of human beings, and in that sense it is only an accidental cause. His views on God's determination of events (qadar) show that he is fully supportive of the notion of divine omnipotence, regardless of the ethical consequences for holding human beings accountable for their actions. Ibn Rushd shares views on possibility and necessity with Aristotle and al-Fārābī, and does not state that every existing thing is necessary. With regard to chance, he holds that it is an accidental cause related to the efficient cause. On the subject of God's determination of events, he believes that our actions are influenced by external causes which are ultimately determined by God.

In medieval Islamic theology and philosophy, we find a variety of positions on the question of free will and determinism, which remains a central question within debates on ethics. Some theologians and philosophers defend the notion of free will, such as the Mu'tazilites and al-Fārābī, while other stress God's omnipotence, such as the Ash'arites, the Jabarites and Ibn Sīnā.

References

Alfarabi, *Al-Farabi on the Perfect State: Abū Naṣr al-Fārābī's Mabādī' Arā' Ahl al-Madīnah al-Faḍīlah*, (ed. and trans.) Richard Walzer, Oxford University Press, New York, 1985.

Alfarabi, *Al-Farabi's Commentary and Short Treatise on Aristotle's De Interpretatione*, (trans.) F.W. Zimmermann, Oxford University Press, Oxford,1991.

Aristotle, *The Complete Works of Aristotle: The Revised Oxford Translation 2 vols,* (ed.) Jonathan Barnes, Princeton University Press, Princeton,1984.

Aristotle, *Physics*, ed. W. D. Ross, Oxford University Press, Oxford, 1998.

Averroes/Ibn Rushd, *Faith and Reason in Islam: Averroës' Exposition of Religious Arguments,* (trans.) Ibrahim Najjar; Majid Fakhry, Oneworld, Oxford, 2001.

Averroes/Ibn Rushd, Al-Kashf 'an-manāhij al-adilla fi 'aqā'id al-milla Kashf, ed. by Muṣṭafā Ḥanafī with Introduction and Comments by Muḥammad 'Ābid al-Jābirī, Center for Arab Unity Studies, Beirut, 1998.

Averroes/Ibn Rushd, *Long Commentary on the Metaphysics, in Tafsīr mā ba'd al-ṭabī'a,* (ed.) M. Bouyges, Imprimerie Catholique, Beirut, 1938.

Averroes/Ibn Rushd, *"Long Commentary on the Physics", Aristotelis de Physico Auditu libri octo cum Averrois Cordubensis variis in eosdem commentariis,* vol. 4 of Aristotelis Opera quae extant omnia Venice, Venetiis apud Junctas, Venice, 1562.

Averroes/Ibn Rushd, *Tahafut al-tahafut (The Incoherence of the Incoherence) 2 vols.,* (trans.) Simon van den Bergh, E. J. W. Gibb Memorial Trust, London, 1954.

Avicenna/Ibn Sīnā, *Lettre au Vizir Abû Sa'd,* (ed. & trans.) Y. Michot, Albouraq, Beirut, 2000.

Avicenna/Ibn Sīnā, *The Metaphysics of The Healing,* (trans.) Michael E. Marmura, Brigham Young University Press, Provo, 2005.

Avicenna/Ibn Sīnā, *Physics of the Healing II vols. (Books I–IV),* (trans.) Jon McGinnis, Brigham Young University Press, Provo - Utah, 2009.

Avicenna/Ibn Sīnā, *Al-Samā' al-ṭabī'ī (Al-Shifā'),* (ed.) Ja'far Āl Yasīn, Beirut, 1996.

Avicenna/Ibn Sīnā, *Al-Ta'līqāt,* (ed.) Badawī, The General Book Organization, Cairo, 1973.

Belo, Catarina, *Chance and Determinism in Avicenna and Averroes*, Brill, Leiden, 2007.

De Cillis, Maria, *Free Will and Predestination in Islamic Thought: Theoretical Compromises in the Works of Avicenna, al-Ghazālī and Ibn 'Arabī*, Routledge, London and New York, 2014.

Al-Ghazālī, *Abū Ḥāmid Muḥammad, The Incoherence of the Philosophers,* (trans.) Michael E. Marmura, Islamic Translation Series, Brigham Young University Press, Provo-Utah, 2000.

Al-Ghazālī, *The Incoherence of the Philosophers,* (trans.) Michael E. Marmura, 2nd edition, Brigham Young University Press, Provo-Utah, 2000.

Goodman, L. E., "Did al-Ghazālī Deny Causality?", Studia Islamica, no. 47 (1978), pp. 83–120.

Káldy-Nagy, Gy., "Ḳaḍā'," Encyclopaedia of Islam, (ed.) P. Bearman, Th. Bianquis, C. E. Bosworth, E. van Donzel, W. P. Heinrichs, Second Edition, Consulted online on 15 August 2022.

Kant, I., *Critique of Pure Reason (The Cambridge Edition of the Works of Immanuel Kant),* (eds.) P. Guyer & A. Wood, Cambridge University Press, Cambridge, 1998.

Mattila, Janne, *The Eudaimonist Ethics of Al-Fārābī and Avicenna,* Brill, Leiden, 2022.

The Meaning of the Holy Qur'ān, (trans.) 'A. Yūsuf 'Alī, Amana Publications, Beltsville-Maryland, 1997.

Mourad, Suleiman Ali, *Early Islam between Myth and History: Al-Ḥasan al-Baṣrī (d. 110 H/728 CE) and the Formation of His Legacy in Classical Islamic Scholarship,* Brill, Leiden/Boston, 2006.

Watt, William Montgomery, *Free Will and Predestination in Early Islam,* Luzac, London, 1948.

A World Without Nuclear Weapons: Is It Possible

Şafak Oğuz

Introduction

With their enormous destructive potential exceeding all weapon systems in history, Nuclear Weapons (NWs) represent a crucial breakthrough in weapon systems, as well as a game changer in the history of warfare. Their deterrence capability for states that possess them is so great that none of these states' adversaries ever contemplated or dared to attack them, due to the possibility of retaliation that could annihilate adversaries' territory and population in a very short time. And yet, none of these weapon systems has provided safety for their possessors, but do, at the same time, create a huge threat for the extinction of human beings and the planet.

The realist theory, which explains international relations in terms of power, advises states to maximize their power, especially military power, in order to prevail in the international theater. NWs became one of the main tools, perhaps the most important one, to endow possessor states with deterrent power. Therefore, states tend to acquire NWs, and nuclear states sought to increase their nuclear stockpiles, in order to maximize their military power, despite the horrendous effects of NWs that the world has witnessed, and their threat of annihilation. Possession of NWs provided the image of being a great power, while superpower status, especially during the Cold War, stemmed from possession of a massive NWs stockpile.

Per the Nonproliferation Treaty (NPT) of 1968, the US, Russia, the UK, France, and China rank as nuclear states and have the right to produce, acquire and possess NWs. However, despite strong non-proliferation norms and efforts, India, Pakistan, Israel, and allegedly North Korea also acquired NWs and gained nuclear deterrence capability. Iran has embarked on a NWs project, but international efforts continue to convert Iran's facilities and activities to a peaceful nuclear energy program. The nuclear program of states such as

South Africa and Libya were forcibly abolished by the international community in recent history.

In addition to non-proliferation efforts, efforts to free the world of NWs have been on the agenda of the international community since the first bombs dropped on Hiroshima and Nagasaki in 1945. Even scientists who contributed to the invention of NWs expressed their regret and proclaimed the importance of a world free of NWs, for the sake of humanity and the planet. However, nuclear states have been reluctant to give up such power and deterrence capability, so that they have mainly focused on nuclear non-proliferation activities, in order to prevent other states from acquiring these weapons. The Cold War continued under the shadow of NWs competition and a massive nuclear arms race, and the dream of a nuclear-free world survived into the post-Cold War era.

The early post-Cold War era witnessed close cooperation between the US and Russia in non-proliferation as well as in containing Weapons of Mass Destruction (WMD) inherited by the successor states of the former Soviet Union. This cooperation was accompanied by the gradual efforts to reduce the strategical and tactical NWs of both states, with the new security environment providing hope for a nuclear-free world. US President Obama's speech in Prague in 2009 laid out a vision for this scenario, which triggered new discussions on a nuclear-free world and nuclear-free future among the international community.

Obama's vision was considered an important and hopeful step toward a world without NWs, in that the concept was articulated by the world's highest-level official for the first time. Just a decade after his speech, though, recent developments, especially the Russia-Ukraine war under the shadow of Russia's nuclear threat, and the renewed nuclear arms race between the US and Russia, have dashed hopes for such a glorious vision. Once again, the world began to discuss the concept of Mutual Assured Destruction (MAD), or first-strike and second-strike capabilities, as had been the case during the Cold War.

Replete with uncertainties as it was, the new security environment propelled states again toward a massive and dangerous arms race, possibly far more dangerous than the Cold War period. As occurred before WWI and WWII, the world has been dragged into an atmosphere in which nationalism, militarism and patriotism are reaching a dangerous level. The danger of major crises with the existence and readiness of massive stocks of nuclear weapons form the chief difference between the world of history and the world of today.

Nuclear Weapons: Do They Help Ensure Peace?

NWs came into existence through America's Manhattan Project, launched in 1939 out of concern that Germany might acquire its own NW. President Roosevelt agreed to invest a great deal of money in this project, which was at the beginning but a theory, largely at the advice of Einstein, who sent him letters from scientists who fled Europe before WWII and feared that Germany might have a NW relatively quickly.[1] The US conducted its first atomic bomb test in 1945, when President Truman was attending the Potsdam Conference to discuss the course of the war with Churchill and Stalin. The message sent to the President to herald the success of the world's first NW changed his status relative to other states, without knowing, however, that Stalin had been following America's NW activities through Soviet spies.[2] The US dropped two atomic bombs on Japan, Little Boy (a uranium bomb) in Hiroshima and Fat Man (a plutonium bomb) on Nagasaki, resulting in the death of more than 220,000 people. Having rejected surrender after the first atomic bomb, Japan acquiesced after the second, ending WWII.

Discussion about the deterrence capability of NWs began with their role in forcing Japan to surrender, thus ending WWII. We cannot know if Japan would have eventually surrendered without the use of NWs, but one can state that surrender would not have occurred anytime so soon as after the use of atomic bombs. Therefore, it is clear that NWs do have a role in deterrence, but at what cost? Was there another way to spare the lives of some two hundred thousand people in Hiroshima and Nagasaki?

Arguments have been made that the use of atomic bombs was primarily based on the assessment by the Truman administration that invasion of Japan would cost, at a minimum, a quarter million casualties, and perhaps as much as one million, on the American side alone.[3] Thus the uncertainties about the duration and cost of a possible invasion of Japan by conventional means played an important role in the US decision to use atomic bombs. Yet it is worth noting that Bernstein, as well as many others, argue that there is no evidence that

---

1   The letter can be found at https://thebulletin.org/virtual-tour/albert-einstein-leo-szilard-and-the-letter-that-led-to-the-manhattan-project/

2   "The Potsdam Conference, 1945", https://history.state.gov/milestones/1937-1945/potsdam-conf

3   Kathryn Moore and Dennis M. Giangreco, *Dear Harry: Truman's Mailroom, 1945-1953: the Truman administration through correspondence with "everyday Americans*, Stackpole Books, Lanham, 2017, p. 470.

any top military planner or major policy maker believed that an invasion would cost that many lives, maintaining instead that claim was a post-war creation.[4]

The Soviet Union closely followed America's atomic bomb activities with its spies and acquired its own NWs in 1949, with the successful test code-named First Lightning. They were followed in 1952 by the UK, which had partially participated in the Manhattan Project, in 1960 by France, which op-posed American hegemony in Europe and in NATO, and in 1964 by China. With this nuclear proliferation, the Cold War era, associated with NWs, was in full swing. The new security environment was shaped by five nuclear states who are also permanent members of the UN Security Council, the body that decides the fate of the world in security matters.

Acquisition of NWs by these states within a short period also alarmed them concerning the dangers of nuclear proliferation, which constituted a di-rect threat to their deterrence capabilities. That encouraged them to cooperate in non-proliferation efforts, resulting in the Treaty on the Non-Proliferation of Nuclear Weapons in 1968, known generally as NPT (Non-Proliferation Treaty. The Treaty granted them the legal status of a nuclear state, while prohibiting other signatory states to research, acquire, possess, and use NWs. Despite its unequal and unjust obligations, the treaty was acknowledged as one of the most important steps so far in curbing nuclear proliferation. These states, the key powers in the two camps of competition between East and West, thus main-tained their deterrence capabilities through cooperation with their adversaries.

The first phase of the Cold War witnessed a massive nuclear arms race, in which the US and the Soviet Union, in particular, produced thousands of NWs in addition to their intense conventional, chemical, and biological weapons pro-grams. The invention and production of hydrogen bombs by the US and the Soviet Union, which are much more powerful than atomic bombs, launched a new era in the and threat of destruction by NWs. The Russian hydrogen bomb tested in 1961, known as the "Char Bomb," which unleashed 50-60 megatons of TNT—roughly 2,500-3,000 times more powerful than the atomic bomb used on Nagasaki—underscored the dimension of the threat posed by the new hy-drogen bomb, as well as its role in deterrence.

The deterrence role of NWs altered the security environment during the early Cold War, which experienced a period of proxy warfare across the world,

---

4   Barton J. Bernstein, "A post-war myth: 500,000 US lives saved", Bulletin of the Atomic Sci-ences, 42. No. 6 (June/July 1986), p.38.

rather than direct confrontation between the superpowers. Both the US and the Soviet Union focused on the deterrence strategies of NWs during this period: terms such as "game theories", "first- and second-strike capabilities" emerged as the main terminology involving NW policies. Associated as the Cold War was with nuclear strategies, the works of Thomas Schelling[5], Herman Kahn, and Bernard Brodie shaped US nuclear policies during this period. All their efforts focused on providing deterrence by NWs, because a failure of nuclear deterrence was viewed as tantamount to mutual annihilation, in the coined term "Mutual Assured Destruction" with its cynical acronym MAD.

The 1962 Cuban Crisis, in which the world came to the brink of nuclear warfare, changed the perception of NWs, nuclear warfare, deterrence, and nuclear proliferation. Deterrence by NWs prevented a last-minute nuclear war between the US and the Soviet Union, which most probably would have resulted in annihilation of the Earth. The crisis prompted both states to discuss and negotiate the threat of nuclear warfare, inaugurating a new phase of the Cold War, the "Détente Period", in which international cooperation outweighed international confrontation, especially concerning nuclear issues. Beginning already before the Cuban Crisis with a symbolic Treaty, the 1959 Antarctic Treaty, which banned testing NWs in the Arctic, many international treaties were signed to limit and ban testing, acquiring, possessing and deploying NWs.

In addition to the international agreements, the US and the Soviet Union also signed several bilateral treaties to limit production of NWs and to reduce their numbers, having been prompted to do so due to the logic behind deterrence, the international security structure, and pressure from domestic and international populations. The Strategic Arms Limitation Treaty (SALT) of 1972 restricted the manufacture of missile systems capable of carrying nuclear warheads, thus playing a crucial role in reducing the number of NWs.

Despite severe tension between the East and West, during the late Cold War the world experienced a period of relative peace, termed "The Long Peace" by

---

5   See: Thomas Schelling, *The Strategy of Conflict* 1960, *Arms and Influence*, Yale University Press, 1966.
     Herman Kahn, *On Thermonuclear War*. Princeton University Press, 1960: *Thinking about the unthinkable*. Horizon Press. 1962: *On escalation: metaphors and scenarios*. Praeger, 1965.
     Bernard Brodie, *The Absolute Weapon: Atomic Power and World Order*. Harcourt, 1946: *Strategy in the Missile Age*, Princeton University Press, 1959: *From Cross-Bow to H-Bomb*. Dell, 1962; *Escalation and the Nuclear Option*. Princeton University Press, 1966.

historian John Lewis Gaddis[6]. The lack of major wars during the Cold War, in particular the period of relative peace overall was considered by many scholars as the result of the deterrence capability of nuclear weapons. Proxy warfare— regional conflicts or civil wars supported by the major powers without direct involvement—emerged as an outcome of the strong competition between East and West. Similarly, conflicts such as the Korean War, the US invasion of Vietnam, and the Russian invasion of Afghanistan erupted in which only one major power was directly involved while the other preferred to support the attacked state secretly rather than directly. In line with the theory of nuclear deterrence, indirect competition prevented a major conventional war, as well as nuclear warfare.

The core of the discussion stands here: Did NWs prevent a major war or conflict between superpowers, and did nuclear deterrence work as Gaddis argued? Did the logic of Mutual Assured Destruction (MAD), named by strategist Donald Brennan, hold true, by which each side will possess enough nuclear weaponry to destroy each other and both sides will definitely be annihilated in a nuclear war? Or was the peace period a result of the new and international security environment after the horrifying death and destruction of WWII? The question cannot be answered easily and definitively, but the lack of a major war between East and West during their indirect confrontation in the Cold War serves as a crucial indicator of the working logic of deterrence by NWs.

The second question remains: Is a nuclear-free world possible? Would it be more dangerous than the current world with NWs? Or more may be better as argued by Kenneth Waltz?[7]

A Nuclear-Free World: One Possible Vision

We have seen that the early post-Cold War era witnessed close cooperation between the US and Russia on controlling WMD proliferation, and then on the safety of WMDs inherited from the former Soviet Union. This was accompanied by further treaties to reduce the number of tactical and strategic nuclear weapons and their delivery vehicles. The Strategic Arms Reduction Treaty (START) of 1991, which aimed to reduce the existing NWs of the US and Russia, launched a crucial process for the reduction of the excessive stocks of

---

6   John Lewis Gaddis, *International Security*, Vol. 10, No. 4 (Spring, 1986)

7   Kenneth N. Waltz "The Spread of Nuclear Weapons: More May Be Better: Introduction ", *The Adelphi Papers*, Vol., 21, No. 171, 1981.

NWs, although it did not target the complete elimination of all of these weapons in the world. The treaty did, however, create new and fresh hope for a world without NWs, and without threat of MAD, leading into an atmosphere of peace in which cooperation, especially on nuclear issues, outweighed competition, and confrontation on international security.

Despite confrontation that arose over the NATO membership discussions of Georgia and Ukraine, US/NATO-Russian relations remained good, with Russia participating in some NATO activities, and with NATO-Russia cooperation reached a peak through the NATO-Russian Council. Despite crises, such as the Color Revolution, in states that Russia regards as its backyard, Russia did not vehemently oppose NATO's major expansion in Eastern Europe in 1999 and 2004; this period witnessed landmark cooperation between East and West.[8]

Upon gradually increasing crisis, both parties pursued a double-track nuclear policy: on the one hand, cooperating on nuclear matters, such as the NEW START Treaty that provided further reduction in both the American and Russian nuclear arsenals, and on the other hand embarking on a massive nuclear arms race and works on missile defense systems based on new technologies.

In the midst of this cooperation-confrontation dilemma, a nuclear-free world has remained on the agenda of many politicians and scholars. Four former US politicians, George P. Shultz, William J. Perry, Henry A. Kissinger and Sam Nunn, for example, published an opinion piece entitled *A World Free of Nuclear Weapons* in the Wall Street Journal in 2007, and outlining the importance of, and the requirement for, a nuclear-free world. As they put it:

> *Nuclear weapons were essential to maintaining international security during the Cold War because they were a means of deterrence. The end of the Cold War made the doctrine of mutual Soviet-American deterrence obsolete. Deterrence continues to be a relevant consideration for many states with regard to threats from other states. But reliance on nuclear weapons for this purpose is becoming increasingly hazardous and decreasingly effective.*[9]

The atmosphere ensued in which advocates for a nuclear-free world gained support all around the world. European states, including Germany, the

---

8   Russian authorities repeatedly underline that further enlargement of NATO creates a crucial threat against Russian national security and they are determined to use all available means, including nuclear weapons to deter NATO.

9   George P. Shultz, William J. Perry, Henry A. Kissinger and Sam Nunn, "A World Free of Nuclear Weapons", *Wall Street Journal*, January 4, 2007.

Netherlands, and Belgium urged the US to remove the American TNWs stationed in Europe, so to create a nuclear-free Europe. Similarly, states such as Kazakhstan emerged as leaders in the endeavor to create regional and global nuclear-free zones. US President Barack Obama's speech in Prague in 2009 emerged as a crucial step toward the dream and vision of a nuclear-free world:

> *So today, I state clearly and with conviction America's commitment to seek the peace and security of **a world without nuclear weapons**. . . . This goal will not be reached quickly—perhaps not in my lifetime. It will take patience and persistence. But now we, too, must ignore the voices who tell us that the world cannot change. We have to insist.[10]*

Is such a goal possible? Is it a realistic vision that can be achieved over a long period? Would nuclear states, especially the US and Russia (and China) agree to relinquish the most important weapons system the world has known, one regarded as a game changer in history?

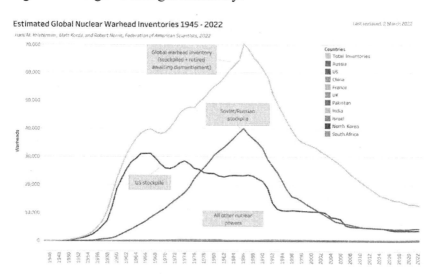

Table 1. Estimated Global Nuclear Warhead Inventories 1945-2022
Source: https://fas.org/issues/nuclear-weapons/status-world-nuclear-forces/

The story of the nuclear arms race and nuclear arms control may tell us much to answer these questions. The estimated inventories of global nuclear warhead (Table-1) shows that there has been a sharp decrease in the number of NWs since its peak in the mid-1980s. This indicates that bilateral treaties

---

10   Remarks By President Barack Obama in Prague as delivered, April 5, 2009, https://obamawhitehouse.archives.gov/the-press-office/remarks-president-barack-obama-prague-delivered

between the US and Soviet Union/Russia enabled elimination of a very large number of NWs globally. Today, we are still far from zero, but the number of existing weapons is considerably lower than at the peak, which gives hope for a nuclear-free world in the future. In particular, the Strategic Arms Reduction Treaty (START) of 1993 and its successors (the latest, NEW START was signed in 2016 by the US and Russia) asked both states to reduce their strategical NWs. Although there has not been any legally binding treaty that asked both states to reduce Tactical Nuclear Weapons (TNWs), several initiatives by both states, as President Bush and Yeltsin agreed in 1991, provided non-binding reduction for TNWs.

This period was accompanied, however, by several developments that directly and negatively affected nuclear cooperation and the vision of a nuclear-free world. America's unilateral withdrawal in 2002 from the 1972 Anti-Ballistic Missiles (ABM) Treaty opened a new phase, which can be termed *The New Cold War*. The US embarked on a comprehensive project, National Missile Defense (NMD)[11] that will protect American territory from the threat of nuclear missiles fired from anywhere in the world, but especially from Russia. The US deployed missile defense systems in Europe under the project European Phased Adaptive Approach (EPAA)[12] against the ballistic missile threat from Iran, and in Pacific states against the threat by North Korean missile systems.[13] It also accelerated development of hypersonic missile projects, such as Conventional Prompt Global Strike (CPGS), which can hit any target in less than one hour without being detected by a missile defense system.[14] Thus, Obama's vision was accompanied with dangerous nuclear and ballistic missile projects.

Russia regarded the American actions, along with NATO's enlargement, including the aspirations of Georgia and Ukraine for membership, as a major imminent threat against its national security, and concomitantly intensified its projects on missile systems and NWs. Putin revealed the Russian modern weapons systems on March 1, 2018,[15] clearly highlighting the extent of a nuclear warfare threat. SARMAT missiles, for example, which according to Russian

---

11   Detailed information about NMD can be found at https://www.mda.mil/

12   About EPAA, see https://www.armscontrol.org/factsheets/Phasedadaptiveapproach

13   In essence, these systems are intended to intercept Russian missiles.

14   Detailed information about the CPGS can be found at https://sgp.fas.org/crs/nuke/R41464.pdf

15   "Russia's Putin unveils 'invincible' nuclear weapons", *BBC*, https://www.bbc.com/news/world-europe-43239331

authorities can annihilate most of France[16] and the UK[17] with a single missile and cannot be stopped by any existing missile defense system, underlines the level of threat posed by the new Russian weapon systems.

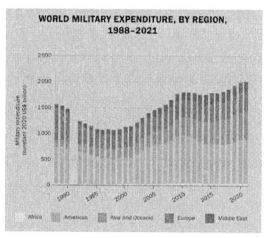

Table 2. World military Expenditure, By, Region, 1988-2021.
Source: https://www.sipri.org/media/press-release/2022/world-military-expenditure-passes-2-trillion-first-time

Military expenditure has always served as a reliable indicator of the international situation and security environment. As Table-2 shows, after a sharp decline at the beginning of the Cold War the world's military expenditure has been increasing gradually in the post-Cold War era. The September 11 attacks and the subsequent invasion of Iraq and Afghanistan accelerated the increase. We see a slowdown of the increase in 2009-2014, beginning with Obama's speech, until the Russian-Ukrainian crisis in 2014. That crisis, which the former Secretary General of NATO described as a "wake-up call"[18] for the Alliance, altered the perception of security in Europe and resulted in the expenditure of 2 trillion USD in 2022, an all-time record. The table shows the world in a crisis in which states choose to invest in the military rather than in peace. The table is consistent with the new nuclear weapons projects pursued by the US and Russia, as well as with the political crises internationally.

---

16   Rachael Bunyan, "Russia is planning to flight test new missile with a range of 6,200 miles and capable of destroying an area the size of France", *Daily Mail*, 4 January 2021.

17   Thomas Kingsley, "Putin threatens to deploy Satan II nuclear missile which can reach UK in three minutes by end of the year", *The Independent*, 22 June 2022.

18   Karen de Young, "Russia's moves in Ukraine are 'wake-up call,' NATO's Rasmussen says in speech", *The Washington Post*, March 19, 2014.

Along these lines, cooperation between the US and Russia on the legally binding nuclear arms control and disarmament treaties has been scrapped under the shadow of the increasing crises between the two. The unilateral American withdrawal from the 1972 ABM Treaty in 2002 allowed the US to embark on the Ballistic Missile Systems without restriction, while US withdrawal from the 1987 Intermediate Nuclear Forces (INF) Treaty enabled both sides to deploy intermediate nuclear forces in Europe. Finally, Russia has declared that it will pull back from the NEW START Treaty[19], the last remaining nuclear weapons arms control treaty between Russia and the US. That move will end the nuclear arms control regime between the US and Russia and will allow both to produce NWs without limitations.

Conclusion

The end of the Cold War provided new hope for peace and security in the international arena, in which international cooperation was expected to prevent conflicts and increase cooperation between states. The first phase of the post-Cold War era created this atmosphere, with the US and Russia cooperating in non-proliferation of WMD, especially in nuclear non-proliferation. That period also provided hope for an era in which the role and impact of NWs in international politics would diminish.

This atmosphere also provided a new vision, as articulated by US president Obama in 2009, of a world without NWs. Recent developments, however, have dimmed this hope, while crises between the US and Russia on nuclear arms control and armament has altered the trend within a short time, as the world entered a NEW COLD WAR era with more sophisticated, dangerous, and devastating weapon systems. Mutual Assured Destruction is now a more likely scenario. The lives of billions of people, indeed the survival of life on earth depend on decisions by leaders of all nuclear states, especially the US and Russia.

That does not mean the international community should give up hope. Priorities and perception of international relations and international politics change over time. Scientists who worked on the Manhattan Project expressed their regret after they witnessed the horrendous effects of the atomic bomb in Hiroshima and Nagasaki and stated that NWs should never be used again. Realist

19   David E. Sanger, "Putin's Move on Nuclear Treaty May Signal End to Formal Arms Control", *The New York Times*, February 21, 2023.

hardline American politicians, including Henry Kissinger, laid out a vision of a world without NWs, while the American president clearly expressed his dream of a nuclear-free world. The world has witnessed a period in which nuclear states cooperated on many issues, including the massive reduction of NWs.

Therefore, we have many reasons to look forward to better international cooperation to improve the international security environment. Temporary crises should not destroy the dream for peace, security, and international cooperation. We should have a common vision for humanity and the planet of a world without nuclear weapons.

References

Bernstein, Barton J. "A post-war myth: 500,000 US lives saved", Bulletin of the Atomic Sciences, 42. No. 6 (June/July 1986), pp.38-40

Brodie, Bernard, *The Absolute Weapon: Atomic Power and World Order.* Harcourt, 1946

Brodie, Bernard, *Strategy in the Missile Age*, Princeton University Press, 1959

Brodie, Bernard, *From Cross-Bow to H-Bomb.* Dell, 1962;

Brodie, Bernard, *Escalation and the Nuclear Option.* Princeton University Press, 1966.

Bunyan, Rachael "Russia is planning to flight test new missile with a range of 6,200 miles and capable of destroying an area the size of France," *Daily Mail,* 4 January 2021.

DeYoung, Karen, "Russia's moves in Ukraine are 'wake-up call,' NATO's Rasmussen says in speech", *The Washington Post*, March 19, 2014.

Gaddis, John Lewis, *International Security*, Vol. 10, No. 4 (Spring, 1986), pp. 99-142

https://thebulletin.org/virtual-tour/albert-einstein-leo-szilard-and-the-letter-that-led-to-the-manhattan-project/ https://www.armscontrol.org/factsheets/Phasedadaptiveapproach https://sgp.fas.org/crs/nuke/R41464.pdf

https://www.mda.mil/

Kahn, Herman, *On Thermonuclear War,* Princeton University Press, 1960.

Kahn, Herman, *Thinking about the unthinkable.* Horizon Press. 1962:

Kahn, Herman *On escalation: metaphors and scenarios.* Praeger, 1965.

Kingsley, Thomas, "Putin threatens to deploy Satan II nuclear missile which can reach UK in three minutes by end of the year", *The Independent*, 22 June 2022.

Moore, Kathryn and Dennis M. Giangreco, *Dear Harry: Truman's Mailroom, 1945-1953: the Truman administration through correspondence with "everyday Americans*, Stackpole Books, Lanham, 2017.

Remarks By President Barack Obama in Prague as delivered, April 5, 2009, https://obamawhitehouse.archives.gov/the-press-office/remarks-president-barack-obama-prague-delivered

"Russia's Putin unveils 'invincible' nuclear weapons", *BBC*, https://www.bbc.com/news/world-europe-43239331

Sanger, David E., "Putin's Move on Nuclear Treaty May Signal End to Formal Arms Control", *The New York Times*, February 21, 2023.

Schelling, Thomas, *The Strategy of Conflict* 1960, *Arms and Influence*, Yale University Press, 1966.

Shultz, George P. William J. Perry, Henry A. Kissinger and Sam Nunn, "A World Free of Nuclear Weapons", *Wall Street Journal*, January 4, 2007.

"The Potsdam Conference, 1945", https://history.state.gov/milestones/1937-1945/potsdam-conf

Waltz, Kenneth N., "The Spread of Nuclear Weapons: More May Be Better: Introduction", The Adelphi Papers, 21:171, 1981.

The "Newest" World Order, Uncertainty, and a Futuristic Approach[1]

Hasan Ali Karasar

Introduction

The development of international order has been in progress for a long time, in particular over the last few centuries. Long and bloody confrontations and competition around the world, especially in Europe, were accompanied by the colonization of other parts of the world, which led to the birth of new states such as the US. The late 19th century witnessed the development of the nation-state order in the West while the rest of the world, namely Asia, Africa, Oceania, consisted largely of colonies ruled by the Western world. The mindset of colonization, however, has never ended.

The early 20th century witnessed a new world order with the collapse of empires and the emergence of nation-states after two bloody World Wars, in which millions of people lost their lives. WWI and WWII reshaped the world map and restructured the international order. The rise of nation-states and the successful establishment of the UN, despite its drawbacks, created hope for an international order based on international law.

The 20th century figured as a sort of arena in which utopias of the previous century challenged each other and fought unnamed wars. Capitalism, socialism, nationalism, anarchism, libertarianism, federalism, confederalism, communism, imperialism, liberalism, idealism, utilitarianism, corporatism, collectivism, nihilism, conservatism, social Darwinism, monarchism, fascism, syndicalism, revolutionism and other similar isms, shaped human life in this era.

The Cold War era (1947-89) created its own kind of world order. Neither static nor immune to constant change, it had a rough structure. Many observers were reluctant to call it an "order." There was a pattern, though: two main camps on the

---

1 This article is a revised version of "Yeni Dünya Düzeni, Belirsizlik ve Gelecekbilici (Fütürist) bir Deneme" published in Türk Yurdu Dergisi (Vol. 110, Nu. 404, April 2021)

political, economic, and social fronts. The two camps pursued their own ideologies and their ideas of utopia, competing not only in the intellectual sphere but also in the industrial-technological development sphere.

The post-Cold war era provided hope for the development of an international order based on human rights, democracy, and international law, a goal of which many scholars and thinkers have dreamed for a long time. Despite a period of relative peace in the early post-Cold war era, emerging crises around the world, including genocide and ethnic cleansing in places such as Bosnia-Herzegovina and Kosovo, made it clear that the world and humanity were not yet ready for the development of an ideal and decent international order.

The Failure of the Development of International Order

The end of WWII, which had reshaped borders mainly in Eurasia, became a turning point for the continuing development of the international order. The early Cold War era witnessed a fast recovery of ruined Europe, the beginning of massive decolonization in Africa and Asia, and the emergence of two superpowers, the USA and the Soviet Union. This world order—the Cold War[2]—represented a new era in which the two superpowers confronted each other through bloody proxy warfare in Korea, Vietnam, the Middle East (Palestine and Israel), Asia (Pakistan and India, Afghanistan) and Africa (Angola).

The competing utopias of the 19th century evolved into strong competition between the socialist ideology of the Soviet Union and the "liberal and free world" utopia represented by the US and its allies. The US expanded its influence over the Western world with the motto of "a liberal economy-capitalism and democracy". On the other hand, the Soviet Union and subsequently China promised socialism and decolonization as an alternative utopia to imperialism and capitalism. Massive decolonization during 1960s and 1970s provided hope for a better world order, one that was equal and fair.

Crucial developments in the technological, scientific, social, and political areas, accompanied by continuous uncertainties, urged scholars to question the future of the world in terms of international order. As one example, the distinguished American futurist and writer Alvin Toffler studied the possible impacts of technological

---

2   The term "Cold War" was used first by George Orwell to describe the period after the World War II. He published an article, "You and Atomic Bomb", right after the use of atomic bombs in Hirohisma and Nagazaki and pointed out to the Dynamics of the new period. See: George Orwell, 'You and the Atom Bomb', *Tribune* (19 October 1945).

innovation and developments in information technologies on our life. He predicted that humans may face a wide of array of problems such as digitalization, asymmetric warfare, or immigration in the future due to the technological developments.[3] He also bluntly predicted in 1980 that in the three short decades between then and the 21st century, millions of ordinary, psychologically normal people will undergo an abrupt collision with the future.[4]

Thus, issues we describe today as "uncertainties" were topics of discussions in futuristic books, including bestsellers during the Cold War. Futurists such as John McHale,[5] John Naisbitt[6] or Frank Feather[7] aimed to clarify these uncertainties by providing a horizon for the future of humanity, and a possible international order based on current analysis of technological, social, economic or scientific developments.

The fall of the Berlin Wall, the symbol of the two-block system, was followed by the disintegration of the Soviet Union and marked the beginning of the post-Cold War era. The end of the Cold War order increased uncertainties about the future of the world, for which scholars and politicians strived to offer predictions. Francis Fukuyama, an official in the US Department of State, named the new period "The End of the History," based on the clear triumph of the US and values supported by the West, and pointed to the beginning of a new unipolar world order. Fukuyama aimed to clarify the new "uncertainty" with his influential essay that argued "the very prospect of centuries of boredom at the end of history will serve to get history started once again."[8] His theory, however, did not hold true. History did not end, the unipolar world order did not come about, and globalization could not declare victory.

The search to describe the new period of uncertainties continued. Samuel Huntington forecast in his article "The Clash of Civilizations" that ideological and economic competition will be replaced by new competition based on culture.[9] He ar-

---

3   Alvin Toffler, *Future Shock*. Random House, New York, 1970.
4   Ibid.
5   John McHale, *The Future of the Future*, George Braziller, New York, 1969.
6   John Naisbitt, *Megatrends: Ten New Directions Transforming Our Lives,* Warner Books, 1982.
7   Frank Feather, *G-Forces: Reinventing the World : The 35 Global Forces Restructuring Our Future*, Summerhill Press, 1989.
8   Francis Fukuyama, "The End of History?" *The National Interest*, No. 16 (Summer 1989), pp. 3-18
9   Samuel Huntington, "The Clash of Civilizations?", *Foreign Affairs*, Issue. 72, No. 3 (Summer, 1993). pp.22-49

gued that "the clash of civilizations will dominate global politics. The fault lines between civilizations will be the battle lines of the future".[10] Instead of bringing new ideas to tackle the uncertainty issue, he created more and complex uncertainties.

The uncertainty of the global system has been lingering since the end of the Cold War. This period can be analyzed in three different decades. We have witnessed many bloody civil wars and traditional wars in the first decade of this thirty-year period, including Gulf War I, the war in Bosnia, the Chechen wars, the war in Kosovo, and civil wars in Afghanistan, Rwanda, and Somalia. All these events thwarted the development of a new post-Cold War international world order in the way that many people had envisioned and hoped for.

The second part of this period, the "War on Terror" era, started after the September 11 attacks. Global and regional terror organizations such Al Qaida, the Taliban, El-Shabab and Boko Haram emerged as main actors in the international area. The American-led invasion of Afghanistan and Iraq (the Second Gulf War), the Color Revolutions, the Russian-Georgian War, the Gaza War, and swine flu emerged as the main events impacting development of a new international order between 2001 and 2011. It was not possible, again, to talk about a new world order during this period.

The main events in the last decade of this period included the civil war in Syria, the rise of DAESH, the Arab Spring, the rise of China, Islamophobia, coup attempts around the world, the election of Trump in the US, the COVID-19 pandemic and BREXIT. Considering the failure of an international order to develop, "uncertainty" remained the only term to describe the future, after COVID-19 pandemic impacted the entire world in 2020.

Finally, the Russian-Ukrainian war, which attempted to change the borders of a European state by force for the first time since the end of the World War II, under the shadow of the threat of nuclear weapons, started a new phase that once again increased uncertainties in the international order. The war reshaped the security environment globally and in Europe especially was regarded as a "warning call"[11] for the NATO Alliance, as articulated by Anders F. Rasmussen, former Secretary General of NATO, and intensified competition between the East and West similar to as it had been during the Cold War.

---

10   Ibid, p.23.

11   "Ukraine crisis 'wake up call' for Nato, says Rasmussen", BBC, 03 June 2014, https://www.bbc.com/news/av/world-europe-27690320 (last accessed on 03 June 2023)

Political disorder was not the sole reason for the failure of the development of a new world order. The anthropocene, the term coined to describe the era in which the accelerated accumulation of greenhouse gases has impacted the climate and biodiversity, and the irreversible damage to the planet caused by over-consumption of natural resources,[12] also emerged as a factor increasing instability in the world, one of the main sources of uncertainties.

Throughout history, the world has witnessed horrifying pandemics. The "Black Death" of the 1300s, for example, killed up to fifty percent of Europe's population[13] as well as millions of people in Asia. We recently experienced swine flu or bird flu, which was not associated with the death of millions of people, but the COVID-19 pandemic emerged as one of the main threats to human beings in recent history, affecting every aspect of daily life from education to economics.

It is worth noting that pandemics have taught us many things. It turned out that national capabilities are as important as international capabilities to fight against pandemics. The importance of national resilience in the fight agains pandemics has been better understood..

We also witnessed that the pandemics triggered a transformation for which the world has long been waiting. We have witnessed revolutionary and fast changes and transformation in all aspects of our life, including education, tourism, production modellings, finance, and work life. Online education, work at home, the redundancy of bureaucracy, the emergence of small production systems and the rise of cryptocurrencies, especially the rise of BITCOIN, and the digital economy have emerged as main products of the pandemic period. We are not sure about their long-term effects, but they have changed and shaped our life.

Digitalization cannot be described as a technological breakthrough although it has changed the rhythm of life[14]. We are living in an age in which long-standing prejudices could be changed in a very short time. We are speaking of a period that emerged as a weapon of capitalism; an ideology that forces societies to make a choice between freedom or security, and democracy and wealth or stability.

---

12   https://en.unesco.org/courier/2018-2/anthropocene-vital-challenges-scientific-debate (last accessed on 22 May 2023)

13   William G. Naphy and Andrew Spicer, *The Black Death: A History of Plagues, 1345-1730*, Tempus, 2004.

14   Bekir Ağırdır, *Hikayesini Arayan Gelecek*, Doğan Kitap, İstanbul, 2020, p. 25.

At this point, the arguments of philosopher Byung-Chul Han, which inspired neo Marxists, play an important role. In his 2014 book *Psycholopolitics*[15], he discusses biopolitics and data. According to Han, ruling elites who used to threaten populations with death now reward them with life, based on realities of biopolitics.[16] Dataism is a form of data fetishism, as we might infer from the term.[17] Regarding the size and dimension of the data of the world population, our digital footprint represents all of us.[18]

Developments in information technology resulted in the manipulation of societies, whereby cartels in the information domain can manipulate our minds. Invisible hands lead the fate of young populations or leave them unguided, while traditional centers of guidance disappear. Social media centers use artificial intelligence that produces algorithms to influence preferences[19], which scholars term "algorithrocracy".[20] As French mathematician Poincare[21], the famed theorist of chaos, pointed out 130 years ago, some events we regard as chaos might be, in essence, part of systems we cannot understand. In other words, a situation we regard as chaos or uncertainty might have an order in mathematical formation that we cannot see. The most recent theories, such as "Butterfly Effects" or "Quantum Physics" date back to one century ago. None of them, however, are regarded as an alternative to classical positivism. Post-modernism lost its explanatory power after the pandemics and given the new realities.

The new and modern version of Space Wars is also expected to bolster the misuse of the information sphere. Space has consisted another important component in the development of the international system. It has been more than 60 years since the Soviet Union launched Sputnik, the first human-made satellite. The number of active satellites in the orbit was 464 in 1990, 769 in 2000, 997 in 2010 and

---

15 Byung-Chul Han, Psikopolitika: *Neoliberalizm ve Yeni İktidar Teknikleri*, Metis, İstanbul, 2019.

16 Ibid, p. 29-30. (For example with health systems, medicine or vaccines)

17 Ibid, p. 65.

18 Ibid, p. 81.

19 It was revealed that 50 million Facebook profiles harvested for Cambridge Analytica in major data breach in 2015 for use of political proposes and this was just a tip of the iceberg.

20 Şeref Oğuz, "Dünya Algoritokrasi çağına mı giriyor?," *Dünya Gazetesi*, 13 Nisan 2020, https://www.dunya.com/kose-yazisi/dunya-algoritokrasi-cagina-mi-giriyor/467552 (last accessed on 01 March 2021)

21 Christos Skiadas (ed.), *The Foundations of Chaos Revisited: From Poincaré to Recent Advancements*. Springer, Genoa, 2016.

reached 3,368 in 2020 and 6905 at the end of the 2022[22], a six-times growth in the last decade. Two thousand of them are commercial satellites while 700 are used for civilian purposes, and 600 satellites are used for military and intelligence activities. Russia still uses facilities inherited from the Soviet Union, while China has been increasing its capabilities in recent decades. The US transferred most of its activities in space to the SpaceX company, which is known for its reusable rocket systems. Russia became the leading state for space transportation because of the reliability of proton rockets. China has been pursuing a double track policy: first, increasing military-intelligence capabilities and secondly, establishing a basis for an independent telecommunication and internet system through satellite systems.

Google started the Loon[23] project, which aimed to provide high-speed internet connection in areas that have problems with connection (mainly in South America and Africa) through giant helium balloons deployed in the stratosphere. However, Google canceled it in early 2021 after SpaceX's Starlink project increased its activities. SpaceX aims to become the main fast-speed internet provider around the world via a low-orbit satellite network. They placed 800 satellites into orbit in 2 years and aim to place 12,000 satellites at three different orbit levels by 2025. In addition to providing massive internet connection capability, these projects will enable states to closely follow, watch, listen and track most of the activities of other states and people around the world. Most importantly, these projects will provide the capability to change, lead and guide the minds of people.

The Pessimist Future Scenario

We cannot name the period that includes the last decade of 20th century and first two decades of the 21st century. Major failures and mistakes by the US destroyed expectations about a unipolar world. Capitalism as an economic system seemed to win hegemony across the world, but its liberal values did not meet expectations. Global peace was not achieved and conflicts in the MENA region contributed to this failure. Conflicts in Afghanistan, Bosnia-Herzegovina, Chechenia, Nagorno-Karabakh, Iraq, Syria, Libya, Yemen, Arakan, and Kashmir resulted in the death of millions of people. Migration has a new meaning today, creating new dynamics across the world.

Several factors have thwarted the establishment of an international order based on human rights, democracy, international cooperation and the just distribution of

---

22 "Number of active satellites by year 1957-2022", https://www.statista.com/statistics/897719/number-of-active-satellites-by-year/ (last accessed on 10 June 2023)

23 https://loon.com/ (last accessed on 22 May 2023)

income: recent crises between nation states, the increasing competition between the US and Russia accompanied by revitalized nuclear challenges, the lingering effects of COVID-19 in economic, social and psychological spheres, the rise of populism across the world, and the effects of high inflation affecting billions of people. It seems that humanity and the planet will be not better in the future than they are today.

The rapid increase of world population will accelerate problems. World population expanded from 2.7 billion in 1955 to 7.8 billion in 2020.[24] Providing food, shelter, health care, and education for this population, as well as satisfying the needs of the consumption economy, can only be possible by destruction of habitat, over-consumption of natural resources, and exploitation of people.

The increasing difference between wealthy and poor economies, as well as uneven income distribution in them, will accelerate mass movements of population. This, in turn, will trigger another wave of legal and especially illegal immigration in the near future. Fortified borders, strict customs controls and tough visa measures will not be enough to prevent this process.

It seems that we will lose control of many things in this century. To start with the family, we will not be able to educate our children based on our values. Our culture, our civilization with its history of more than one thousand years, our language, our religion will face domestic or international challenges which we have never seen in history. Algorithms will rule in the new age.

Decentralized or multi-centered organizations will weaken the values that bring us together. Algorithms will question values such as truth, intelligence, morals, justice, or decency, and lead us to behave contrary to our values. Digitalized economies and crypto-currencies will nullify the values of traditional currencies that derive their power from their states of origin. States will not be able to collect taxes unless they accept the new situation and reality. Digital education will have doubled yields with the help of artificial intelligence. Digital health systems have been providing concrete solutions for a long time. Digitalized finance and retirement systems are in progress.

We are at the crossroads of a major transformation of the world. Those kinds of changes have taken place only once or twice in a millennium in history. The question here is a very simple one: **Are we ready?**

---

24 https://www.worldometers.info/world-population (last accessed on 19 March 2023)

References

Ağırdır, Bekir, *Hikayesini Arayan Gelecek*, Doğan Kitap, İstanbul, 2020.

Feather, Frank, *G-Forces: Reinventing the World: The 35 Global Forces Restructuring Our Future*, Summerhill Press, 1989.

Fukuyama, Francis, "The End of History?" *The National Interest*, No. 16 (Summer 1989).

Han, Byung-Chul, *Psikopolitika: Neoliberalizm ve Yeni İktidar Teknikleri*, Metis, İstanbul, 2019.

https://en.unesco.org/courier/2018-2/anthropocene-vital-challenges-scientific-debate (last accessed on 22 May 2023)

https://loon.com/ (last accessed on 22 May 2023)

https://www.worldometers.info/world-population (last accessed on 19 March 2023)

Huntington, Samuel, "The Clash of Civilizations?", *Foreign Affairs*, Vol. 72, No.3 (Summer, 1993). pp. 22-49

McHale, John, *The Future of the Future*, George Braziller, New York, 1969.

Naisbitt, John, *Megatrends: Ten New Directions Transforming Our Lives,* Warner Books, 1982.

Naphy,William G., and Spicer, Andrew, *The Black Death: A History of Plagues, 1345-1730*, Tempus, 2004.

Number of active satellites by year 1957-2023, https://www.statista.com/ (last accessed on 10 Haziran 2023)

Oğuz, Şeref, "Dünya Algoritokrasi çağına mı giriyor?", *Dünya Gazetesi*, 13 Nisan 2020, https://www.dunya.com/kose-yazisi/dunya-algoritokrasi-cagina-mi-giriyor/467552 (last accessed on 01 March 2021)

Orwell, George, "You and the Atom Bomb", *Tribune* (19 October 1945).

Skiadas, Christos (ed.), *The Foundations of Chaos Revisited: From Poincaré to Recent Advancements.* Springer, Genoa, 2016.

Toffler, Alvin, *Future Shock*, Random House, New York, 1970

"Ukraine crisis 'wake up call' for Nato, says Rasmussen", *BBC*, 03 June 2014, https://www.bbc.com/news/av/world-europe-27690320 (last accessed on 03 June 2023)

In Lieu of a Conclusion

Hasan Ali Karasar
Şafak Oğuz

Humanity and our planet have been passing through hard times. Despite a partially effective international system, in which the UN is tasked with providing and maintaining international peace and security, the Russian-Ukrainian war continues under the threat of the use of nuclear weapons, a threat the world has not heard since the 1962 Cuban Crisis. Russia's membership in the UN Security Council and its right of veto derailed a decision and resolution in the UN to resolve the crisis and end the war. Thus, despite strong international support for Ukraine, not even the UN, with the participation of 193 states, could find a solution to stop the killing, and the suffering of millions of people in Ukraine.

The crisis has affected most of the world's population, not just the people of Ukraine. The war, the first to change the borders of a European state by force since World War II, has also impacted the flow of natural gas to Europe and the flow of grains around the world, threatening millions of people with famine. Türkiye's efforts, in coordination with the UN, launched a Black Sea Grain Initiative, which allowed the resumption of Ukrainian and Russian grain exports via the Black Sea, enabling millions of people to reach food they desperately needed. The initiative, and international cooperation with the involvement of the fighting states, staved off famine worldwide in the first year, but the crisis looms in the future.

Ongoing and protracted civil wars around the world have resulted in the displacement of millions of people domestically and internationally, people who have been living under harsh conditions. There has been a flow of millions of people from Latin America to the US and Canada as well as from Africa and Asia to Europe in search of better living conditions. Most of them, especially women and children, failed to reach to their destinations, dying at sea or on the way. People who reached their destinations have been subjected to racist reactions both by officials and ordinary citizens in the states in which they settled. The situation on the ground is becoming more difficult for them day by day. The flow of irregular migrants is regarded as one of the most serious threats to the security of the developed states to which they head, a growing threat that exacerbates ethnical and religious hatred, discrimination, and racism against minorities.

People tend to forget or ignore that irregular migration is a result of the policies of developed states. The colonization and slavery of the past, and the exploitation policies of modern times, prompt these people to leave their homes, for security and for higher living standards. The increasing disparity in income distribution and living standards between developed and undeveloped states as a result of failed policies turn these people into a weapon that targets developed states.

Racism has been recurring and increasing around the world, especially in developed states associated with democracy, freedom, and human rights. Tolerance against others has diminished nearly to zero and hatred based on diversities in religion or ethnicity has reached a peak, while support for racist parties is gradually growing. Economic crises, unemployment, and unequal income distribution fuel racist feeling among the population. The term "coexistence" has ceased to hold much meaning.

The COVID-19 pandemic killed millions of people, impacted the lives of nearly everyone in the world. Its psychological and sociological effects still linger, while most people wonder when they will have to wear masks again. News of the emergence of new variants of viruses and bacteria constantly summons to mind living conditions during the COVID-19 pandemic. The possibility of emergence and dissemination of a genetically engineered or genetically modified virus that might kill millions of people is considered high. Such a scenario, previously in only science fiction novels or movies is not fictitious anymore and the threat is real, imminent, and serious.

Terrorism and the war against terror have been on the agenda of the international community for a long time, although many states that describe terrorism as a threat are the main sponsors of terrorist organizations that target their enemies or allies. Terrorism and terror organizations have been around for centuries as threats to local and regional security. As highlighted by the September 11 attacks, the attacks of the PKK Terrorist Organization in Türkiye's, in the Middle East or in Europe, the threats and attacks by Al-Qaida and DAESH, among other examples around the world, terrorism has become a serious international threat, and success and triumph over terror can only be achieved through international cooperation. That includes a common understanding of the threat and effects of terrorism, stopping the sponsoring of terrorism that targets other states or populations, intelligence sharing, and respecting human rights.

Islamophobia, which arose through events not related to the Islamic world or to Islamic values, has been increasing gradually, gathering wide support. It was manifested as discrimination and stigmatization of Muslims living in non-Muslim states and widened the gap in mutual understanding between Muslim and non-Muslim states. Recent events, including burning the Quran in several European states, heralded new crises from Islamophobia, crises that might trigger social disorder.

Climate change, with its devastating effects on the humanity and our planet, have emerged as major crises that we and other species have been experiencing for a long time. It has been regarded as causing misery-inflicting events including floods, drought, fires, global warming, the extinction of species, and other natural disasters, and the expectation is that if there no effective effort to curb it, the ecosystem will be impacted to the extent that even human life will be under threat in the long run. Climate change has global effects, and it cannot be solved through local and regional measures or implications. There is not a local or global ozone layer hole or depletion, and it effects the whole world wherever it happens or whatever causes it. The fight against the change can only be won through international cooperation, with the participation of each individual actor.

There have been other major crises suffering in the world. It is worth noting, as Prof. Keane pointed out in the previous chapter, that this situation is not unique to our times, considering the crises, devastation, and suffering throughout history. Except for the climate crisis, which has worsened e in recent decades because of heavy industrialization, human beings have experienced most of these malignant events in past eras, sometimes far worse than today's crises. World War Two alone resulted in the death of more than 80 million people, in addition to by millions of people around the world. The Black Death which killed one third of Europe's population in the 14th century, was a continuation of the plague that killed millions in China, India and other parts of Asia.

The sticking point for contemporary crises, however, is their global scale, and the necessity for global cooperation to solve the problems, due to the globalized structure of the world today. Events in the Middle Ages, or the French

Revolution, the Renaissance, and the Reformation in Europe, impacted other countries or empires gradually, but to a limited degree. Limited interaction between different parts of the world prevented dissemination of the effects of crises and did not require global cooperation and action. Globalization, however, shrinking and interconnecting the world, changed that situation.

The rapid dissemination of information as a result of breakthroughs in information technologies and globalization changed the nature of the world, making it more interconnected. As we have witnessed, local or global events in the world affect other parts of the world more deeply, sooner, and to a larger degree. No one has the chance anymore to prevent the effects and isolate themselves from the effects of regional or global developments. Neither heavily fortified castles nor strictly controlled borders can protect against threats emanating from other parts of the world.

In international relations, the classic realist approach urges states, as the sole effective international actor, to maximize their power, and highlights the role of power rather than cooperation. That has been and still is the main policy of many states including the big powers. Idealism, on the other hand, is mainly associated with international cooperation and highlights the importance of effective international organizations for peace and security either local, regional, or international.

Although idealism has been regarded as "too ideal" for realists, it is worth noting that recently the international order has been shaped on the idealist approach, at least visibly. The United Nations, despite its drawbacks and problems, is the only platform, and the largest, that brings all states to the table and encourages international cooperation. Despite the veto power of the UN Security Council, which is responsible for security matters and includes only the US, Russia, China, the UK, and France, the UN succeeds in bringing states together for cooperation in international matters.

Recent events, however, have proved that the classic realist approach has reached its limit, and remind us of the urgent need for stronger and more effective international cooperation. It is crystal clear that none of the contemporary problems can be solved by a single actor on its own. Peace and security can be provided only through solidarity, cohesion, and cooperation of all actors in the international community. *No one is safe until everyone is safe.*

According to the System Approach, which provides a framework for effective interaction between parts of the system in a specific way to reach their target, a problem of a subsystem would result in the malfunctioning of the entire system. This is also valid for the international system composed of international actors, namely states and international organizations. The international system, including the ecosystem, can only work if all subsystems work properly and in coordination with other actors, including actors of the ecosystem.

Therefore, we need *a Common Horizon for Humanity and the Planet* if we desire to live in a safer world. Contemporary problems can only be solved by international cooperation based on a realistic and widely accepted Common Horizon. All actors of the international system should be included in the development and application of this common horizon.

We need a Common Horizon which ensures that "Everyone is entitled to all the rights and freedoms set forth in the Universal Declaration of Humans Rights and other documents related to human rights, without distinction of any kind, such as race, colour, sex, language, religion, political or other opinion, national or social origin, property, birth or other status."

We need a Common Horizon in which states have, in accordance with the Charter of the United Nations and the principles of international law, the sovereign right to exploit their own resources pursuant to their own environmental and developmental policies, and the responsibility to ensure that activities within their jurisdiction or control do not cause damage to the environment of other States or of areas beyond the limits of national jurisdiction, as stated in Rio Declaration on the Environment and Development in 1992.

We need a Common Horizon which accepts and stresses that life without war serves as the primary international prerequisite for material well-being, development, and progress of countries, and for the full implementation of the rights and fundamental human freedoms proclaimed by the UN, as stated in the Declaration on the Right of Peoples to Peace by the UN in 1984.

We need a Common Horizon that will enable a safer, peaceful, and livable world that we can transfer to our children. We need a Common Horizon that will provide a world all humans deserve.

We need a Common Horizon that will enable a safer, peaceful, and livable world that we can transfer to our children. We need a Common Horizon that will provide a world all humans deserve.

Index